Wole Soyinka
Plays: 2

A Play of Giants, From Zia, With Love, A Scourge of Hyacinths, The Beatification of Area Boy

Wole Soyinka is 'a writer who in a wide cultural perspective and with poetic overtones fashions the drama of existence . . . His writing is vivid, often harrowing, but also marked by an evocative, poetically intensified diction.' Citation, Nobel Prize for Literature 1986

The Beatification of Area Boy: 'A beautifully crafted piece of theatre that takes what it needs from Western dramatic conventions and then does what it wants to do – which is to commemorate and commiserate with the daily life of Nigerians. On the surface it's a straight slice of life, eavesdropped and reported – one day in the vibrant and violent, cruel and colourful life of a street corner in post-oil-boom Lagos . . . He does it with consummate skill, drawing threads of social observation, political passion, emotional tension and tough intellectual debate into the complex rhythms of a jazz symphony . . . Both accessible and poetic, very warm and funny and deeply moving in its tragic, complicated argument . . . a masterpiece.' *Guardian*
'Witty, wise and uplifting, this is a beautiful play whose message steals up on you and lingers on.' *Financial Times*

A Play of Giants paints a savage portrait of a group of African dictators with pronounced resemblance to recent 'supermen'; *From Zia, With Love* is a stinging indictment of Nigerian society in the early eighties, where the brutality and injustice of military rule is parodied by life inside prison; and *A Scourge of Hyacinths*, a radio play, presents variations on the same themes.

Wole Soyinka was born in Nigeria in 1934. Educated there and at Leeds University, he worked in British theatre before returning to Nigeria in 1960. In 1986, he became the first African writer to win the Nobel Prize for Literature. His plays include *The Jero Plays* (1960, 1966), *The Road* (1965), *The Lion and the Jewel* (1966), *Madmen and Specialists* (1971), *Death and the King's Horseman* (1975), *A Play of Giants* (1984), *A Scourge of Hyacinths* (1991) and *From Zia, With Love* (1992). His novels include *The Interpreters* (1973) and *Season of Anomy* (1980). His collections of poetry include *Idanre* (1967), *A Shuttle in the Crypt* (1972) – composed during a period of over two years in prison without trial, most of it in solitary confinement – and *Mandela's Earth* (1990). In 1988, his collection of essays on literature and culture, *Art, Dialogue and Outrage*, was published. He has also written three a *Childhood* (1981), *Ìsarà: A Vo 4*).

D1581778

by the same author

Poetry
Idanre and Other Poems*
A Shuttle in the Crypt*
Mandela's Earth*

Plays
A Dance of the Forests
The Lion and the Jewel
The Road
Kongi's Harvest
The Swamp Dwellers
The Strong Breed
Madmen and Specialists*
Camwood on the Leaves*
The Bacchae of Euripides*
The Jero Plays*
Death and the King's Horseman*
Opera Wonyosi*
A Play of Giants*
Requiem for a Futurologist
From Zia, With Love*
A Scourge of Hyacinths*
The Beatification of Area Boy*

Essays, Fiction and Memoirs
The Interpreters
Season of Anomy
The Man Died
Aké: The Years of Childhood*
Myth, Literature and the African World
Art, Dialogue and Outrage*
Ìsarà: A Voyage Around Essay*
Ibadan: The Penkelemes Years*

*published by Methuen

WOLE SOYINKA

Plays: 2

A Play of Giants
From Zia, With Love
A Scourge of Hyacinths
The Beatification of Area Boy

Methuen Drama

METHUEN CONTEMPORARY DRAMATISTS

1 3 5 7 9 10 8 6 4 2

This collection first published in 1999 by Methuen Publishing Ltd
20 Vauxhall Bridge Road, London SW1V 2SA

Peribo Pty Ltd, 58 Beaumont Road, Mount Kuring-Gai, NSW 2080, Australia,
ACN 002 273 761
(For Australia and New Zealand)
Random House South Africa (Pty) Ltd
Endulini, 5A Jubilee Road, Parktown 2193, South Africa

A Play of Giants first published in Great Britain in 1984
by Methuen London Ltd
Copyright © 1984 by Wole Soyinka
From Zia, With Love and *A Scourge of Hyacinths* first published
in Great Britain in a volume together in 1992
by Methuen Drama
From Zia, With Love copyright © 1992 by Wole Soyinka
A Scourge of Hyacinths copyright © 1992 by Wole Soyinka
The Beatification of Area Boy first published in Great Britain in 1995
by Methuen Drama
Copyright © 1995 by Wole Soyinka

Collection copyright © 1999 by Wole Soyinka

The right of the author to be identified as the author of these works has been asserted by
him in accordance with the Copyright, Designs and Patents Act, 1988

A CIP catalogue record for this book
is available from the British Library

Methuen Publishing Limited Reg. No. 3543167

ISBN 0–413–73260–6

Typeset by Deltatype Ltd, Birkenhead, Merseyside
Printed in Great Britain by
Cox & Wyman Ltd, Reading, Berkshire

Caution
All rights whatsoever in these plays are strictly reserved and application for
performance, etc., by professionals and amateurs, should be made before rehearsals
begin to: Morton Leavy, 11 East 44th Street, 10th Floor Suite, New York, NY10017,
USA. No performance may be given unless a licence has been obtained.

Contents

Wole Soyinka
A Chronology

Note: Only first or specially notable productions of plays are given.

1934   Born in Abeokuta, of Ijegba parentage.

1938–43   Primary education – St Peter's School, Ake, Abeokuta.

1944–45   Abeokuta Grammar School.

1946–50   Government College, Ibadan.

1952–54   University College, Ibadan (now University of Ibadan).

1954–57   University of Leeds, obtained degree in English. Short stories published: *Madame Etienne's Establishment* and *A Tale of Two Cities*.

1957–59   Attached to the Royal Court Theatre, London, as playreader. *The Invention* (never published) performed at the theatre in November 1959. On the programme were poems from the play-in-progress, *A Dance of the Forests*, and other poems.

1959   *The Swamp Dwellers* produced for the *Sunday Times* Student Drama Festival. *The Swamp Dwellers* and *The Lion and the Jewel* (first version) produced in Ibadan, Nigeria.

1960   Langston Hughes' *African Treasury* published, containing Soyinka's poems. Back in Nigeria, Soyinka formed the 1960 Masks drama company. *A Dance of the Forests* produced with that company, the play winning the *Encounter* award.

1961–62   Rockefeller Research Fellow in Drama, University of Ibadan.

1962   Frances Ademola's *Reflections* published, containing pieces by Soyinka.

1962–64   Lecturer in English, University of Ife.

1963   Satirical revue, *The Republican*, performed by the 1960
       Masks. Later in the same year, *The New Republican*
       performed. *The Lion and the Jewel* and *A Dance of the
       Forests* published. *Modern Poetry from Africa* (ed.
       Gerald Moore and Ulli Beier) published (Penguin),
       containing Soyinka's poems.

1964   Orisun Theatre (drama group) formed. March: twenty-
       five minute adaptation of *The Strong Breed* filmed in
       Nigeria for American Television (Esso World Theatre).
       The Strong Breed and *The Trials of Brother Jero*
       produced at Greenwich Mews Theater, New York.

1964   *Five Plays* published (Oxford University Press).

1965   *Before the Blackout*, satirical revue, produced in Lagos
       and Ibadan in September. *The Road* directed by David
       Thompson at Theatre Royal, Stratford, East London.
       October: Soyinka arrested in connection with a 'pirate'
       broadcast made from the Western Region studios of
       the Nigerian Broadcasting Corporation, following dis-
       puted election results. Charged with armed robbery of
       two tapes from studios. December: acquitted. *The
       Road* published (OUP). *Camwood on the Leaves* (radio
       play) broadcast BBC, London. *The Interpreters* pub-
       lished. *Kongi's Harvest* directed by the author, Lagos.

1965–67 Senior Lecturer in English, University of Lagos, and
       Acting Head of Department.

1966   *Kongi's Harvest* performed at the Dakar Festival of
       Negro Arts. *Rites of the Harmattan Solstice* (unpub-
       lished) celebrated at University of Lagos. June: *The
       Trials of Brother Jero* produced at Hampstead Theatre,
       London. December: *The Lion and the Jewel* produced
       at Royal Court Theatre, London.

1967   *Kongi's Harvest* published (OUP). *Idanre and Other
       Poems* published (Methuen). Awarded the John Whit-
       ing Drama prize. Appointed Head of Department of

Theatre Arts, University of Ibadan. August: detained by
the Federal Military Government of Nigeria.

1968   Awarded the Jock Campbell *New Statesman* Literary
        Award. *The Forest of a Thousand Daemons*, Soyinka's
        translation of D. O. Fagunwa's novel *Ogboju Ode
        Ninu Igbo Irunmale* published (Nelson).

1969   *Three Short Plays* published (OUP). *Poems from Prison*
        published (Rex Collings). October: released from
        detention. Assumed position as Head of Department of
        Theatre Arts, University of Ibadan.

1970   *Madmen and Specialists* (early version) produced at the
        Eugene O'Neill Theater Center, Waterford, USA.

1971   January: complete version of *Madmen and Specialists*
        directed by the author in Ibadan and Ife. *Before the
        Blackout* published (Orisun Editions).

1972   *The Man Died* (prison notes) and *A Shuttle in the
        Crypt* (poems) published (Rex Collings).

1973   *The Jero Plays*, including *The Trials of Brother Jero*
        and *Jero's Metamorphosis*, and *Camwood on the
        Leaves* published (Methuen). *Collected Plays I* pub-
        lished (OUP). *Season of Anomy* published (Rex Col-
        lings). *The Bacchae of Euripides* performed at the
        National Theatre, London.

1973–74 Visiting Fellow, Churchill College, Cambridge.

1974   *Poems from Black Africa* (Soyinka ed.) published
        (Secker and Warburg).

1974–75 Visiting Professor, University of Ghana, Legon. Editor
        of *Transition* (later *Ch'Indaba*).

1975   Elected Secretary-General of the Union of Writers of
        the African Peoples, newly formed. *Collected Plays II*
        published (OUP). *Jero's Metamorphosis* performed
        Lagos. *The Detainee* (radio play) broadcast by BBC,
        London. Returned to Nigeria to take up appointment

as Professor of Comparative Literature, University of Ife.

1976 *Death and the King's Horseman* performed in Ife. *Ogun Abibiman* (long poem) published (Rex Collings). *Myth, Literature and the African World* (essays) published (Cambridge University Press).

1977 *Opera Wonyosi* (adaptation of *The Threepenny Opera*) performed in Ife, directed by author.

1978 Head, Department of Dramatic Arts, University of Ife. Created the Unife Guerrilla Theatre, performing satirical revues.

1979 *Death and the King's Horseman* performed at the Goodman Theater, Chicago and J. F. Kennedy Center, Washington, the author directing.

1980 *Rice Unlimited* (satirical revues) performed Ife, Ibadan, Lagos.

1980–81 Visiting Professor, Yale University.

1981 *Aké: The Years of Childhood* published (Rex Collings). *The Critic and Society* (essay) published (University of Ife Press).

1982 *Die Still, Dr Godspeak* (radio play) broadcast BBC, London. *Priority Projects* (satirical revue) toured in Nigeria.

1983 *Requiem for a Futurologist* performed in Ife and on tour.

1984 *A Play of Giants* published (Methuen). April: *The Road* directed by author, Goodman Theater, Chicago.

1985 *Requiem for a Futurologist* published (Rex Collings).

1986 Awarded Nobel Prize for Literature and the CFR (Commander of the Federal Republic), one of Nigeria's highest awards.

1988 *Art, Dialogue and Outrage* (essays) published. *Mandela's Earth and Other Poems* published (Methuen).

1989   *Ìsarà: A Voyage Round Essay* (memoirs) published
        (Methuen).

1991   *A Scourge of Hyacinths* (radio play) broadcast on BBC
        Radio 4.

1992   *From Zia, With Love* (an extension of *A Scourge of
        Hyacinths*) premiered in Siena, Italy.

1994   *Ibadan: The Penkelemes Years – A Memoir 1945–1965*
        published (Methuen).

1995   *The Beatification of Area Boy* premiered at West
        Yorkshire Playhouse, Leeds, and published (Methuen).

1996   Forced into exile because of threats by the military
        government of General Abacha.

1997   Charged with treason by the Abacha regime, and
        placed on trial *in absentia*. Becomes Woodruff Profes-
        sor at Emory University, USA.

A PLAY OF GIANTS

To Byron Kadadwa

ON THE HEROES OF OUR TIME:
SOME PERSONAL NOTES

No serious effort is made here to hide the identities of the real-life actors who have served as models for *A Play of Giants*. They are none other than: President for Life Macias Nguema (late) of Equatorial Guinea; Emperor for Life (ex) Jean-Baptiste Bokassa of the Central African Republic; Life President Mobutu Sese Koko etc., of Congo Kinshasa (just hanging on); and – the HERO OF HEROES in the person of Life President (ex) the Field-Marshal El-Haji Dr Idi Amin of Uganda, DSc, DSO, VC etc., etc., who still dreams, according to latest reports, of being recalled to be the Saviour of Uganda once again.

It is obvious that no single play should even attempt to contain such a gallery of Supermen. I therefore shift the blame for this act of hubris to Jean Genet (*The Balcony*) who suggested the idea, that is, provided a model of form which might possibly attempt the feat. Naturally I absolve Genet of the short-comings in execution.

Unlike many commentators on power and politics, I do not know how monsters come to be, only that they are, and in defiance of place, time and pundits. According to some of these last, our grotesqueries are the product of specific socio-economic histories, yet no one has ever satisfactorily explained why near-identical socio-economic conditions (including a similar colonial experience) should produce, on the one hand, a Julius Nyerere and on the other, an Idi Amin. What we are able to observe more confidently (in addition to their mechanisms for first acquiring power) is how our subjects succeed in remaining entrenched in power long after they have been unambiguously exposed for what they are. Mobutu, to take our surviving example, should have received his *coup de grace* at least a decade ago but for the resolute interests of the Western powers – Belgium, France and West Germany most directly.

Such a seemingly straightforward identification of interests fails to apply however when we come to the figure of Idi Amin. This certified psychopath was sustained in power at various periods by group interests and ideologies as varied as those of Great Britain (which installed him in power in the first place), the United States, the Soviet Union, the Organisation of African Unity, Cuba, Libya, the PLO and Israel, not to mention the vociferous support accorded him by the cheer-leaders among the intelligentsia of the African continent and the Black Caucuses of the United States.

That genuine ignorance accounted for part of this phenomenon is not to be denied. As Secretary-General of the Union of Writers of the African Peoples and the editor of a journal, both of which organs were mobilised to confront the tyranny of Amin's regime, I did however have the opportunity of engaging, at first hand, politicians, intellectuals and even Heads of State in the effort to expose the truth about Uganda under Idi Amin. My experience in the majority of cases was that such ignorance was willed, not fortuitous. The tone, the varied disguises of their 'ignorance' left me with the confirmation of a long-held suspicion that power calls to power, that the brutality of power (its most strident self-manifestation) evokes a conspiratorial craving for the phenomenon of 'success' which cuts across all human occupations. This may be one of the many explanations why some of the most brilliant men of science and the humanities bend their skills and intelligence to ensuring the continuity of power even in its most brutal, humanly exorbitant manifestation. (Hitler, Stalin are our notorious examples.) It certainly makes it easier to understand why some of our own colleagues, including those of the Left, could find it possible to rationalise and applaud the crudest barbarities of an Idi Amin – their 'success' is reflected and consummated in the Colossal Success which Amin's power symbolised, even in its very excesses!

Pinochet, Galtieri, Pol Pot (who will have us believe he is now reformed and a patriot to boot), d'Aubuisson and his Right-wing murder squads, confidently striving for the ultimate legitimation of his innate propensities ... all masters of the statecraft of 'disappearance' whose magnitude acts inversely to magnify their own appearance. Yes, we do know what is at stake, what is being fought over. The puzzle which persists is why some, but not others, actually enjoy, indeed *relish* the condition of power, why certain individuals would rather preside over a necropolis than not preside at all, why, like the monkey in the folk tale, some would rather hold on to the booty of power through the gourd's narrow neck than unclench the fist and save themselves.

Power, we have suggested, calls to power, and vicarious power (that is, the sort enjoyed by the politically impotent intelligentsia) responds obsequiously to the real thing. Apart from self-identification with success, there is also a professed love (in essence a self-love) which is perverse, being also identical with the 'love' of the slave-girl for her master. Often, on listening to the rationalisations of this group, I feel that I am listening to a slave-girl in a harem, excusing the latest sadisms of the seraglio, exaggerating the scattered moments of generosity, of 'goodness', forgetting that even the exceptions to the rule merely emphasise the slave relations between herself and the Master. Our friends professed to find in Idi Amin the figure of a misunderstood nationalist, revolutionary and even economic genius – after all, he did boot out the blood-sucking Asians, and was he not always to be relied on for a hilarious insult against one super-power imperialist chieftain or another and their client leaders on the continent? And so the Organisation of African Unity remained deaf to all objections and proceeded to honour him with the chairmanship of that body, an honour later denied Colonel Ghadafi, his erstwhile protector, when it came to that maverick's turn. That irony would not have been lost on the Ugandan survivors of

Amin's reign of terror, but I doubt if many of them shed any tears over the injustice.

In human terms, what happened in Uganda was this: that nation lost its cream of professionals, its productive elite. That much is no longer denied, the pitiful list of the notable 'desaparecidos' is no longer disputed except by the deaf and the blind. But Uganda also lost tens of thousands of faceless, anonymous producers, workers and peasants who were ghoulishly destroyed by this mindless terror; the attendant economic disaster is still with Uganda, compounding her political instability. Even more sobering is the continuing horror of daily existence, the brutalisation of normal sensibilities which is apparent in the conduct of the ongoing resistance to Milton Obote's rule and in the government's pattern of repression on sections of the populace. What is being claimed here, in effect, is that the longer a people are subjected to the brutality of power, the longer, in geometric proportion, is the process of recovery and re-humanisation.

Byron Kadadwa to whom this play is dedicated is representative of the many thousands whose contribution to the nation of their birth was brutally cut short by Idi Amin. He led his theatre troupe to the Festival of Black and African Arts (FESTAC) in Nigeria, 1977. Shortly after his return to Kampala, he was arrested – for reasons which are ultimately unimportant, dragged from rehearsals by the notorious State Research Bureau and later found murdered. His successor, Dan Kintu, met a similar fate, together with playwright John Male. The relations of all three had to pay substantial bribes to the police before their bodies were even released for burial. Need one add the footnote that, following these warnings, the rest of the troupe fled into neighbouring countries?

Now why does one say that the 'reasons' for Byron Kadadwa's arrest are ultimately of no importance? That the reasons why any one of the missing thousands came to the 'notice' of Idi Amin at all did not really matter? Only because this was the reality, as testified to by Ugandans themselves, including one of the most notable survivors, the late Robert Serumaga. Robert was, to start with, one of the most ardent supporters of Idi Amin. It is no exaggeration to say that he actually prospered under his regime. Shortly after Amin's seizure of power, we met in a European capital where we café-crawled one night till nearly dawn, while he bombarded me with arguments (buttressed by Ministry of Information tracts), in favour of the coup. I was equally adamant in my negative view which was based on my knowledge of Idi Amin's history as a cold-blooded killer and my partiality (then) to Milton Obote who appeared to be embracing the socialist creed just before the coup. Serumaga's faith in Idi Amin was based on a genuine assessment, by him, of Idi Amin's leadership qualities and what he saw as a relaxing of constraints on individual liberty imposed by Obote. The 'excesses' which, even then, were already gaining publicity, he defended as genuine accidents which Idi Amin himself regretted and deplored. Over-enthusiastic subordinates were, in Serumaga's view, mostly to blame.

Robert Serumaga was then a member of the editorial board of *Ch'Indaba* (formerly *Transition*), whose editorship I had recently assumed. So convinced was I of what Robert refused to accept that I took the precaution, not merely of removing him from the editorial board, but of writing him a formal letter to that effect. I quoted his glowing statements of support for Idi Amin, commenting that these were incompatible with *Ch'Indaba*'s editorial position, and wished him luck.

My next meeting with Serumaga took place about two years later at Victoria Station where he had gone to see off his theatre company on their way to Gatwick Airport and home. They were just returning from a tour of the Soviet Union. I plunged straight into the apology which I had rehearsed for our next face-to-face encounter, explaining the brusqueness of my letter as a deliberate insurance for his own life which I knew would be endangered, sooner or later, like all others. Robert cut me short by confirming the worst.

He was convinced that the letter had indeed enabled him to survive. It had been intercepted and, first the Head of Amin's Security Service, then Idi Amin himself, summoned him to discuss its contents. Our Hero even tried to persuade Robert to try and recover his position on the journal where he could keep an eye (and perhaps some control) on our activities which, I was informed by the then Head of Ghanaian Security, had already come to the attention of Idi Amin. (He had sent a protest through his ambassador about the Union's use of Ghana as a base for 'subversive' activities against his government.) Serumaga said, 'I told him, sir, but you see what is in the letter. The man has sacked me; he didn't simply ask for my resignation, I've been given the boot.' The incident assisted Robert in remaining secure in Idi Amin's trust for a long while, compared to others who never even served on the editorial board of *Ch'Indaba* or contributed to its activities. But inevitably, even Robert discovered that he was living on borrowed time. He was seeing off his troupe but had decided to remain behind to look for an apartment in London. Then a quick trip home to evacuate his wife, family and immediate dependants, after which – self-exile. Robert's explanation for this reluctant decision was simple but chilling; it has not been possible for me to forget the very words he used:

'At the start,' he said, 'you more or less knew what to do and what to avoid if you wanted to stay alive. You knew when to speak, when to shut up and what to say or not say. Now there are no longer any rules. What saved you yesterday turns out to be your death-warrant today. I have no friends, no colleagues left. They are all dead, or escaped. But mostly dead.'

Robert Serumaga later joined the Liberation movement against Idi Amin, broadcasting from Tanzania during the struggle. Those same intellectuals we have spoken of began to raise the academic issues of the role of the Tanzanian Army in that war. They had

9

found Idi Amin's prior bombings and incursion into Tanzanian territory, boastfully publicised in the familiar Aminian cacophony, mainly amusing, certainly no worse than 'naughty'. But now Tanzania mobilised itself, counter-attacked, and those same cheer-leaders suddenly recalled issues of 'territorial integrity', 'external interference', etc., etc., as the Tanzanian Army, motivated in the way Idi Amin's could never be, swept the latter aside in a record time for any military disintegration in recent times.

Robert Serumaga died of illness. He had at least the satisfaction of participating in the successful end to a repellent dictatorship. I do not know if, were he still alive today, he would consider Uganda truly liberated – that is a question which a Ugandan playwright will, I hope, he moved to tackle before long. For now . . . (*Enter brass band, ringmaster, up platforms, hoops, and trampolines.*) . . . 'Ladies and gentleman, we present . . . a parade of miracle men . . . (*Cracks whip.*) . . . Giants, Dwarfs, Zombies, the Incredible Anthropophagi, the Original Genus Survivanticus, (alive and well in defiance of all scientific explanations) . . . ladies and gentlemen . . .'

WOLE SOYINKA, 1984

CHARACTERS

BENEFACIO GUNEMA
EMPEROR KASCO
FIELD-MARSHAL KAMINI
GENERAL BARRA TUBOUM

} *African heads of state*

GUDRUM, *a Scandinavian journalist*
CHAIRMAN OF THE BUGARA CENTRAL BANK
SCULPTOR
BUGARAN AMBASSADOR
MAYOR OF HYACOMBE
PROFESSOR BATEY
TWO RUSSIAN DELEGATES
TWO AMERICAN DELEGATES
TASK FORCE SPECIALS
GUARDS
SECRETARY-GENERAL OF THE UNITED NATIONS

The action takes place at the Bugaran Embassy to the United Nations, New York. The time is a few years before the present.

PART ONE

*Three figures are seated in heavy throne-like chairs at the top of a
wide, sweeping stone stairway. Behind them runs a curving
gallery, with framed portraits, really the balcony of the upper
floor, windows overlooking a park, across which is a skyscraper,
the UN building, in silhouette. The balcony railing is opulently
gold-gilt. One of the figures, a huge man (KAMINI) is in military
dress uniform, its massive frontage covered in medals. On one
side of him is a comparatively dwarfish creature (KASCO) who
appears to be a deliberate parody of the big man. His costume is
the same, down to the last medal. In addition, however, he wears
a cloak of imperial purple. Flanking the central figure on the
other side is a tall, thin man (GUNEMA) in tails of immaculate cut.
His own decorations consist simply of a red sash and blue rosette,
plus a medal to two.*

GUDRUM, *a stout, florid and rather repulsive Nordic type sits half-
way up the steps, gazing in obvious adoration at* KAMINI. *From
time to time she inspects the* SCULPTOR's *labour.*

*The ground floor is a lounge which has been turned into a studio.
A* SCULPTOR *is working at a life-size group sculpture of the three
'crowned heads', on which any likeness is hardly yet apparent.
When the sitters speak, they do so stiffly, in an effort to retain
their poses. But first the tableau is revealed in silence, the*
SCULPTOR *adding putty here and there or scraping away.*

GUNEMA. Ah, *el poder, amigos*, to seek the truth of the matter,
these subversives, *guerrilleros*, they do not really seek to rule,
no, not to administer a space, not to govern a *pueblo,
comprendo?* No, mostly they seek power. Simply power.

KASCO. But that is obvious, no? It is not the lust for responsibility
which makes the social misfits to become guerrillas. If you
think first of responsibility and governing, you give up search

for power. Lust for power, *oui*. But lust for responsibility – I never hear of it.

GUNEMA. Ah, but I have not finished. Beyond *la responsabilidad*, beyond politics lies – ah – power. When politics has become routine, organised, we who are gifted naturally with leadership, after a while, we cease to govern, to lead: we exist, I think, in a rare space which is – power.
Es verdad, no?

KAMINI. Only one thing to do to subversive – khrr! (*A meaningful gesture across his throat.*) I used to have subversives too. The Western press like to call them guerrillas. I say, I have no guerrillas in my country. Only bandits. We call them *kondo*. I catch any *kondo*, I make him smell his mother's cunt.

GUDRUM. I know all about subversives. My over-permissive country is full of them, hiding from their failure to cope with reality. Unfortunately we Scandinavians still take a spurious pride in our so-called liberal ideas, open our doors to all sorts of ne'er-do-wells from the Third World who ought to be in their countries, contributing something to development. As a journalist I get to meet many of them. Effete youngsters who hang around the cafés and wine-bars and disco joints, useless to themselves and to their nation.

KAMINI. Gudrum very good friend of African leaders. She writing book about me with many photographs. She calling it *The Black Giant at Play*. It show Kamini very very jovial family man. Big uncle to everybody in country.

GUDRUM. It would be finished by now if I didn't have to take time dealing with the slander spread by those Bugaran runaways in my country. They spread the most disgusting libel against the Field-Marshal. They are poufs, most of them. Faggots.

GUNEMA. What mean poufs? Or faggots.

GUDRUM. Cissy. Homosexuals. They don't know what it is to be a man. They are terrified of virility.

KAMINI (*laughing*). Gudrum, I think you tell me, they even run away from real woman. Like you.

GUDRUM. Of course Your Excellency. They have become part of the culture of drug dependency. A continent of the future, which Africa is, does not need their type. They would only contaminate its soul, its history. You have your heroes, Excellency, nation-builders. Today, we are lucky to have in you their reincarnation. Those statues my Life President – a very brilliant idea. It will serve to prick the conscience of the United Nations.

KAMINI. You very good lady Gudrum. Just remember to give names of these subversives. Even if they refuse to come home, we find their villages. Only one treatment good for family which support guerrillas hiding in Scandinavia and other American-type countries.

GUNEMA. *Si.* For my country also. But sometimes I look at country like Italy. Red Brigade. Or Germany. Or these new people, the Armenian Brigade who assassinate and bomb airport no matter where. I do not think they seek government. Because why? Because they already enjoy power. Secret power. They strike, hold hostage, bomb office, kill person they do not know before, total stranger – is that kind of power I talk about. I think that kind, he only seek to redress history, not take government. But he enjoy secret power.

KAMINI. All subversives bad people. Mostly imperialist agents. Better you kill them first.

GUNEMA. Of course, of course. Very definitely. I am not sentimental, no.

KASCO. Sentiment? No. Was Saint-Just sentimental?

KAMINI. Saint-Just? Who was Saint-Just?

KASCO. Executioner of the French Revolution. He take care of Danton – guillotine. Saint-Just was a soul-brother to the immortal Robespierre. But they all make mistake. Too many people drink this power. Every riff-raff from *poubelle* – the sans-cullottes, Girondists, Jacobins, Montagnards, bakers, tavern-keepers, even forgers and convicts. Opportunists. That is what destroy Robespierre. Power was debased. Power is indivisible.

GUNEMA. Is why I like voodoo. That also secret power. *Misterioso, pero amigo, también – muy peligroso.* For those who are not chosen, very dangerous. Is not suddenly that it manifest itself, like Red Brigades. All of them very sudden, like ejaculation. Voodoo power is tranquil, *extendido*, like you making love to woman you really love or possess. You dominate her but still you make the love prolong, not to body alone but to her soul.

KAMINI. Ah, now I understand. Before you talk like all those my Bugara professors. When they want to think subversive, they talk in that way to make confusion. But the woman matter, oh yes, Kamini in full agreement. That is why is good a leader should have many wives.

The door opens gently and a face peeks round.

CHAIRMAN. May I come in Your Excellency?

KAMINI. Who? Ah come in, come in. Why you take so long Mr Chairman? (*He turns to his companions.*) You excuse me while I talk some business. Is my chairman of Bugara Central Bank. When I travel, I take Bank of Bugara with me, then nobody can steal money behind Kamini's back. Too many *kondo* wearing European coat and tie and forging signature of this and that bank manager. When Kamini not home, only chairman can sign cheque, and he here with Kamini. (*He guffaws.*)

KASCO. *C'est sage, mon vieux.*

KAMINI. So what happen? How much loan they give us?

CHAIRMAN. Your Excellency, it was a difficult meeting. The World Bank was not very cooperative.

KAMINI. They don't give loan?

CHAIRMAN. Not exactly, Your Excellency. They simply insisted on certain conditions . . .

KAMINI. What I care about conditions? Agree to any conditions, just get the loan.

CHAIRMAN. It is not quite so easy as all that Your Excellency. They want to mortgage Bugara body and soul . . .

KAMINI. I say what I care about body and soul? If they can loan Bugara the two hundred million dollars, I give them body and soul. Go back and agree to any condition they want.

CHAIRMAN. There is more to it, Your Excellency. They don't even want to hand over the money directly. In fact, the Board dismissed that request outright. There was no discussion.

KAMINI. What they mean by that? You not tell them Bank of Bugara is here with President in person?

CHAIRMAN. Your Excellency may rest assured that I explained the position very thoroughly. But their decision is that they would only fund specific projects with the loan.

KAMINI (*flaring up*). So they can come and send their stinking spies into Bugara saying they come to supervise loan project? No deal. Kamini wise to their game of infiltrating Third World country with their syphilitic spies. Go back and tell them either they loan ready cash direct, or I take over all remaining foreign business in Bugara. Any member country of World Bank with business in Bugara, we nationalise.

CHAIRMAN. Your Excellency, I did outline that possibility to them. I left them in no uncertainty of such a consequence.

KAMINI. And still they say no?

CHAIRMAN. I'm afraid so Excellency. (KAMINI *falls silent, chewing his lips.*)

GUDRUM. It's a plot my Life President. It is part of their deliberate economic sabotage.

KAMINI. I know. Is dirty capitalist plot all over. World Bank belong to everybody. Why they are discriminating against

Bugara alone? Why they give Hazena loan? You tell me Hazena still owe them more money than Bugara, not so?

CHAIRMAN. That is a fact Your Excellency. I pointed it out to them.

KAMINI. Aha! So what they say? What they say to that enh?

CHAIRMAN. They replied that Hazena had been paying interest regularly Your Excellency.

KAMINI (*angrily*). What I care about rotten interest? Bugara promised to pay everything all at once, in five years. So what I care about stupid interest enh? Taking interest and taking interest and finishing up all Bugara foreign exchange.

GUDRUM. Bugara has more than contributed its quota to the World Bank, that is a fact, Your Excellency. When the economy was buoyant Bugara never missed a payment.

KAMINI. Is what am saying and is all discrimination and dirty imperialist plot. I make complaint to Secretary-General today and raise matter in General Assembly. Let World Bank tell us once for all if it is just for rich countries and neo-colonial bastards like Hazena or it belong to Third World countries who need loan. As for you, get back to Bugara right away and start printing more Bugara bank notes. I show the bastards at least they can't control Bugara sovereign currency.

CHAIRMAN (*aghast*). I beg your pardon Dr Life President?

KAMINI. I said go back and get cracking with government mint. When I return I want to see brand-new currency notes in circulation, not hearing all this grumble of shortage of money and so on and so forth.

CHAIRMAN. But Your Excellency, that's why we came to seek this loan in the first place. Now that we haven't got it, there is nothing to back the new currency with.

KAMINI. What the man talking about? You short of good currency paper at government mint?

CHAIRMAN. I'm trying to explain, Your Excellency. Even now, at

this moment, our national currency is not worth its size in toilet
paper. If we now go ahead and print more, it would . . .

KAMINI. What? What you say just now?

CHAIRMAN. Your Excellency?

KAMINI. I say, what you talking just now about Bugara currency?

CHAIRMAN. Just that all currency needs backing Your Excellency.
It must be . . .

KAMINI. No, you said Bugara currency only worth something this
and that.

CHAIRMAN. Oh. I was trying to explain that any paper money is
only worth what . . . (*He trails off.*)

KAMINI (*rising*). You saying Bugara currency only worth shit
paper? Is that what I hear you say just now? Is that what I hear
you say just now?

CHAIRMAN. Your Excellency, I was only trying to illustrate . . .

KAMINI (*to* KASCO *and* GUNEMA). You see, is this kind of traitor I
have in charge of Bugara Central Bank. This syphilitic bastard
talking worse than imperialist propaganda.

CHAIRMAN. Your Excellency . . .

KAMINI. Is no wonder Bugara getting broke all the time, when this
kind of chairman insulting Bugara national currency, calling it
shit paper to everybody. This the kind of person going to
important meeting of World Bank to ask for loan. You think
World Bank give Bugara loan when you calling national
currency shit paper?

CHAIRMAN (*falling on his knees*). My Life President, I assure Your
Excellency I never . . .

KAMINI. Today I make you eat good old Bugara shit. (*He reaches
for the bell.*)

CHAIRMAN (*abject with terror*). Your Excellency, my Life President . . .

KAMINI. Taking around with me sneaking traitors left and right
talking bad about Bugara. Today I make you smell your
mother's cunt . . .

Enter a TASK FORCE SPECIAL.

TF SPECIAL. Your Excellency?

KAMINI. Take this coat-and-tie *kondo* inside that toilet room there and put his head inside bowl. (TF SPECIAL *proceeds upstairs.*) Each time the tank full, you flush it again over his head.

> TF SPECIAL *hauls up the pleading* CHAIRMAN *by the shoulders and shoves him towards a door leading from the balcony.* KAMINI *follows, he stands just outside the doorway giving instructions as the* CHAIRMAN, *struggling, is forced to his knees.*

Push his head deep inside. I say deep inside. Put your bloody foot on his neck and press it down. (*Sounds of gurgling.*) That's better. Now pull chain. (*Noise of rushing water follows.* KAMINI *beams broadly.*) Good. Call Bugara currency shit money, not so? So you drink some shit water for now until Kamini ready for you. (*Returning to his seat.*) You leave door open so I can hear water flushing his stinking mouth.

> *From now on until towards the end of the play, the sound of the emptying cistern will be heard, periodically.* KAMINI *resumes his seat. He turns to his companions.*

I'm sorry my brothers. I hope you excuse that little interruption while I taking care of business.

KASCO. *Mais pas de quoi, mon frère.*

GUNEMA. *Si, comprendido.* Discipline must be imposed.

KAMINI. Is no wonder he fail to get the loan. He already go there with bad attitude of mind to subvert Bugara economy. Now if I go and complain that World Bank refuse Bugara loan, they will just tell me, your chairman of Central Bank already admit your currency is shit money and so on and so forth.

GUDRUM. We could send the Minister of Finance next, my Life President.

KAMINI. Yes, but I wait now until my statue goes up in the United

Nations. When everybody see it standing there I think it give the World Bank something to think about. Is they who will come this time and beg me to talk business all over again.

The AMBASSADOR *enters, opening the door with the greatest deference and speaking almost apologetically.*

AMBASSADOR. Your Gracious Excellency, I think I have found the right spot to display the sculpture.

KAMINI. Yes?

AMBASSADOR. I think not only Your Gracious Excellency, but your comrade Presidents, their Excellencies, will be pleased. The position is not too dissimilar to this present one. It is the top of the stairs dominating the passage which all delegates must pass through on leaving the General Assembly for the committee and public reception rooms. Vistors who come to consult the delegates cannot fail to see your Excellencies' commanding figures.

KAMINI turns to his companions one after the other. KASCO *responds with a wide grin of approval and a nod.* GUNEMA *slightly inclines his head.* KAMINI *resumes his pose.*

KAMINI. My brothers approve. See that the Secretary-General is informed. The protocol officer will see me to arrange the unveiling ceremony. Gudrum, you will give him advice? I think you have informed the world press.

GUDRUM. Of course Dr President. I am looking forward to the historic moment. In fact, maybe I ought to go and inspect the location myself.

KAMINI. Very good idea. Go with Ambassador and bring me report.

The AMBASSADOR *bows and leaves, accompanied by* GUDRUM. *Again a brief period of silence as the* SCULPTOR *continues his work, the trio having resumed their stiff postures.*

I like the Secretary-General. He's a nice man.

KASCO *grins and nods.*

GUNEMA. *Si. Pero,* him *niño.* Baby. No, him like child, *pequeño.*
Not understand power. Not use power. Good man, *si, muy
simpatico pero,* not man of power.

KAMINI. It is good like that. He is to carry out our orders. We
come here to give him orders. We have the power, not him.

KASCO. *Oui, oui. Le pouvoir, c'est à nous.*

KAMINI. What?

KASCO. Power, is we. We have ze power.

KAMINI. Is good like that.

Some moments silence. Suddenly GUNEMA *sighs.*

GUNEMA. Sometimes I dream . . . *El Caudillo.*

The others turn to him puzzled.

El Caudillo, General Franco. Yes, Franco I think he make
better Secretary-General. Is good for world peace. Spain very
peaceful for forty years. Now everybody make trouble.

KAMINI. Franco? Was he not friend of Zionists?

GUNEMA. *El Caudillo?* No no no. If General Franco Secretary-
General, first he finish off the Zionists.

KAMINI *nods approval.*

KASCO. What you think of Papa? I think he makes good
Secrétaire-General.

GUNEMA. Papa Doc? Papa Doc Duvalier? Si, he is man of power
but er . . .

KASCO. No, Papa de Gaulle, the saviour of modern France. He
was like a Papa to my people. I wept when he died.

GUNEMA. I think first you meant the strong man of Haiti. Now
that was *un hombre!* The power! *Misterioso.* He was Franco of

the Caribbean. But I don't think he make good *Secretario*, oh no!

KAMINI. Why?

GUNEMA. Voodoo. Too much voodoo. It give him power, plenty power. He will put voodoo over all the delegates and make them zombie.

KAMINI. Even you my brother? Oh you are making joke. Everybody knows you are a man of voodoo yourself.

GUNEMA. Not like Papa Doc. He was *maestro. El uno, y unico.* He turn nearly half of Haiti into zombie and the rest – (*He makes a slashing gesture across his throat.*) he send his Ton Ton Macoutes. Even the Ton Ton are zombie. Papa Doc can give them order from anywhere. He can be one end of island and *think* to them – do this or do that. And they do it. Distance no importance. Now that is power. But too much for *Secretario. Muy peligroso.*

KAMINI. You think Papa Doc can put voodoo on somebody like me?

GUNEMA. Impossible! *Jamás*, never! My friend, you are not *un hombre ordinario.* Like me and our *camarade* the Emperor Kasco, we are not *ordinario.* Why you think we rule our people? Some people are born to power. Others are – cattle. They need ring in their nose for us to lead.

KASCO. *Oui oui.* There are persons, individuals who are born with the imperial sign here (*He taps his forehead.*) on head. Me, I think – de Gaulle. Robespierre. But the prime, the leader of them all in history, in all the world history – the *sans pareil* of all time is Napoleon Bonaparte!

GUNEMA. No, is Franco.

KASCO. Franco is like midget in history when you compare with Bonaparte. Franco! Franco was – he did not even have a presence. No command in personality.

GUNEMA. Is Franco, is Franco. You do not know history, you only know French.

KASCO. My friend, to know French is to understand history. In Napoleon Bonaparte you have the entire history of modern Europe and its civilisation ... even North Africa entered history with Napoleon.

KAMINI. My brothers, what are we fighting about? What about our very own brother, Chaka? For me, Chaka is greatest. Only Hitler can compare to Chaka. Even then, if Chaka had aeroplanes and flying bomb, he would have conquered Hitler. I know, because I am descended from the great Chaka.

> KASCO *and* GUNEMA *turn to look at him, then at each other.* KASCO *gives an embarrassed cough while* GUNEMA *lifts a cynical eyebrow.*

GUNEMA. Of course *amigo.* If you are not descended from the great Zulu, who is?

KAMINI. The history department of my university trace my family tree for me. They announce it in the newspapers and give lecture on television. It make my people very happy.

KASCO. *Naturellement!*

KAMINI. Even our lives are very similar. I too, I kill my first lion at seven years old, with a spear. It is part of our tradition. The test of manhood. At thirteen years, the young boy must go into the bush, all by himself. He takes a spear and a *panga* – cutlass you know – and he lives in the bush until he can come home with a kill. For other people it is always a small antelope, or a baby water-buck. Me, after five days, I track down a lion and kill it.

KASCO. But my brother, you said you did this at seven years!

KAMINI. Yes, at seven. Others thirteen, but me, I could not wait. Like Chaka, I could not wait.

The door begins to open, very gingerly. Again the AMBASSA-*DOR's head appears, this time naked fear showing on her face. She looks steadfastly at* KAMINI, *then withdraws without shutting the door. Seconds pass, then the door is pushed firmly open.* GUDRUM *enters first, then beckons and more or less drags in the* AMBASSADOR. *She musters some measure of resignation which does not disguise the very real terror beneath. She coughs to attract* KAMINI's *attention.*

AMBASSADOR. Your Gracious Excellency . . .

KAMINI. What is it? Why do you continue to disturb?

AMBASSADOR. They've gone, Your Excellency. The rest of the delegation, they've gone.

KAMINI *sits bolt upright, grasping the arms of the chair.*

KAMINI. What did you say?

GUDRUM. Some more traitors have shown their true faces, Your Excellency.

AMBASSADOR. They left straight after the working session of the Foreign Ministers' Committee. The Foreign Affairs Minister, his secretary, the two specialists on the Palestinian and South African problems – Dr Wamue and Mrs Olanga, and that new . . .

KAMINI. My speech! What happen to speech he prepare for me to address General Assembly tomorrow. He suppose to read it to me over lunch.

AMBASSADOR. I shall assign it immediately to the Third Secretary, your Gracious Excellency.

KAMINI. The Third Secretary. The Third Secretary to write address of Bugara's Life President which he make to United Nations?

GUDRUM. Actually he is very bright, Dr President. A young graduate but very bright.

KAMINI. The Third Secretary! You, Madame Ambassador, you have been mistake in appointment. Why can you not write the address? Why? Because you are ignorant! If I have no expert why are you ambassador if you are not expert? Why can you not represent my opinion and put it correctly if I am not here.

GUDRUM. Of course she can Your Excellency. I could lend a hand too if Your Excellency wishes. But this young graduate has studied all the Life President's speeches at the university. He did his doctorate on the very subject. I have read some of the briefings he prepared for the delegation.

KAMINI (*relaxing somewhat*). Is that so? I know that my political philosophy and so on are studied in the university but I did not know that somebody has been getting doctorate degree from them. Did he get this doctorate from our own Bugara University?

AMBASSADOR (*eagerly*). Certainly Your Excellency. And he has given many public lectures on the subject since he took up position here.

KAMINI. Very good, very good. But where is the First Secretary?

AMBASSADOR. That position has been vacant for two years Your Excellency, same thing for the Second Secretary. If Your Excellency will be kind enough to recall the several memos I sent to the Minister of Foreign Affairs on the subject, copied to Your Excellency . . .

KAMINI. All right. What is the young man's name?

AMBASSADOR. Seli Metatu, Your Excellency.

KAMINI. Promote him First Secretary and tell him to get on with my speech. Still, I don't like idea of Third Secretary writing speech for a Life President. Promote him today.

AMBASSADOR. But, if er . . . if I may make bold to remind Your Excellency, the reason why the post of First and Second Secretaries, plus that of Commercial Attaché have been vacant is that, well, according to the Foreign Affairs Minister, there are no funds to pay anyone in those grades.

KAMINI (*screams*). I remember very well. I do not forget. And is that not the same minister who has now run away in the middle of his international mission? Why did he run away? Why do they all run away? Because they steal Bugara money, that's why. They smuggle goods and do black market, ruining Bugara currency! You tell me, why that traitor, the one who calls himself professor, why he run away instead of leading my team

of delegation to this meeting here? He embezzle money and he
suspect that Kamini find out. He know I want to disgrace him
before his international friends at the United Nations Assembly
– a common thief like that. With all his grey hairs he is so
shameless. So everybody thinking him a great scholarship man,
a brilliant man and so on and so forth. A brilliant man to be
embezzling money and running away. Thank you very much
for brilliance, I take stupid man any day. I promote that young
man, today. When he come back to Bugara, see that he go to
university and make him professor. But if he try to be brilliant
like Kiwawa, he will smell his mother's cunt before he can run
away. Now I find new Foreign Minister who will find money
and pay salaries instead of running away with Bugara money.
Perhaps I make you the Foreign Minister, you are useless as
ambassador when you cannot write my speech in emergency.

AMBASSADOR. Your Gracious Excellency's orders will be carried
out.

KAMINI. How did they get away? I want the names of my Task
Force Specials who are watching their movement hand and
foot. How did all of them escape without being followed? I tell
them to watch carefully even when they go toilet to shit.

AMBASSADOR. I have already set up an inquiry Your Excellency.
They must have planned it very carefully. They pretended they
were still holding their meeting in the committee room but in
fact they had all escaped through the lavatory window. It
opened into a passage used only by the cleaners in the building.
The Presidential Task Force guards kept waiting at the door for
over an hour before . . .

KAMINI. What fools! Did they not notice that they can no longer
hear anything? Did they think the delegation was sleeping or
what?

AMBASSADOR. Your Gracious Excellency, they were clever. They
left on a tape recorder of conversations which must have kept
running for an hour or more.

KAMINI. You see. Is it not a disgrace? A whole minister of state, he is playing tricks like 007 James Bond in order to run away with national funds. That is the kind of ministers left in Bugara. James Bond. That is what result from imperialism and neo-colonialism and the culture they teach our people. Syphilitic culture. Mental syphilis. How you explain a thing like this? An educated man, a cabinet minister playing like James Bond in the United Nations.

AMBASSADOR. Your Excellency, if I may . . .

KAMINI. Don't interrupt. You are not a good ambassador or this would not happen under your nose. Have you telexed Bugara for the Task Force to go to these people's villages?

AMBASSADOR. Your Gracious Excellency, I was about to suggest that I run over to a friendly embassy and use their telex.

KAMINI. Why a friendly embassy? Why not our own telex?

AMBASSADOR. It was cut off months ago, Your Excellency. We . . . could not pay . . . we had no funds to settle our bills. (*Speaking more hurriedly.*) The Foreign Minister was aware of . . .

KAMINI. The Foreign Minister! I do not want to hear the name of those traitors – any of them. Just get a message any way you like to my Presidential Task Force Specials and dispatch them to their villages. You have already lost precious time Madame Ambassador. And report the matter to the Secretary-General of the United Nations. Let him know what bad things his people have done to me.

AMBASSADOR. I will attend to it Your Excellency. (*She hurries out followed by* GUDRUM.)

KASCO. *Mes condolences, camarade.* But these are the tiny thorns that trouble the head of crown.

GUNEMA. *Si. Que lástima.* But, it is nothing. Traitors breed like maggots, no? They are rotten to the bone, to the tissue inside the bone. Their souls fester with corruption. They infect others.

KASCO. I see you send to the village. That is good. The root may have poisoned the surrounding soil.

GUNEMA. My subjects, they are very careful how they plot against Benefacio Gunema. When I look at each one of my ministers, or army officer, he knows I am looking into the heart, into the very soul of his village. He know that I see through his head into the head of his wife, his children, his father and mother and grandfather and uncles and all his dependents, all his kith and kin, living or dead . . . yes, including the dead ones. It is he who must choose whether they lie in peace in their graves because, *la culpabilidad* the – er – guilt, it extends beyond the grave.

KAMINI (*still agitated*). I think it is difficult now to sit and pose for artist. We take a break now and fill the stomachs a bit, what do you say?

KASCO. *Oui, d'accord.*

GUNEMA. Agree. My bottom of spine is beginning to feel mighty cramp.

KAMINI. Good. My good friend Mr Sculptor, we take break now. You too, I think, you take break. All work and no play . . . not so? When my ambassador lady comes, you tell her I say she give you taxi money because I like you.

SCULPTOR. Oh there will be no need for that Your Excellency. I get paid all my expenses.

KAMINI. What is the matter? You don't like me? You don't take my money?

SCULPTOR (*hurriedly*). No Your Excellency, on the contrary . . .

KAMINI. Maybe you don't like American dollars. Bugara money good enough for you? (*He takes out thick wads of notes and thrusts them at the* SCULPTOR.) There. Good Bugaran currency.

SCULPTOR. Mr President sir . . .

KAMINI. Dr President.

SCULPTOR. Your Excellency, Dr President is most generous.

The door is flung wide open by the AMBASSADOR *who ushers in a visitor.*

AMBASSADOR. Your Excellencies, His Excellency the Life President of Nbangi-Guela.

Enter LIFE PRESIDENT BARRA TUBOUM. *He is dressed in a striped animal skin 'Mao' outfit with matching fez-style hat. He sports an ornately carved ebony walking stick. At his waist is strapped an ivory-handled side-arm stuck in a holster which is also made of zebra skin.* KAMINI *rushes at him, arms outstretched. The other two follow more slowly.*

KAMINI. Alexander! Welcome, welcome.

TUBOUM *stops short, seems to recoil.*

TUBOUM. Tuboum, my brother, Barra Tuboum.
KAMINI. Barra Tuboum?
TUBOUM. Barra Boum Boum Tuboum Gbazo Tse Tse Khoro diDzo. I have abandoned all foreign names.
KAMINI. My brother, I congratulate you.

They embrace.

TUBOUM. You did not hear about it? I have begun a vigorous campaign to eliminate all foreign influences from our people. I took the lead and changed my own names. Even the names of my father's headstones, I changed. All names on our cemeteries will be changed.

The others applaud mildly and embrace, French-style.

GUNEMA. Alexander was an African. You must study your history. It has been proved conclusively that he was African.
KASCO. But surely the name . . .
GUNEMA. African to the core. But, it does not matter. The rebellion is what I want to hear about. Is it finish?
TUBOUM. You see me here, do you not? Of course it is finished.

Crushed. All the ring leaders? -- Tsch! (*He makes expressive gesture.*) Except three. I brought them with me to exhibit before the General Assembly. They have confessed that some foreign powers were behind the rebellion. After public confession, perhaps we serve them up at cocktail party.

GUNEMA. *Hijos de puta!*

KASCO. Imperialist swine!

KAMINI (*leads with the general back-slapping*). I congratulate you my brother. I congratulate you again.

KASCO. Bravo! You have served good lesson on our enemies.

GUNEMA. I still wish you do not change name. After this, everybody will have call you Alexander the Great. Who will remember name of Barra Tuboum?

TUBOUM. Oh yes they will. After this victory it is a name no one will ever forget. I led my forces in person, the famed striped leopards of Mbangi-Gwela.

GUNEMA. Ah yes, *amigo*, I always mean to ask, a striped leopard, is a real animal? It really exists?

TUBOUM. A chimera perhaps. A phantom, a sphinx. But it is a fearsome part of our lore, a mystery creature which stalks at night. Nobody see it and returns to tell the tale. Yet the tale is there, terrifying. My elite troops must be fearless and mysterious. Do they exist? They appear. They complete their task, they vanish – back to their camp at Lake Gwanza. They do not mix with the populace. In action they eat with their leader, the only being whose orders they understand. They know they are the elite, they bathe in the same ambiance of power, terribly invincible. They train in secret, far from the prying eyes of the common herd. Their secrecy is their power, like the hair of Samson; the eyes of any stranger at the mysteries of their self-preparation is a corrosion of that power. They kill such strangers, and they eat them.

KASCO. Eat them!

TUBOUM. Eat them – white, black or yellow. Is it not the only way to ensure the re-absorption of that power of yourself which has been sucked away by profaning eyes? Oh they are as fearsome as they are fearless, my striped leopards of Gwanza. The rebels were desperate too, the tribe of Shabira, mean, cruel, unscrupulous. What is the Geneva Convention to them? They took hostages, workers at the mines of Shabira, their families, priests, nuns, children, foreigners and citizens alike. Our allies the French paratroops arrived. What to do about the hostages? Nothing. The Belgian commanders had no qualms – the eggs must be broken before the omelette. Rebellion is a cancer, worse than death, worse than rape or mutilation. Rebellion is an enemy of growth. Better the loss of a few children than the poisoning of their growth by the horror of rebellion. The Belgians asked no questions, they took orders and filled in the gaps. My leopards were mean and taut. I propelled them like a fine-honed shaft along River Butelewa. We swept down on the rebel stronghold at dawn; they were sated from plunder and rape but for all that, fierce and savage. The hostages? What does a violated nun hope for? Many fell before our own bullets, the rebels had turned coward, hiding behind the very habits they had defiled. We moved from street to street, from square to square. They retreated. We followed. They moved into their last redoubt, a fortified hill, riddled with bunkers, oh, they had been a long time preparing this rebellion. In their confusion they no longer could be certain who was friend or foe. We pinpointed them by their own voice: '*Qui va là?*' a voice would cry, and my canons responded: 'Boom, Boom Tuboum'. '*Qui va là?*' again and again. 'Boom, Boom Tuboum. Boom, Boom Tuboum.' Till at last, covered in masonry and blood, they began the surrender.

KAMINI. Ah yes? You take many prisoners?

TUBOUM. Only a handful, enough for the celebration feast of my striped leopards. The rest, had they not committed murder and rape? We did not even give them a soldier's death. We hanged them, and left them hanging.

> *One by one they go up to* TUBOUM, *embrace him and kiss him formally on both cheeks.*

KASCO. *C'est vraiment héroïque. Félicitations!*

GUNEMA. I envy you *amigo*. A brave man, a leader of enormous courage.

KAMINI (*grips him by the shoulders*). As you speak, I wish I am there by your side. A man comes to life, in middle of battle, not so? He feel power beating through his blood, like madness.

GUNEMA. I envy you three, *amigos*. Warriors. You take power through army. You fight. You conquer. It is different for me. I feel like odd man out. Power is something I must experience another way, a very different way. Your method is straight-forward, it has a clarity, *muy hermoso*, mathematical. I inhabit, I think, the nebulous geography of power. That is why, always, I am searching to taste it. You understand, really taste it on my tongue. To seize it *a la boca*, roll and roll it in the mouth and let it trickle inwards, like an infusion. Once, only once, I think I succeed.

KASCO. Courage does not come only in war, *mon ami*. In matter of courage, it is clear you are *pareil* with all of us. I fight for the French wars in Indo-China, but on the battlefield, an enemy is just an enemy. We fight, we kill, or we die. I have been thinking, what you say before, I agree with you. Power comes only with the death of politics. That is why I choose to become emperor. I place myself beyond politics. At the moment of my coronation, I signal to the world that I transcend the intrigues and mundaneness of politics. Now I inhabit only the pure realm of power. I fear, *mes amis*, all three of you have chosen to remain in the territory of politics. But – is it choice? Or are you trapped?

KAMINI (*shakes his head in bewilderment*). Lunch my brothers, lunch! Are we hungry or not?

The door is flung open again and the AMBASSADOR *announces:*

AMBASSADOR. Your Excellencies, the Honourable Mayor of Hyacombe and his party!

Preceded by a beadle (PROFESSOR BATEY) *who carries a golden key on a red velvet cushion, the* MAYOR *enters in full regalia, chain and all. He makes a low bow, sweeping the floor with his hat, and suddenly freezes. He comes up very slowly, his eyes popping.* GUDRUM *squeezes her way past them.*

MAYOR. Your Gracious Excellency, we did not know that you had guests. I mean . . . and such guests. Your Excellencies! The entire continent of Africa is here!

KAMINI. My friend Mr Mayor, these are my brothers. They are not guests.

MAYOR. So His Excellency General Barra Tuboum was able to visit us after all. The media said there were some problems . . .

GUNEMA. Imperialist conspiracy. He crush it – boom boom. Like Alexander the Great.

KASCO. No. Like Napoleon!

MAYOR. Your Excellencies, you will have to excuse me. I feel rather embarrassed. You see, we did not expect to meet . . . I mean, we only have one key.

TUBOUM (*looking round in puzzlement*). Key? What key?

MAYOR. The key to the city of Hyacombe Your Excellency. We had made an appointment with President Dr Kamini to make a presentation today. Freedom of the city of Hyacombe. Now we find four of you. My heart is bursting. All leaders who have given us our pride of race. You who have uplifted us from the degradation of centuries of conquest, slavery and dehumanisation. Your excellencies, the city of Hyacombe will never forgive me if I fail to maximise this unique occasion. All four Excellencies must be presented with the freedom of the city. We shall make this an annual public holiday in Hyacombe.

BATEY (*tugs him by the sleeve*). Mr Mayor . . .

MAYOR. Yes? Oh, do forgive me Your Excellencies. I should have begun by introducing my delegation. This is Professor Batey, one of our councillors, in charge of protocol. He is of course our link with his Excellency Dr Kamini.

KAMINI. Of course I know my good friend professor. (*He hugs him, to* BATEY's *physical discomfort.*) Come and meet my brothers. My brothers, this is Professor Batey, very good friend. He is writing book on me which he call *The Black Giant at Work*. You know Gudrum is doing the other one, *The Giant at Play*. People think Big Uncle Kamini never play, but Miss Gudrum will show them. This is President-for-Life Signor Gunema of . . .

BATEY. Let me save you the trouble Your Excellency, I know every one of their Excellencies, although I have not had the honour until now. Sirs, I cannot tell you . . . I am overwhelmed. I mean, all at once. When we tell them back in Hyacombe, no not just Hyacombe, when the entire nation gets to know this, that we were able, at one and the same time to shake hands with . . . I mean, to stand within the same four walls in the presence of . . . please, forgive me, I am a very emotional person . . . (*He turns away, whipping out his handkerchief.*)

KAMINI (*turning to his guests*). Professor Batey is like that, a very kind person. When he visited me in Bugara too, he cried, just like that. And you know why he cried? Because of all the bad propaganda which the imperialist press was making against me. They said I killed people, that I tortured people and lock them in prison – all sorts of bad things about me because I, Life

President Dr Kamini, I tell them to go to hell. No black man ever tell them like that before.

BATEY. You did sir. You told them the way we like to hear it here.

KAMINI. Professor Batey, he come, he see with his own eyes. He travel throughout the country and he not see any single person being killed, not one person being tortured. He return to his country and he write nice things which he has seen with his own eyes.

BATEY (*recovered*). Your Excellency, it was my duty as a scholar to present the truth. The problems of Bugara were purely economic – as a sociologist, I saw that only too clearly. Bugara has not only inherited a discredited economic system from its colonial history, she is still being exploited by a neo-colonial conspiracy of multi-national conglomerates which continue to prey on developing countries in the Third World. It is an outrageous and inhuman situation Your Excellencies, and I hope you lay it on them again when you address the General Assembly tomorrow. What sickens one most of all is the hypocrites who raise the diversionary scarecrow of human rights when in this very country . . .

MAYOR. Professor . . . Professor Batey . . .

BATEY. What?

MAYOR. We have an immediate problem.

BATEY. I beg your pardon.

MAYOR. That's all right. It's all in your address, so save it. Your Excellencies, I have thought up a solution – if you will be so kind as to indulge us. We must fix a new appointment. Give us time to get more keys. And Professor Batey of course will have to include all Your Excellencies in his address.

GUDRUM. With your permission, Your Excellency, just what I was going to suggest. We must use the occasion to make history. The embassy will fix a new time which gives us time to invite the press and television.

KAMINI (*turns to his colleagues*.) Does this meet with your

approval my brothers? (*They chorus 'Si, si', 'D'accord' etc.*)
We are all agreed Mr Mayor. Everything, we like to do
together. Like statues there. I insist we present united, collective front in all matters. We show these super-powers.

MAYOR. It is an inspiring example Your Excellency.

KAMINI. Goodbye my friend. Oh, perhaps while you are here, you
can help me look at the speech which I am making in the
General Assembly tomorrow. My ambassador will show you a
copy. It had to be written by one of the junior secretaries in our
embassy and I have not yet tested him properly.

BATEY. A junior secretary? What about my friend Dr Kiwawa? I
was looking forward to seeing him here – at the head of your
delegation as usual.

KAMINI. Dr Kiwawa, he turn bad. He disappeared the very day
we ready to travel here for the Assembly. In fact three of my
team of advisers disappeared with him. They run away after
they embezzle money from the Treasury. My police could not
find them till now, perhaps they have run to the neighbouring
country.

BATEY. Dr Kiwawa! But that is incredible Your Excellency! I
thought I knew him so well. Oh, but this is most discouraging,
Dr President.

KAMINI. And then since we arrive here, five more have disappeared from United Nations. I know they have been bribed to
run away by capitalist money. Soon they will start to write bad
things about me in the capitalist press when the truth is that
they ran away from guilty conscience. I know they were in this
embezzlement plot with Dr Kiwawa.

BATEY (*firmly*). You must contact Interpol Your Excellency. I
regret that I ever placed such reliance on him.

KAMINI. I have sent to inform the Secretary-General. After all, I
come here on the affairs of the United Nations. I want him to
know what bad things the imperialists are doing to me just
because I champion the cause of our people.

BATEY. It is sad Your Excellency, very sad. I shall certainly lend a hand with your delegation while you are here, sir. It is an honour. I gratefully accept.

KAMINI. My friend, I cannot thank you enough. Goodbye Mr Mayor.

The Mayoral delegation leaves, ushered out by the AMBASSA-DOR. GUNEMA *shakes his head.*

GUNEMA. Nobody on my delegation will ever run away.

KAMINI. Anybody can run away.

GUNEMA. No. Not my delegation. And you know why?

KASCO. You keep them happy with women?

GUNEMA. No. Voodoo. They know if they desert on duty, something bad will happen to them. They will fall sick with horrible disease. They will die very slowly.

TUBOUM. Yes, the whole of Africa knows of your reputation in that direction. Does it work all the time?

GUNEMA. You had better believe it.

TUBOUM. It is simpler just to take their family hostage. At home, anyone who gets sent on an official mission leaves his family behind, under strict surveillance.

KAMINI. I do that too. But sometimes they bribe the guards and smuggle out the families. There is so much corruption. One man cannot supervise everything.

GUNEMA. You can, with voodoo. From here I am surveillancing everything at home. Every one of my subjects, I see. The ones who are plotting, who think they can overthrow Benefacio Gunema, I see them. And the plots of my supercilious aristocracy, the mestizos, I see. They think they superior to Benefacio, because I, I am full negroid, and I arise from low background, poor environment – I see them. Fools! They do not understand yet that some am born to rule. It is there, in the signs since I am born. I am different being from everybody else. I wipe my feet on their necks, mestizos, aristocrats and conspirating negritos alike. (*His eyes become progressively hard, staring into the distance.*) Power is the greatest voodoo and voodoo is greatest power. I see, I surveillance all of my subjects – wherever I am. Nobody stage coup d'état for Gunema and live to tell the story. No public servant steal money from Benefacio and nobody run away when I send him on important mission.

KASCO. Never?

GUNEMA. Never. It never happen. Even my political prisoners I see when they begin to plan escape from prison.

TUBOUM. Lucky for you. You've only got a small island, easily patrolled by a canoe or two with outboard motors. Do you know the sheer size of Mbangi-Gwela? Even I don't know half of what is inside it.

GUNEMA. Size is not important. I know everything.

KASCO. Well, I have no problems of escapees. We are French. My government people are proud to be French, all my officials. To try to escape from la France – *mon Dieu* – who ever heard of such a thing?

KAMINI. My brothers, let us go and eat. It is long past time for food. We continue our discussion of politics over a good dinner, not so?

KASCO. *Ah oui. Moi, j'ai faim.*

As they leave, the SCULPTOR *stares after them in exasperation. He flings down his implements and begins to take off his overalls.* GUDRUM *has remained behind.*

GUDRUM. When will your work be completed? That is, tomorrow what time?

SCULPTOR. Tomorrow what time? Are you being funny? May I just remind Your Excellency that when I came here, it was only to sculpt the President and the President only. No one said anything about the other two. They were never even considered back at headquarters – I mean, I have no doubt that they are very important in their own country, probably more important, but they don't make quite the same splash on world headlines as your President Kamini.

GUDRUM. His Gracious President invited the others. It's a brilliant fraternal gesture.

SCULPTOR. Fraternal gesture? Very good. I am not arguing. My bosses are not arguing, I mean, they agreed to it didn't they? But don't come and expect me to perform miracles when a single sculpture suddenly becomes a family portrait. An extended family portrait – if you'll excuse the racial joke.

GUDRUM. It must be completed tomorrow, that is our understanding. The discussions I held with your bosses in London made that quite clear. Their Excellencies are unveiling the work jointly before the closure of the ongoing session of the General Assembly – that's the day after tomorrow.

SCULPTOR. Did you tell them that in London? As far as I recall, you only told them that you would like it exhibited at the UN before it goes over to London for our own exhibition.

GUDRUM. Your own exhibition?

SCULPTOR. Hey, what's the matter with you? Madame Tussaud's waxworks exhbition. That's what brought me here in the first place, isn't that right?

GUDRUM. Oh, that. That has been overtaken by events; I should have thought that was obvious.

SCULPTOR. Obvious my God! Not obvious to me it isn't. And certainly not obvious to them in London. Madame Tussaud's want to open their new Africa section – it's part of our anniversary celebrations. That's why we made contact with the embassy. We made the contact, remember?

GUDRUM. I shall speak again to your London office. You've got it all wrong.

SCULPTOR. No, you've got it all wrong. And let me tell you something else, if their Excellencies keep bobbing up and down the way they've been doing all this week, and adding more and more Excellencies to the group, I will never get it finished, not even for our own exhibition. I may as well pack it all up and go home for all the good I'm doing here.

GUDRUM. Please get this into your head. First, that sculpture is going on permanent exhibition in the United Nations. Next, you had better get it ready so we can move it there latest tomorrow night.

SCULPTOR. Are you giving me orders? Christ, you don't even know the first thing about this sort of thing do you? You don't exhibit any damned sculpture in this state, not with this stuff you don't. This is just the model. At Madame Tussaud's, we make a wax mould of it and that is what we exhibit. We are a waxworks museum. Strictly between you and me, this one should go into the Chamber of Horrors – that's where it belongs. Personal opinion, that's all. But if you want to exhibit it permanently at the United Nations I expect you'll be wanting it cast in bronze or something. So one way or the other, this object here can't stay as it is in no damned United Nations.

GUDRUM. I see. So it is your opinion that His Excellency belongs in the Chamber of Horrors?

SCULPTOR. Hey, you are not offended are you? Oh come on . . . what are you anyway? His mistress? What does he do to you eh?

Without a change of expression, GUDRUM *storms out of the room.*

SCULPTOR (*his laughter dies abruptly*). Oh my God, I hope she doesn't go and report to the Ambassador. Or even to the Life President himself. (*He shrugs.*) To hell with that. They won't dare sack me till I finish the job. Ah well, better keep this moist. No knowing when we get to start again.

He begins to cover the sculpture in plastic. The door opens slightly but no one enters for some moments. Then KAMINI's *bulk slowly pushes its way in.*

KAMINI (*beaming broadly*). Ah my good friend, how's the work going?

SCULPTOR (*startled*). Oh I didn't hear you come in. Er . . . to be honest your Excellency, this thing doesn't look like it will be ready on time.

KAMINI. But why not? You are very good worker. I like you.

SCULPTOR. Well, now that you ask me your Excellency, I shall try to explain something about this job. It is not always clear to laymen you see.

KAMINI. Explain? Explain what?

SCULPTOR. It's about this commission you see, sir. For one thing, that lady – not the Ambassador, the white one, she was just telling me it must be ready tomorrow.

KAMINI. Oh I am sure. You are a good worker. I watch you. Some time you come to my country. I invite you. You meet other artists like yourself. Traditional. European. The lot. You ever see a Makongo carving?

SCULPTOR. I can't say I have, Your Excellency. I am really not an artist as such. I just copy the original so to speak.

KAMINI. Nonsense. You great artist. I like you. Tell that Ambassador to remind me, I invite you to Bugara. You and our Makongo carvers, you exchange ideas. I know they will like you. When they see how their President like you, they will like you like a member of the family. You will become one of the family. Perhaps you even marry one of our girls eh? Good for world peace I always say. I like inter-marriage between all races.

SCULPTOR. I shall be honoured to visit Mr President.

KAMINI. Dr President, Field-Marshal El-Haji Dr Kamini, Life President of Bugara.

SCULPTOR. I beg your pardon, Dr President. As I was saying sir, I shall be very honoured.

KAMINI. You like, I promise you. So, you hurry up and finish work and you come as my special guest. Right, you finish tomorrow.

SCULPTOR. Dr President sir, Your Excellency, there is something I have to explain. I mean, you just don't understand!

KAMINI (*freezes*). You say what?

SCULPTOR. I know how it is, I mean, I don't expect a layman to understand. You see, there are so many stages to making that kind of statue you see in Trafalgar Square or in Times Square if you like. If I may just explain, as I was saying to that lady . . .

KAMINI. You are telling me I can't understand? You tell His Excellency, Field-Marshal El-Haji Dr Kamini he can't understand! You telling me I stupid.

SCULPTOR. Mr President, I swear, I did not mean any such thing. As God is my witness, if I can just explain . . .

KAMINI. You say I cannot understand. That means you call me stupid! Me, you common Makongo carver, you call head of state a stupid man. In Bugara own embassy. On Bugara sovereign territory!

SCULPTOR (*resigned*). Well, Your Excellency, I cannot deny that charge more than I have already. I very humbly apologise, sir. You have taken the wrong meaning, I swear to that. It could happen to anyone. You are more powerful than me, I know you can report me and get me sacked . . .

KAMINI. Report you? Report you? To whom, you Makongo carver?

SCULPTOR. To my bosses in London of course.

KAMINI (*breaks into a loud guffaw*). Report you to your bosses? What for? I may as well report you to the Secretary-General of the United Nations. Ho, listen my friend, because I like you so much, I tell you of project. Sit, sit . . .

SCULPTOR. Actually, if you don't mind, sir, I'd rather remain standing.

KAMINI (*bellows*). I said SIT!!!

Hurriedly, the SCULPTOR *uncovers one of the chairs and sits.*
KAMINI *remains standing, staring at him.*

So? And where you want me to sit?

The SCULPTOR *leaps up again, looks round the room at the several chairs, finally up the stairs towards the three heavy armchairs.*

SCULPTOR. Do you want me to bring one of those Your Excellency?

KAMINI. Ha, so you remember I am His Excellency. Good. It is good you sit in same chair as Excellency? That makes sense of protocol to you? If your people have no culture, we have.

KAMINI *watches the* SCULPTOR's *confusion for a while, then takes the chair the* SCULPTOR *was about to use, and points to the floor. The* SCULPTOR *quickly squats down.* KAMINI *beams broadly.*

Now my friend, is that not looking better? In our country a young man never sits on same level as his elder. If you coming to Bugara, maybe marry Bugara girl, is good you learn something of Bugara culture, not so? (*He looks round.*) Maybe is even better I find seat much much higher than this. After all, you common Makongo carver while Field-Marshal El-Haji Dr Kamini full Life President of sovereign state. (*He begins to climb the stairs.*) Also, I have unfinished business so to speak. Must try to kill two birds with one stone as you say in Queen Elizabeth English, not so? I like Queen Elizabeth, the royal family is my very good friend. Is why I like Gudrum. She remind me something like the Queen Mother.

KAMINI *has taken off his jacket. He lays it very carefully over the back of his chair. He unbuckles his belt and moves towards the toilet door. When he gets to the door he gestures to the* TASK FORCE SPECIAL *who emerges, dragging his prisoner, his head dripping wet and spluttering.*

KAMINI. You wait outside till I finish private business.

KAMINI *is seen lowering his trousers, then his bulk onto the toilet seat, remaining visible from the waist up through the door. He raises his voice.*

Hey my friend, white Makongo carver, you still hearing me?

SCULPTOR (*his gaze rivetted on the dripping* CHAIRMAN, *he swallows hard*). Yes, Your Excellency.

KAMINI. Good. Because I want to tell you of project which I make from your carving. I am looking at this statue and I think, is time to make new Bugara currency. Same thing as I beginning to tell my chairman of Bugara Bank but instead he prefer to insult our sovereign currency. So, as I am thinking, is time to change the picture on our currency and I am thinking I use photo of that statue for the currency. What you think of that eh?

SCULPTOR. I think it's a very good idea Your Excellency.

KAMINI. You think is good idea enh? Better Kamini statue be on face of currency than sit in Madame Tussaud Chamber of Horrors, is that what you say?

SCULPTOR (*clutches his head*). Christ! She told him! The bitch! She went and told him.

KAMINI. What you say my friend? You think Kamini belong in Chamber of Horrors, not so? Not very good thing to say about Life President the Field-Marshal El-Haji, Dr Kamini, DSO, VC, LLD, PhD, DSc and so on and so forth from universities all over the world. But I like you. Perhaps some day I visit you in Queen Elizabeth England. You show me round London, take me to Madame Tussaud waxwork exhibition and we see Chamber of Horrors where you say Kamini belong. What you say about that my friend?

The SCULPTOR looks round wildly, trapped. He half rises, as if thinking of flight, looks up to see the TASK FORCE SPECIAL watching him closely, and changes his mind. The door opens diffidently and the AMBASSADOR enters. She takes a look at the SCULPTOR, then upwards at the TASK FORCE SPECIAL on the balcony.

AMBASSADOR. Have you seen His Excellency? I can't find him anywhere.

KAMINI. Who's that?

AMBASSADOR. It's me, Your Excellency. I have been looking everywhere for you. Your Excellency. Your guests are waiting to . . .

KAMINI. You! If you are not careful I dismiss you. I am looking everywhere for you and you tell me now you are looking for me. Where you go all this time? Why you are not looking after my brother Excellencies?

AMBASSADOR. Your Excellency, I was on the phone talking to the Secretary-General. He called on the emergency number over the matter of Your Excellencies' statues.

KAMINI. I have no emergency when it is my lunch time, how many times I tell you that?

AMBASSADOR. But I know that, Your Excellency. That is why I undertook to discuss the matter with him myself. He has been in contact with the Russians and the Americans over the proposal.

KAMINI. Good. The Secretary-General is a civil servant, that is all. I should be calling him, not that he should call me. Next time he wants to call, tell him he must make an appointment.

AMBASSADOR. I will Your Excellency.

KAMINI *rises, pulling his trousers up, and emerges fully, zipping up and adjusting his belt.*

KAMINI. Is best I can do now but maybe I have more for you when I have finished lunch. (*He jerks his head towards the toilet. The*

CHAIRMAN, *horrified, is prevented from flinging himself at* KAMINI'S *feet and is frog-marched into the toilet, blubbering.*)

KAMINI (*to the* AMBASSADOR). What you doing there waiting? Go and tell my brother Excellencies I coming now. Serve them drinks.

AMBASSADOR. They've been served Your Excellency. I shall inform them you are on your way. (*She goes.*)

KAMINI *carefully puts on his jacket, adjusts his medals and descends the stairs.*

KAMINI (*standing over the* SCULPTOR). So you don't know even to stand up when Head of State enter in room. Is that how you do when Queen Elizabeth or Richard Nixon enter room in England or America?

SCULPTOR (*scrambles up, confused and scared*). I am sorry Your Excellency, very sorry. I just didn't know whether . . . I mean you yourself ordered me to sit down Your Excellency.

KAMINI. Still no get sense, you white Makongo carver. Not get sense at all. (*He goes.*)

The SCULPTOR *stands still for some moments. He looks up in the direction of the toilet from which very strange sounds are coming. He walks back to the statues and completes the task of covering them up in plastic sheets. He exits slowly. He is hardly half out through the door when his body is forcefully propelled from outside. His muffled scream is followed by blows and the sound of stamping boots. Further groans and blows, then the sound of a body being dragged along the ground. Upstairs, the toilet is flushed.*

PART TWO

Voices coming in from outside. Enter a GUARD *who carries in another chair which is brother to those already on the top landing. He climbs the stairs and rearranges the others to make space for the fourth.* KAMINI *enters, followed by his three brother Heads of State and the* SECRETARY-GENERAL. KAMINI *speaks as he leads the way up the stairs, begins to fiddle with the chairs for a more satisfactory arrangement, positioning the other three crowned heads, changing his mind, then trying something else. The* SECRETARY-GENERAL *remains at the foot of the stairs.* KAMINI *shows all the signs of having dined well; picking his teeth and belching from time to time.*

SECRETARY-GENERAL. It's all a great pity Your Excellency. I don't quite know what we can do about it.

KAMINI. You are a clever man Mr Secretary-General. If you are not, we will not make you Secretary-General. You solve big problems. I not see why you cannot solve simple matter of culture. (*Turning to the others.*) Is matter of culture, not so?

KASCO. *Ah, oui. Évidemment.*

GUNEMA. *Si si, verdaderamente.*

KAMINI. Or maybe you send for UNESCO of Paris to solve the matter.

SECRETARY-GENERAL. I don't think that will be necessary Mr President.

KAMINI. Perhaps is because you have not had your lunch? Why you not let my ambassador give you quick snack of lunch? You know, sometimes big problems which seem BIG, BIG, they disappear like that when I have eaten good dinner. Is true the brain is here (*He taps his head.*) but, as we say in Bugara, sometimes, when a man is body tired, the brain fall down (*He pats his stomach.*) – here. (*He guffaws, joined by all three.*)

SECRETARY-GENERAL. Well, I am glad Your Excellency is in such excellent spirits. We also have a saying in Bogotá, 'Laughter is the tequila which corrodes the machete of anger.' I take it Your Excellency is no longer angry – no, in fact that is too strong a word – let us say, no longer disappointed with the United Nations.

KAMINI *has stopped fiddling with the chairs. He gives the* SECRETARY-GENERAL *a long studied look.*

KAMINI. You have proverbs in your country too?

SECRETARY-GENERAL. You forget Mr President, we are also a Third World country. We have many meeting-points in our cultures.

KAMINI. Hn-hm. Then I tell you another lesson of our culture. Do you notice what time you arrive at our embassy?

SECRETARY-GENERAL (*puzzled*). No, I did not particularly notice the time.

KAMINI. No, think. Try and remember when ambassador bring you in, what do you find me and my President brothers doing?

SECRETARY-GENERAL. Well, I think you had just finished lunch. Yes, you were just rising from the table.

KAMINI. There you are. In Bugara, a man who come to your house unexpectedly when you are just beginning or in middle of meal, with your family or your friends, that man is a good friend. He means well with you. But the man who arrive when you have finished, when the pots have been emptied and you are picking your teeth, that man is to be watched. It means the man has done something bad to you or will do so before the end of the day.

KASCO. *Ah oui? Chez nous aussi*!

GUNEMA (*nodding*). El Colonel Aranja, my late *capitan* of the Palace Brigade of Guards, it happens like that with him. One day he come my house as my family finish . . . yes, I remember, we eat paella that afternoon. We finish eating, he enter the dining-room unceremoniously, over urgent matter. We talk, I watch him. That very night, I dream he plan coup d'état against me. I arrest him in the morning and the tribunal find him guilty. I give him firing squad.

SECRETARY-GENERAL. Your Excellencies, I can see that you've all had a good lunch. Shall we just agree then that this has been just a misunderstanding? I promise I shall look for a solution.

KAMINI. But when, Mr Top Civil Servant?

SECRETARY-GENERAL. Naturally in due course Your Excellencies. Nothing can be done during this present session.

GUNEMA. *Caramba*!

KAMINI. My people will be disappointed. The black peoples will be disappointed all over the world, and especially in this country. The whole of the Third World will be disappointed. . My ambassador has already make press release, all the television networks have been invited to make record of the historic day. How can you do this thing when we were only helping you in your work to make United Nations better?

SECRETARY-GENERAL (*in despair*). Helping me! (*As he turns round in despair, he sees for the first time, the covered group of statues. Eyes popping, he turns back slowly to* KAMINI *and Co.*) Dr President Kamini, is this the thing you propose we put up in the Delegates' Passage of the United Nations?

KAMINI. Is not finished. My Life President General Tuboum has just arrived and now he is to join the group.

SECRETARY-GENERAL. When the ambassador spoke to me about statues, I somehow thought she meant statuettes.

GUNEMA. Statuettes? What that?

SECRETARY-GENERAL. Small statues – (*Indicating.*) like that. The kind of small busts which are made in factories. For distribution.

KAMINI. Small busts?

SECRETARY-GENERAL. Like the bust of Beethoven. Or Shakespeare. Or Lenin. The kind you place on bookshelves.

KAMINI. Small bust is not dignified for big place like United Nations. Later, I make small bust copies to distribute to all my people and sell internationally. Maybe that bring some foreign exchange to Bugara.

SECRETARY-GENERAL. Oh my God! Mr President, sir . . .

KAMINI. Dr Life President.

SECRETARY-GENERAL. Excuse me, Dr Life President, let us go back a little.

KAMINI. Yes, good idea. It was your idea in the first place, you agree? You make request of all nations.

SECRETARY-GENERAL. For the international gallery Dr President, for the United Nations international gallery. I invited all permanent delegations to bring with them one work of art representative of their culture, one work of art only, to be exhibited in the international gallery.

KAMINI. So why now you making problem? Our three brother countries . . .

TUBOUM. Four.

KAMINI. I am sorry, now four. Four of our countries have come together to present your United Nations with one work of art. What now your problem Mr Secretary-General?

SECRETARY-GENERAL (*exasperated*). Have you seen the size of the International Gallery Dr President?

KAMINI. My ambassador see it, that is why she recommend different place. Top of stair. Delegates' Passage. We are all agree.

TUBOUM. I was not consulted, but I am in full agreement with the wishes of my brothers. It is your duty, Mr Secretary-General, to bow to the wishes of our collective voice. We are firmly together in this.

SECRETARY-GENERAL. Your Excellencies, I do not understand why you have set out to embarrass my Secretariat in this way.

KASCO (*fuming*). Embarrass? *Mon Dieu*, embarrass? Who is

embarrass? Who is create the embarrassment? Is better for –
one, two, three, four heads of states to be embarrassed or for
one *fonctionnaire, oui,* even if *haut fonctionnaire,* to be
embarrass? You wish to embarrass me, *mon ami,* and that is
NOT HAPPEN – *non, jamais!*

TUBOUM. I mean, what do we tell the world press? It is
intolerable.

GUNEMA. We do not permit, no.

KASCO. *C'est de la lèse-majesté, n'est-ce pas?*

KAMINI. I think now we resume sitting. Give time for sculptor to
finish work. (*He presses the bell.*) You spend too much time
talking Mr Secretary-General. Time you go back and start
finding solution to simple matter.

    Enter the AMBASSADOR.

AMBASSADOR. Dr President?

KAMINI. Tell the artist man we are ready for him.

AMBASSADOR. Yes, Dr President. And er, Professor Batey is here,
Dr President. He has brought a revised draft of your speech
with him. Would you like him to come in and give you a
summary?

KAMINI. Good man, my friend Professor Batey. Tell him to come
in. He read the whole speech to us while we sit for that artist
man to finish his work. My brothers, you will give me your
opinion of the speech, I beg you.

    Exit the AMBASSADOR.

TUBOUM. My pleasure.

KAMINI. Mr Secretary-General, perhaps you like to hear speech
too, then you contribute your opinion? But you must promise
not to steal Kamini's ideas for your own. Too much of this
stealing of idea in United Nations. Not good for world peace.

    An armed GUARD *enters, holds the door open for the*

SCULPTOR. *He is swathed in bandages from head to toe. Only his arms appear uninjured. His eyes barely peep out through a mummified face. The* SECRETARY-GENERAL *stares.*

SECRETARY-GENERAL. What on earth happened to him?

KAMINI. Oh him? I know he look like something from Chamber of Horrors. (*Convulses with laughter.*) He fall off ladder I think. Not serious accident. We take good care of him. Well Mr Secretary-General, I expect you to settle everything at the United Nations.

On hearing the words 'Secretary-General', the SCULPTOR *raises his head, stares hard and limps as fast as he can towards him. He tries to speak through the bandages but only muffled sounds emerge. In desperation he attempts to tear off the bandages.*

Stop that bloody man!

The GUARD *rushes forward and pinions the* SCULPTOR's *arms behind him, making him wince in pain.* KAMINI *then stomps down the stairs, his face contorted in fury. As he faces his victim however, his manner suddenly changes, and he breaks into a big, paternal grin. He wags a playful finger at the man.*

KAMINI. You are a bad boy, a very naughty boy. You know the doctor say you must leave the bandages on for rest of week. How else you going to get healed if you continue to remove dressing. We take good care of you after your accident. But if you continue to tamper with dressing, what happen? The wounds become infected. Perhaps your leg get gangrene and then the doctor must do amputation. Perhaps even your head get infection and gangrene and then the doctor must do amputation. You want Bugara embassy to get blame I do not take good care of you? You will make me angry if you try that again. Even Egyptian mummy get more sense.

A bewildered SECRETARY-GENERAL *looks from the injured man to* KAMINI *and back again, completely at a loss.*

SECRETARY-GENERAL. You are sure he should be working? Perhaps he should be in hospital.

KAMINI (*taking his arm and piloting him to the door*). He is very conscientious artist. Want to finish work in record time then go back to England, to his wife and children. He is my friend, he likes his work too much, like Makongo carver. (*To the* GUARD.) See that the Secretary-General is escorted to the gates.

Ignoring the SCULPTOR *completely as he walks past him,* KAMINI *resumes his place at the top of the stairs to encounter the questioning stares of his companions. The* SCULPTOR *shuffles back to his work.*

KASCO. *Mais qu'est-ce qu'il arrive?*

KAMINI. He is a very bad man. A spy. I think that Madame Tussaud Museum of England one big spy organisation, perhaps branch of MI5 of British Intelligence with support of CIA. My guards catch him climbing in a window with a ladder. When they challenge him, he fall down from ladder.

TUBOUM. You should have shot him immediately.

GUNEMA. *Hijo de puta!* It is an international outrage. Expose him. Call press conference!

TUBOUM. What for? Everything will be denied. He will be disowned. You should shoot him and fling his body in the streets.

KAMINI. Perhaps I will shoot him. (*Looking pointedly at the* SCULPTOR.) It will depend on whether or not he finish sculpture in time for unveiling in UN. Then perhaps we give him reprieve.

GUNEMA. *Si, si.*

KAMINI. We have to teach all these super-powers that they cannot be sending their spies to be committing espionage with impunity. This is Bugaran sovereign soil. I will not allow foreign spies to get away scot-free. They will be tried and punished under Bugaran laws because we are on Bugaran sovereign territory.

KASCO. *Bravo mon frère, bravo*!

KAMINI. You do good statue, and you do it in time, perhaps I exercise good old Bugara clemency for you. If not . . .

The AMBASSADOR *ushers in* PROFESSOR BATEY *with papers.*

BATEY. Your Excellency, Dr Life President.

KAMINI. My good friend Professor Batey, you are welcome once again. And by the way, from now on, even if I am not here, this embassy is your own home. You must use it as if it is your own home. Madame Ambassador, I hope you are taking good notice. I want Professor Batey to have everything he wants any time day and night.

AMBASSADOR. Yes, Your Excellency. (*The* AMBASSADOR *leaves.*)

BATEY. You are very kind Your Excellency. (*He glances curiously at the* SCULPTOR, *hesitates and appears to wait for instructions.*)

KAMINI. Well, read on, Professor Batey. I want to hear my speech, how it sounds. My brothers will tell me whether I will make impressive speech.

BATEY. Of course Your Excellency. But er . . . (*He glances pointedly at the* SCULPTOR.)

KAMINI. Oh him, he is just common spy but he good Makongo carver now. Like good brass monkey, he hear nothing, he see nothing and he speak nothing. You read out my speech, perhaps he learn plenty from it.

BATEY. Very well Your Excellency. I have er . . . tried to touch on the general world situation, especially the trouble spots and the position of the Third World vis-à-vis such crisis-torn spots. I remembered from our last discussions in Bugara, Your Excellency, that your burning concern above everything else is the total liberation of apartheid South Africa.

KAMINI. Oh yes. You still remember the famous air, land and sea military exercise I make to demonstrate how I will defeat South Africa. I invite all the embassies. It was serious mock battle I tell you. It make Vorster shit in his pants.

BATEY. It was a memorable event Your Excellency. Not only impressive but moving. The commitment behind it all, it was most inspiring.

KAMINI. Yes, yes. But read on, professor. Read me the whole speech. My brothers want to hear how it sound.

BATEY. Of course Your Excellency. (*He clears his throat.*) Mr Chairman, my brother and sister Heads of State, honourable delegates to the United Nations . . .

The AMBASSADOR *re-enters. She coughs to attract attention.*

KAMINI. What is the matter? Why you come here to disturb my speech?

AMBASSADOR. I apologise Your Excellency, but we seem to have an emergency. Two members of the Russian delegation have just called. It would seem that the Secretary-General tried to get them to approve the installation of Your Excellencies' statues in the UN and has met with some difficulties. Finally they insisted on coming to see the work of art itself before coming to a decision.

KAMINI. Very careful people, the Russians. But they are my friends, I know they will support me. Bring them in, bring them in. And get ready to give them lunch.

The AMBASSADOR *goes out.*

GUNEMA. I approve the Russians. But they try to make trouble for my small country.

TUBOUM. All the big powers make trouble. Only the Chinese are different. They come, help to build our railways and factories. They bring their own food and they never make trouble.

KAMINI. The Chinese are my friends. But they have no money.

KASCO. I say any day – *Vive la France*!

BATEY. What of America, Your Excellencies? You all say nothing of the good old US of A.

KAMINI. Oh we discuss America when we eat lunch, and it give us indigestion.

> *Enter* TWO RUSSIANS. *They see the statue almost as soon as they enter, and it stops them dead.* KAMINI *and the others watch them. The* RUSSIANS *then turn slowly and fix their gazes on the four figures above.*

FIRST RUSSIAN (*speaking in Russian*). Fraternal greetings of the government of the Union of Soviet Republics to illustrious leaders of the African continent.

SECOND RUSSIAN. The leader of our delegation brings with them the fraternal greetings of the government of the Union of Soviet Republics and its peoples and declare ourselves greatly honoured to be in the presence of no less than four of the most illustrious leaders of the African continent.

FIRST RUSSIAN (*speaking in Russian*). We are particularly revolted by the unexpected presence of the General Barra Boum Boum Tuboum, the well-known neo-colonial stooge and shameless exploiter of his own African peoples.

SECOND RUSSIAN. Comrade Rostovich especially felicitates Life General Barra Boum Boum Tuboum for his courageous defeat of the imperialist conspiracy launched against him in his country by neo-colonial stooges and agents who are attempting to install puppet regimes all over the continent in order to facilitate their shameless plans for the continuous exploitation of the struggling peoples of Africa.

TUBOUM. You see. I told you. They already know the name which my own people give me after I crush the dirty plotters.

KAMINI. They are our friends. I like the Russians. Please . . .

FIRST RUSSIAN (*speaking in Russian*). How the spirits of the great

Lumumba, Nkrumah, and even Jomo Kenyatta must be squirming in their graves.

SECOND RUSSIAN. It is our great consolation that despite the machinations of the Western world in various guises, the spirit of Lumumba, Jomo Kenyatta, Nkrumah and other great heroes of the African liberation struggle lives on for ever.

> PROFESSOR BATEY *appears to have become agitated. He makes as if to speak, changes his mind and begins instead to take notes.*

FIRST RUSSIAN (*speaking in Russian*). However, let's get to the business of the international gallery.

SECOND RUSSIAN. Now, regarding this proposed contribution to the United Nations International Gallery . . .

KAMINI. Yes, yes, what you say? You see it there before you. Good work of carving, not so. It remain just one more figure and the artist promise to finish tomorrow . . .

SECOND RUSSIAN. Yes, Your Excellency. The comrade leader of our delegation was saying that the Secretary-General has discussed the matter fully with us. Our position will now be stated.

FIRST RUSSIAN (*speaking in Russian*). Ask the buffoon if he really thinks he deserves an honour which is yet to be bestowed on our own national hero, Vladimir Ilyich Lenin.

SECOND RUSSIAN. While we have no objection whatever in principle, our delegation feels that, in order that the United Nations does not appear guilty of discrimination in reverse, the statue of our great genius, the builder of modern Soviet Union Vladimir Ilyich Lenin must first be found an appropriate place of honour in the United Nations building.

FIRST RUSSIAN (*speaking in Russian*). OK, enough of the charade. Give him the Babushka doll.

SECOND RUSSIAN. We have therefore withdrawn the Babushka doll which was our original contribution to the Gallery of

International Arts and Crafts and propose to substitute in its place a life-size statue of our beloved and revered Ilyich.

FIRST RUSSIAN (*speaking in Russian*). Tell the overgrown child to enjoy himself tearing off the Babushka's limbs instead of those hapless Bulgaran workers and peasants.

SECOND RUSSIAN (*opening his briefcase and bringing out a doll*). In the confidence that you will in turn support our proposal, and as a souvenir of yet another example of mutual cooperation, may we have the honour of presenting you with the Babushka doll which was our original contribution to the gallery.

> KAMINI *rises to his fullest height and begins to descend the stairs, beaming broadly.*

KAMINI. My good friends, of course you have my support. And when I return to Bugara and tell my people how you have helped me against that civil servant who was trying to be so troublesome . . .

> KAMINI *has stretched out his hand to take the doll when* BATEY *suddenly strides forward and knocks it off the* RUSSIAN's *hand. Consternation all round.*

KAMINI. What mean this Professor Batey?

BATEY. I speak Russian, Your Excellency. Ask them what they really said. I wrote some of it down – here.

> *He hands over the notebook to* KAMINI. *The* RUSSIANS *exchange furious Russian with* BATEY.

KAMINI (*looking from the notebook to the* RUSSIANS *in mounting fury*). Ha! So, Kamini has mind of a child. Is that what you say? I, Kamini, I have mind of a child and you want to humour me? Thank you very much, thank you very much, thank you very much indeed. I am very humoured. I am laughing, do you

see, I am laughing to death. (*Turning to the stairs.*) My
brothers, you see? They call Kamini butcher. They say me I am
butcher, a buffoon. They say I am reactionary bastard, killing
and torturing my own people. They say while my people are
starving to death in Bugara I am trying to impose my statue on
the United Nations. Over their dead body they say. Look, I
show you. (*He bounds up the stairs, thrusts the notebook at the
others and turns round to face the* RUSSIANS.) So I am not fit to
wipe the dust off Lumumba's shoes, that is what you think.
You say I think myself another Nkrumah or Lumumba but that
everyone knows I am . . . what that word again? (*He snatches
the notebook.*) Yes, I am – cretin? Professor, what mean cretin?

BATEY. You must excuse me Your Excellency. Anything you like,
but don't ask me to soil my mouth with their disgusting
slander.

KAMINI. It does not matter. You call me a vicious child, then you
give me Babushka doll to play with. I, Life President Dr El-Haji
Kamini, DSO, VC, PhD, LLD many times over, you give me
Russian doll to play with! You insult me and you insult my
people.

The RUSSIANS *continue to protest but their protestations are
mostly drowned by* KAMINI's *mounting fury.*

SECOND RUSSIAN. Your Excellency, it is a lie. This man must be
an agent of the US government. This is the typical trick played
by the United States government to ruin the cordial relationship
between the progressive governments and our brothers in the
Third World.

BATEY. How dare you! I detest the US government and what it is
doing to our black brothers everywhere. My credentials are
impeccable.

SECOND RUSSIAN. Oh yes. CIA credentials. No doubt they are
impeccable.

BATEY. You cannot twist your way out of this.

FIRST RUSSIAN (*speaking in Russian*). Remind His Excellency of our constant support for him in the United Nations.

SECOND RUSSIAN. Your Excellency, ask yourself. If what this fiction says is true, why do you think our government has given you so much support? No other government has defended you so stoutly against the slander of the Western press. On the forum of the United Nations our delegation, led personally by Comrade Rostovich here, has constantly voted against and helped to defeat the libellous motions brought against your government by the imperialist regimes. We have defeated all the calls for a commission of inquiry into allegations of genocide and so-called violations of human rights. Human rights! We denounced them all as hypocritical cant, which is all they are. Mr President . . .

KAMINI. Dr President.

SECOND RUSSIAN. Dr President, ask yourself the question. Try and resolve the contradiction if you like.

BATEY. You are very glib, but it won't work.

SECOND RUSSIAN. Your Excellency, when the US and the United Kingdom removed their military experts, we stepped in and re-armed your armed forces. We provided you MIGs and trained your pilots. Who stepped in to train your security forces, enabling you to defeat coup after coup attempt? Our ambassador in Bugara personally exposed to you three attempted coups. Thanks to our information you were able to purge your army of traitors and their quisling collaborators right inside your cabinet. This is nothing but a shabby plot Your Excellency. We are astonished and offended that you should take it seriously for even one second.

> KAMINI *appears to have begun wavering. He eyes* PROFESSOR BATEY *ominously.* BATEY *quietly reaches in his breast pocket and brings out a mini tape-recorder.*

BATEY. Your discussion. I have it all down on tape. We can call in
an independent opinion.

SECOND RUSSIAN. Ha! He moves about with a secret recorder.
Who now says he is no CIA agent?

BATEY. I always work with a tape-recorder. His Excellency
invited me to assist him with his speech to the General
Assembly. Naturally I sent for my tape-recorder. I switched it
on when you went funny on him.

SECOND RUSSIAN. Good. We call in an expert. Your Excellency,
we ask you to take immediate possession of the tape so that
this man cannot tamper with it. The CIA is ruthless in its
operations. Good-day Your Excellencies.

KAMINI. Where you think you go?

SECOND RUSSIAN. Back to our embassy Your Excellency. We will
make an immediate report of this matter so that appropriate
action can be taken against this latest outrage by the CIA.

KAMINI. No. Nobody go anywhere. First we send for independent
expert who listen to tape and make translation. After that . . .

SECOND RUSSIAN. I regret we cannot wait that long Dr President.
We have other things to do in the meantime. If you would be
kind enough to telephone the embassy after you have obtained
an independent Russian linguist . . .

KAMINI. No, you not go anywhere. This matter come first.

SECOND RUSSIAN (*after quickly conferring in a low voice*). I regret
Dr President . . .

KAMINI. You regret only if you insist you go.

SECOND RUSSIAN. Without meaning any disrespect Mr President . . .

KAMINI. Dr El-Haji Life President!

SECOND RUSSIAN. Without any disrespect, Your Excellency, this is
getting ridiculous.

KAMINI. Ridiculous? I am ridiculous you say?

SECOND RUSSIAN. Not you, Mr President . . .

KAMINI. I, Dr El-Haji Field-Marshal . . .

SECOND RUSSIAN. No one has suggested for a moment, Your Excellency, that you are ridiculous. I merely point out that this present situation is ridiculous. It is ridiculous because we are ready to return to our embassy this minute, this very second, and you say we cannot leave. It is ridiculous because that suggests that you wish to keep us here against our will.

KAMINI. What is ridiculous about that?

SECOND RUSSIAN (*pause while he digests this*). You will keep us here by force?

KAMINI. I say you stay here until I bring expert. I say you stay and that means you stay. Enough of this foolishness. (*He reaches for the bell.*)

BATEY (*growing increasingly alarmed*). Your Excellency, if I may intervene, I er ... I don't think it is wise to detain these diplomats against their will.

KAMINI. Why not? We want to make investigation. So, everybody wait until investigation completed. Plenty of food and drink in the embassy. We even have vodka. But no caviare.

BATEY. Please Your Excellency, what I am trying to say is that it may lead to serious international repercussions. When they later complain that they have been detained against their will, I mean, the entire international community will be up in arms.

KAMINI. Why you want them to escape? You make the accusation.

BATEY. Your Excellency, I don't want them to escape or anything. The evidence is here. I merely want to expose the truth, but there is the question of diplomatic usage Your Excellency.

KAMINI. Then let them wait and hear the truth. All of us, everybody including my brothers here. We wait!

SECOND RUSSIAN. This cannot go on. We insist that we take our leave.

BATEY. Do let them go Your Excellency. It's a question of international law . . .

KAMINI. International law! I know my international l

anybody, even professors. This is Bugaran territory. It is Bugara soil where our embassy is standing. That means everybody here subject to Bugara law. Everybody, including diplomats who abuse and insult Bugara Life President. Even if President of United States come here and abuse Bugaran hospitality, he is subject to Bugara law. (*To his colleagues.*) Is that no so?

OTHERS (*dubiously*). *Si, si. Oui, oui.* But of course.

KAMINI (*he has been pressing furiously on the bell*). Where is that ambassador? Always she disappears when I am looking for her. Professor, please look for her in dining-room. Perhaps she stuffing her ears with food.

BATEY. Certainly, Your Excellency.

The door opens before BATEY *gets to it and a* GUARD *enters, a folded sheet of paper in his hand.*

KAMINI. You. Where is ambassador?

GUARD. She gave me this to bring in to you, Your Excellency.

KAMINI. Why she not bring it herself? She knows very well I like her to bring everything to me with her own hand. Where is the idiot? (*Descending.*)

GUARD. I don't know Your Excellency. She rushed in, gave this to me and instructed me to wait ten minutes before presenting it to Your Excellency.

KAMINI. Ten minutes? Why such foolish instructions?

GUARD. She said Your Excellency was having serious discussions with the Russian delegation and should not be interrupted for at least ten minutes.

KAMINI. All right, bring it. I cannot teach these women anything.

He takes the paper, which is a telex, and opens it. He reads. His face hardens as he looks up.

Cow! Female bastard! She tell you wait ten minutes? So she can empty all the money in the embassy and run away? Bastard cow, she want to desert what she think is sinking ship enh? I show her! Call out my Task Force guards and seal up the gates. Round up everybody. Anyone try to leave, shoot him. Nobody to leave this embassy. (*He screws up the telex and flings it on the floor.*) I show them. I show them nobody mess around with Life President Dr El-Haji Field-Marshal Kamini. I take personal charge of embassy now. Sons of stinking imperialist rats, I show them! (*He storms out shouting.*) And keep everybody away from telephone. Anybody try to phone, shoot his mouth!

Several moments silence after KAMINI's *exit. The crowned heads exchange looks, then turn their gaze on the crumpled paper on the floor.*

KASCO. *Monsieur le professeur*, perhaps you will oblige by retrieving that communication and reading the contents to us.

BATEY (*approaches it gingerly, but picks it up and smoothes it out*). Oh my God. There has been a coup in Bugara!

BATEY *continues to stare straight ahead, anguish all over his face.*

(*With intensity.*) It is grossly unjust! (*He covers his face with his hands and turns away.*)

KASCO (*after an exchange of looks between all three*). Is it an epidemic beginning you imagine?

GUNEMA. How you mean?

KASCO. Look the situation. First Tuboum, now Kamini. Who next?

GUNEMA. You think perhaps there is coordination? Time of General Assembly, danger for all absent Heads of State?

TUBOUM. Oh, I think it is just a coincidence. Coup attempts are as common as floods or drought on the continent.

KASCO. Still perhaps I give orders for some general arrests. *Il faut décourager les autres.*

GUNEMA. Me, I lock up all possibles before I leave the country.
Plus their families in case of very bad suspicion.

KASCO. I send telex I think. Imitation is the ambition of weak
minds. I have many in my empire.

BATEY (*sudden outburst*). You slave. You sacrifice. You devote
your entire existence, day after day, hour after hour, with no
rest, no let up, no distraction. From a hundred tribes, tongues,
cultures, religions, animosities and suspicions, you weld a
single, united people. Deprived, reviled, sabotaged and sub-
verted by outside forces, from whose exploiting hands you have
wrested your people, put an end to their centuries of domina-
tion, sometimes through force of arms, but always with your
share of heroic encounters, imprisonments, tortures and depor-
tations. Wars of liberation side by side with your peoples, often
with the crudest weapons of resistance, against the most
sophisticated and lethal weaponry from their diabolical factories. Every new nightmare of destruction, anti-personnel mines,
cluster-bombs, nausea-gas and a hundred other barbarisms of
chemical warfare. Still you resist, yielding no quarter, saying
only, no, singing rather, for our people sing out their souls in
adversity: this land is ours, we shall retrieve it. The wealth is
the people's, we shall restore it. And dignity, the dignity that is
born to every man, woman, and child, we shall enshrine it. The
invader is driven out, but is the battle over? No. You discover
that the greed is still in their eye and they bring new,
camouflaged weaponry to bear in wresting from your hands the
fruits of your people's labour. Eternally vigilant, sifting
through the deceptions of diplomacy and the traps of preferred
friendship, you ensure that the wolf of yesterday does not
parade before you as the sheep of today. And sometimes even
the people you serve must betray you; that is the unkindest cut
of all. Bought, or simply misguided, blinded by their own greed
or incapable of transcending their petty clan loyalties, they
desert the lofty heights of your vision and burrow busily

beneath the mountains of your dreams. Do you think our experience is any different, those of us from the mother continent who were settled here as slaves? We had a man here, a king among men who once declared, 'I have a dream'. He revealed that he too had been to the summit of the mountain of his dreams, your mountain, the Kilimanjaro of every black man's subconscious . . .

Throughout his speech, the trio look at each other in bewilderment. Finally, KASCO *makes a move to stop him.*

KASCO. *Monsieur le professeur* . . .

BATEY. He was cut down by the bullets of an assassin.

KASCO. *Ah oui*, one must always safeguard the bullets.

BATEY. You don't understand. It was a conspiracy. And in such another conspiracy, who do you imagine pulled the trigger that felled Malcolm X? Who provided the guns?

KASCO. *Encore, oui Monsieur le professeur. Il faut toujours sauvegarder les fusils.* You understand? It is an interesting exposition and it make very interesting debate but right now it is important I send instructions about guns to my country. I must safeguard them from potential rebels. Please fetch me the *ambassadeur.*

TUBOUM. You forget. She has escaped.

KASCO. *Ah, oui.* And perhaps most of the embassy staff.

TUBOUM. Oh, you bet. By now the news must have spread.

GUNEMA. Rats! They desert the sinking ship. I despise them.

KASCO (*rises*). I have my aide-de-camp in the ante-room. Perhaps you will be kind to summon him, *Monsieur le professeur?*

BATEY (*unenthusiastically*). Certainly, Your Excellency. (*Under his breath.*) Pearls before swine. Saving their skin, that's all that matters now. (*As he passes by the* RUSSIANS, *he stops.*) And you are all the same. Cynics. You don't really care one way or the other do you?

SECOND RUSSIAN. We are pragmatists. You should practise it
   sometimes.

BATEY. Pragmatists eh? I have another word for it but I won't
   bother you with it.

SECOND RUSSIAN. Mr Professor, I am curious to hear what it is.
   Be assured, quite unlike your dethroned hero, we are not at all
   sensitive.

BATEY. I thought you could work it out yourselves – opportunists.

SECOND RUSSIAN. Oh, is that all? I expected something worse. But
   really professor, to be practical now. As you see, the situation
   has changed. Field-Marshal Kamini has no further use for that
   tape, as you see. It is now a useless piece of potential
   embarrassment . . .

BATEY. You contradict yourself. If it is useless, then it has no
   potential for anything.

SECOND RUSSIAN. I have no time to play with words, professor.
   Do let us have the tape. It is no longer of any value to Kamini
   whom it principally concerns.

BATEY (studies them both for a while). Isn't this interesting? You
   sustain this man in power for years with the most sophisticated
   weaponry. You train his secret service and condone the so-
   called acts of suppression against his own people. Yet in your
   heart of hearts, you despise him.

SECOND RUSSIAN. Yes. A common butcher. We knew him. We
   had close studies of him sent regularly by our own men, not
   just Western reports. But in any case, we did not create him –
   the British did. They sustained him in power, backed by the
   Americans. Then they disagreed. The pupil had more than
   mastered the game of his masters. So we stepped in to fill the
   vacuum. I admitted to you Mr Professor, we are pragmatists.
   Our policy in that part of the continent required his retention
   in power. But you sir, what about you?

BATEY. What about me?

SECOND RUSSIAN. Come, come, professor, you are not naive. You have visited Bugara. An intellectual, you have met many Bugaran colleagues. Progressives, committed to the cause of socialism – authentic socialism, not rhetorical. You have spoken with them. Sometimes, surely you speak to them one day, only to learn that they have disappeared the next? Their bodies devoured by hyenas or floating down the Nile. Did you really believe it was all Western propaganda?

BATEY. You claimed it was! You shouted it loud enough in the United Nations.

SECOND RUSSIAN. What was the word you used, professor? Opportunism. It is our duty to discredit the Western press when it tries to discredit the instrument of our policies. The Western powers do the same – why not? But what about you? You are here to write a speech for this er . . . heroic leader. But what of the peasants and workers he has destroyed at will? You write speeches on their behalf?

BATEY. He is a product of the economic and historical conditions of our people on the continent. There is no such thing as a monster – you, if nobody else, should be the first to acknowledge that. You know it is colonial history which must bear full responsibility for all seeming aberrations in African leadership.

SECOND RUSSIAN. I see. You have promoted these views among the survivors of the Kamini's policies in Bugaran villages and towns?

BATEY. No, I had no opportunity to . . .

SECOND RUSSIAN. On your next visit perhaps. You see, professor, we also believe that there are no eternal virtues. Like honesty. It is a fiction. Or intellectual honesty, its later, bourgeois refinement. Between our position and yours . . . what shall we say? Please, the tape.

BATEY. I suppose you even had a hand in this coup? Maybe that's why you took such relish in insulting him to his face.

SECOND RUSSIAN. My government does not interfere in the internal affairs of other nations. But – there appears to be no longer reason for anything but frankness – you could say that it became necessary to abandon him to his fate. His presence in power no longer coincided with our interests.

KASCO. *Monsieur le professeur, je vous implore* . . .

BATEY. Forgive me Your Excellency, I'm on my way. (*To the* RUSSIAN.) Put your minds at rest. I did take notes, but it never occurred to me to switch on the tape recorder. There is no recording. (*He goes.*)

> KASCO *sinks back into his chair with a sigh, appears to shut his eyes. The other two are equally busy with their own thoughts. The* RUSSIANS *look at each other, come to a decision. Opening the door slightly, one of them looks down the passage, beckons to the other. They go. The* SCULPTOR *continues to work like a wraith.*

KASCO. Ants, ants, what they understand? Gnawing away at the seat of power. Flies, flies, what they care anyway? Buzzing around the red meat of power. The red blood attracts them, but what they do with the meat? Nothing. They lay maggots, the meat fester. You shoo them away, they run, buzzing away like noisy, excited children. What they can do? Nothing. But you turn your back, they come back – bz, bz, bz, bz. Power is the strong wind that drive them away. When the wind fall, when the sail of power is no longer fill, they come back. So, is better to squash them first time. Don't blow them away, no. Squash them the first time, then you are saved later trouble.

GUNEMA. Zombies. Turn them to zombies. Is better. Any fool can understand government, but power! *Amigos*, that is *privilegio*. To control the other man, or woman. Even for one minute. Not many people understand that. When you control from birth to death, when the other man and woman know, in thousands or millions – I control your destiny from this moment, from this consciousness till the end of your life, now that is power. Even the animal world understand power, even the insect world. I have studied the colonies of ants in my garden. I sit down and meditate and collect my power from the night, and I watch the insects. Is very useful. I am not sentimental.

TUBOUM. I like to see the fear in the eye of other man. If he my enemy, it is satisfactory. But it does not matter. If friend, it is better still. Even total stranger. Because I see this man telling himself, Tuboum does not know me, I am nothing to him, so why should he do anything to harm me. But he is afraid, I know it. I can see it in his eyes. I walk into a village, nobody in this village has seen me before but, the moment I arrive, I and my striped leopards – the village head, his wives, the priest, the medicine man, they are afraid. Sometimes I ask what is this fear I see? Have they been discussing treason before my arrival? Have they been holding meetings with the rebellious Shabira tribesmen? But I know this is not the case. My spies have reported nothing, and they are good. They are afraid, that's all. Barra Tuboum has brought fear into their midst.

GUNEMA. I read once in a book – I think the author is Don Guadajara – he write that power is an elixir. So I say to myself, how I taste this elixir, how? That is when I go into voodoo. With power of voodoo, I do many things, many things impossible for ordinary man but still, I know I do not taste this elixir. If I taste it, I know. I watch the execution of these *mesquinos* who think they want to take my power. Firing squad, hanging, the garrotte, but still I do not taste this elixir. I do my own execution, take over gun, pull lever to hang condemned man. I use the garrotte myself but still, I do not taste this elixir. I watch when my zombies torture lesser zombies, I love their cries of pain, the terror before the pain begins. With some I watch the strength become weakness like baby, strong man cry like woman and beg to be put to death instead of suffer. It give the sensation of power but still, I do not *taste* this elixir.

KASCO. It is impossible, *mon ami*. You chase a will-o'-wisp.

GUNEMA. Ah, but it is possible. It happen finally, I tell you. It happen like this. I sentence one man to death who I suspect of plotting against me. While he is in condemned cell, his wife come to plead for him. She is waiting all day in the house and when I am going to dinner she rush through my guards and fling herself at my legs, I am sorry for her. So, I invite her to have dinner with my family. Well, I make long story short. I tell her what her husband has done, that he is an enemy of the state and that the tribunal is correct to sentence him to death. She cried and cried, I feel sorry for her but, justice is rigid span of power, it must not be bent. My wife she is silent, she know she must not interfere in affairs of state. That night, after my family retire, I take her to bed. Perhaps she think by that I will reprieve her husband, I do not know. We did not discuss it. But I take her hand, and she follow me to my private bedroom. When I make love to her, I taste it at last. It is a strong taste on my tongue, my lips, my face, everywhere. It rush through my spine, soak through my skin and I recognise it for that elusive, overwhelming taste. Every night I made love to the woman, the same taste is there, nothing to compare with it. Nothing.

KASCO. So you reprieved the husband?

GUNEMA. Oh no, that cannot be. He was hanged on the appointed day. I pull lever myself. By then the woman had become fond of me and we still meet and made love. But it was gone. After the husband ceased to live, the taste vanished, never to return.

TUBOUM. I like the story. I like the story very much.

GUNEMA. It is true story, *amigo*.

KASCO. *C'est formidable. Formidable!*

TUBOUM. I like the story. So the woman remain your mistress. For long?

GUNEMA. Not for very long. After the taste was gone, I have to do something. I begin to fear she is plotting to take revenge for her husband's death. I ask, why does she still remain my mistress? I had her garrotted. It was better. But it is a sad story, not so?

The door pushes violently open suddenly and the RUSSIANS *rush back inside, move to a corner and try to remain obscure. Moments later, two* US DELEGATES *are pushed in by armed* GUARD. KAMINI *follows, also with a sub-machine gun levelled at the two captives. They are backed against the far wall.* BATEY *enters last, wearily.*

KAMINI. Yes, it is beginning to make sense. First, the World Bank refuse common loan. Then that Secretary-General! Kamini is never wrong. I know it from moment he arrive after we have finish eating, when we were picking our teeth and there is nothing left in the pot but bones. I said, yes, the vultures are gathering somewhere. There is something bad in the air, somebody is abusing Kamini or plotting bad for him. Now I know him plotting with World Bank. And to think I like that civil servant. I think always he is my friend.

US DELEGATE. But he is Your Excellency. We have come on the same mission.

KAMINI. Yes, do I not say it? Same mission. He come here, make espionage, the Russians follow, make espionage and insult Kamini to his face. I go out and I catch you sitting in my lobby with confidential embassy staff.

US DELEGATE. We had been waiting one hour Mr President. We were kept waiting one hour but we waited patiently for Your Excellency to be done with the Russians. We came as soon as the Secretary-General raised the issue of the statues. We fully support the idea.

KAMINI. What statues? Oh yes, I forget all about statues. (*He goes off and appears to remain lost in thought for a while.*)

US DELEGATE. We did not want the Russians to claim credit for promoting the scheme. We rushed here as fast as we could but the Bolshies sneaked here ahead of us – as usual. Your ambassador refused to announce our presence, kept us in the lobby. What could we do? We waited patiently. Then everything started to go haywire. Your madame ambassador rushed in and out again like the embassy was on fire, then the guards came and rounded up everyone. We wanted to leave but were driven back at the point of guns, and then you came in, all armed . . . this is all highly undiplomatic usage Your Excellency. I suppose there must be an explanation.

> KAMINI *is still lost in thought. The* US DELEGATES *look around in amazement at the presence of the other crowned heads.*

US DELEGATE. Good God. Everybody is here. What is going on anyway?

BATEY. Haven't you heard? There has been a coup?

US DELEGATE (*horrified*). Here? In the United States?

SECOND RUSSIAN (*amused*). Oh. You think such a thing is possible in strong powerful democratic country?

US DELEGATE. Don't be so complacent. It will happen over in yours one of these days.

SECOND RUSSIAN. Never!

US DELEGATE. You hope. So it's Bugara. When was this?

> *All eyes turn toward* KAMINI.

KAMINI (*still half-absent*). Is great pity. Is pity I allow that top civil servant to escape. He cause the coup. It is a United Nations coup, sponsored by super-powers with World Bank. Because Kamini is not slave. I say to British, bugger off. I say to Americans, bugger off. Then the Russians came. They think also they own Kamini. I tell them also, bugger off. Now they make coup against me. All of them, join together. They not fit to face Kamini, man to man, one to one inside Bugara, so they make coup from here with all the United Nations super-powers. Is a pity I don't have their stooge here, that top civil servant man whom I think my friend. I know what I do to him, under Bugaran law.

> *The two* DELEGATES *exchange nervous looks.*

SECOND RUSSIAN. Mr President sir . . .

KAMINI. Dr Life President!

SECOND RUSSIAN. Dr Life President, I wish to assure you, at all times . . .

KAMINI. Yes, always you assure Kamini. Always you assure Life President of Bugara, but still, you stage coup. Your KGB take care of my security, not so?

US DELEGATE. Perhaps I may come in, Field-Marshal Dr El-Haji. You need be in no fear that the US government will recognise these rebels who have taken over – whoever they are. As far as my delegation is concerned, the Head of State of Bugara is right here in this embassy standing before me. My delegation will certainly insist that Your Excellency address the Assembly tomorrow as planned and of course, the proposal which we were bringing to Your Excellency regarding your life-size statue, remains in force. We have given it our unqualified support. The only condition we attached to our support was that the statue of our own nation-founder, George Washington, be given appropriate . . .

KAMINI (*swinging the gun dangerously to and fro*). You hear? Always they make condition. Everybody make condition. Who get the idea in first place? Why then you bring me condition? Is idea of Field-Marshal Dr Kamini, not so? You bring condition because you don't want to see Kamini statue standing in United Nations. While you come here talk conditions, you plan coup. You telling World Bank, no loan for Kamini. Is the fine trick of super-powers, we know. When you call conference and everybody is making talk at conference tables, you are undermining talk and giving weapon to all sides. When you are making disarmament talk, you are making more and more atom bomb. Why you not give me atom bomb when I ask you? Why not? All right, answer me. I tell you, I want to destroy South Africa. South Africa is practising apartheid which is wrong. So I want to fight South Africa, but South Africa has

atom bomb. I beg you for atom bomb, all of you. You smile.
You think Kamini big fool . . .

SECOND RUSSIAN. Be fair, Your Excellency. You wanted the atom
bomb, not just for South Africa, but to use against your
neighbour, the President of Hasena. And he is our friend. A
good socialist friend. We were in a dilemma. You put us in a
difficult position. Did we arm even our friend the President of
Hasena with the atom bomb? Look at Cuba, another close
friend of ours and yours, did we give them the atom bomb?

KAMINI. Is bad. Is very bad you don't give Cuba atom bomb.
Cuba help us in Africa. Cuba is my friend. I like Cuba. I like
Fidel Castro very much. He nice man. In fact, if Fidel Castro is
a woman, I will marry him, but he must first shave off his
beard. Why he wear beard like that? Make him look like
guerrilla. I don't like guerrilla. They are bad *kondo* people,
always creating trouble.

US DELEGATE. Precisely, Your Excellency. They foment trouble,
aided and abetted by the Eastern powers, without any
discrimination.

SECOND RUSSIAN. And what of El Salvador enh? What of
capitalist bandits in Nicaragua.

KAMINI. In my country, all so-called guerrillas are bandits, armed
robbers. When I catch them, I take them to their families. Or
hang from tree. Only way to put a stop to that guerrilla syphilis
imported from Western countries.

The RUSSIANS *smirk at the* AMERICANS.

TUBOUM. *Camarade* Field-Marshal, what is the plan?

KAMINI. Plan? What plan?

KASCO. *Oui, il faut prendre la décision.* What to do now? My
aide-de-camp, where is he? I must send message at once to my
head of security. A few heads perhaps must fall, *pour
décourager les autres*, you understand. Rebellion is contagious
disease, *n'est-ce pas?*

KAMINI (*looks at him, surveys all the others*). Nobody going anywhere. Not safe. I shall send for the Secretary-General.

Silent communication between the crowned heads.

TUBOUM. But my brother, when you say, nobody leaves, surely, that cannot include our – entourage?

KAMINI's *eyes shift nervously round.*

KAMINI. Nobody – leaves. If anybody leave now they make propaganda. Tell lies that Kamini's brothers desert him in trouble. Not good for us.

BATEY. Oh my God. My dear, respected, Field-Marshal Dr President, if I may venture to advise. In such a crisis, solidarity based on goodwill is absolutely essential.

KAMINI. Yes, solidarity. I believe in solidarity. My brothers, they are with me. We make statue together for United Nations. That is why nobody leaves.

A dull explosion is heard, close.

KASCO. *Au nom de Dieu!*

GUNEMA. What happen? We are under attack!

TUBOUM *has dived beneath the nearest chair. Footsteps are heard racing towards the entrance. A* TASK FORCE SPECIAL *enters, in suit.*

TF SPECIAL. Your Excellency, the strong room is now open.

KAMINI. Good work. That traitor, the ambassador, she take the combination of the armoury with her, but we blow open the door. Take out all the heavy artillery and position them round the embassy. Two machine guns, grenade launcher and a rocket launcher to be brought inside here. Booby-trap all doors and windows. Anyone break in, we blow the whole of Bugara sky-high. We are not fearing to die like men.

TF SPECIAL (*salutes*). Your Excellency, it will be done.

KAMINI. Wire the entire building. When Kamini says boom, let everything go boom!

TF SPECIAL. Understood Your Excellency.

The TF SPECIAL goes. Alarm deepens all round, but is kept under control. TUBOUM re-emerges from cover.

KAMINI. They will not dare attack this place. I have here both the leaders of the Russian and the American delegations. They will not dare attack.

US DELEGATE. My dear Excellency, I give you the word of the government of the United States, the grounds of every foreign embassy are sacrosanct. Of course no one would even dream of attacking. If such an unlikely aberration occurs, the United States will defend your sovereignty.

KAMINI. I have seen through your tricks. It is a plot of the United Nations. If the Russians agree on the hot line, you will allow Bugaran rebels to take over my headquarters. You agree everything between the two of you. You don't care about anybody else. Pity. If only your top civil servant is here.

Enter uniformed GUARDS with machine guns and other weaponry. The TF SPECIAL follows them.

KAMINI (*indicating*). Machine gun on the balcony, by windows. Rocket launcher through that toilet door. The window overlook the park across to the United Nations. Anybody attack here, we reduce the United Nations to rubble, then blow up Bugara.

The rocket launcher is taken upstairs. The hapless CHAIRMAN is yanked out of the toilet to sprawl on the floor while the launcher takes his place.

TF SPECIAL. I have to inform you, Your Excellency. The Secretary-General is at the gates, demanding to speak to you. I informed

him of your strict instructions that no one was to enter or to go
out . . .

KAMINI. The Secretary-General! Are you mad? Why you not
escort him here immediately!

TF SPECIAL. Your Excellency, we merely carried out your
instructions.

KAMINI. You son of a bastard, you are a traitor. Get him here or I
finish you on the spot.

TF SPECIAL. I shall do so at once, Your Excellency.

KAMINI. Get out and see. (*The* TF SPECIAL *races for the door.*) And
if he has gone, shoot yourself before you come back. (*He turns
to the others in grim satisfaction.*) He come back henh? Now
who can tell me this is not Bugara soil. The gods of Bugara
bring him back to scene of his crime.

GUNEMA (*ingratiating*). *Amigo*, I do not wish to dispute the
honour, but is Benefacio Gunema who bring him back, with
voodoo. I think, if the *functionario* come back, then we your
brothers can go. So, we go now I think, yes?

KAMINI. Is better all remain here – for your own safety. I know
these people, you go out now, they do bad thing to you because
they know you Kamini friend.

KASCO. *Mon Dieu*, we shall be the judge of that. It is important I
make immediate contact with my imperial regent at home.

KAMINI. I tell you is not safe. By now anyway they have close all
airports and cut off communications. I am sure they have set up
roadblocks and shoot anybody on sight. But you are safe in
Bugara. Field-Marshal El-Haji Kamini personally guarantee
your safety.

GUNEMA. Hey! *Es loco, no*? Crazy!

TUBOUM. S-sh! You know, I must congratulate you, comrade
Field-Marshal. How did you manage to accumulate so much
heavy weaponry here? I don't have anything like it in any of my
embassies.

KAMINI. A-ha, you are forgetting that I am supporting all

revolutionaries everywhere. I put weapon in all my embassies so as to fight the imperialists. You ask, my diplomatic bag is always heavy.

TUBOUM. Admirable, truly admirable.

KASCO (*to* TUBOUM). *Il est dangereux, non?*

GUNEMA. *Muy loco, muy loco.*

> Again TUBOUM *signals him not to speak so loud. The* SECRETARY-GENERAL *is ushered in.*

KAMINI (*swings the gun round to him*). So you come back, Mr Top Civil Servant. Welcome.

SECRETARY-GENERAL. I heard the news, Your Excellency. I felt I had to come personally and offer my sympathies. Also to ask what your plans are, if there is anything we can do while you are here . . . Your Excellency, I er . . . would you please point that thing away from me. I am not used to guns.

KAMINI. Sympathy? Perhaps you think Kamini simple child – after all you and these Russians the same, no? You plot together against me with the Americans.

SECRETARY-GENERAL. Your Excellency!

KAMINI. You make war against me, now I make war against you. You think Kamini finish? Ha ha! Kamini get big surprise for you. Now all of you, you move together in one place. You come to ask what you can do for me? I show you. Move. Over there.

> He herds the SECRETARY-GENERAL *with the* RUSSIANS *and* AMERICANS *in a corner.*

SECRETARY-GENERAL. What is going on? This is preposterous.

SECOND RUSSIAN. I think you do as he says.

US DELEGATE. I second that Mr Secretary-General.

KAMINI. You bet your life you do as Kamini say. Now you listen to me. I know there is no coup in the world which is not back by super-power. Ha. How I know? Of course the British and

American help me make my coup. I am living witness. But I kick them out, they and their Zionists, and then is Russia who is helping me all the time. Until they refuse to give me atom bomb, and I am very angry with them. I tell them to go back to Moscow. I lie? Your government angry because I try to boot you out of Bugara. Give you seventy-two hours to pack out your embassy bag and baggage from Bugara.

SECOND RUSSIAN. But that was a minor misunderstanding, Your Excellency. It was all straightened out and you changed your mind.

KAMINI. Changed my mind bloody hell. You changed your mind. You plan coup but Kamini move fast. Round up your stooges and shoot them. Take ring-leaders to their villages and hang them there, then liquidate their regiment in prison. So you had to change your mind and pretend to settle quarrel. But you only wait new chance.

SECRETARY-GENERAL. If I may interrupt Your Excellency, the whole world knows that the United Nations never gets involved in the internal affairs of our member countries.

KAMINI. You tell that to the marines, not to Kamini! What Dag Hammarskjöld doing in Congo all that time Lumumba killed? Not making coup? How he himself get killed if not plotting all over the place and spying from aeroplane. He too Secretary-General before you, not so? You all pretend you are just civil servant but you take your nose in matter which don't concern you. Why don't you go upstairs Mr Secretary-General, see what you find pointing from toilet window. Unless you do as I say, I begin to lobby one rocket every five minutes to United Nations building. As for you two super-powers, you send urgent message to your governments, you tell them to undo their coup, send International Force to Bugara to crush rebellion, otherwise you don't get out of here alive. Nobody get out of here alive. I have wired everywhere with bomb. You know I always travel with my suicide squad and they have

taken over the embassy. You Mr Civil Servant, you will write
to World Bank to bring Bugara loan here, in cash. Then write
the General Assembly to pass motion condemning the coup.
Get support of China – China too hate super-power game like
me. I want United Nations recognise Kamini as President for
Life. How can anybody topple Kamini when he Life President.
Kamini alive and kicking. You send message to General
Assembly or else I bring down that building to complete rubble.

BATEY (*approaching from behind*). In God's name Dr President . . .

KAMINI (*gives him a back-handed swipe that knocks him flat on
his back*). You sneak up behind me again like that and you
soon smell your mother's cunt. Get over there. You are CIA I
think, to come behind a man like that. How I know you did not
come to Bugara to spy for these super-powers? And then you
come here today, like everybody. Everybody coming here
today, coming here today. Why? Because you all coming to
take over Bugara headquarters from me. But there you make
mistake. Kamini good and ready for all of you. You never want
black man to succeed, don't want his statue in United Nations,
don't want him as Secretary-General, don't want him to
become super-power and keeping the atom bomb to yourself . . .

> *Without, the noise of crowds beginning to gather. Occa-*
> *sional bullhorn order of 'move along there', 'keep to the*
> *pavement', 'other side of the road, please', etc., etc.*

Who all these people?

TUBOUM. As far as I can make out, they appear to be
demonstrators.

KAMINI (*big grin*). I knew it. My people have risen to defend the
sovereignty of Bugara. (*To the* TF SPECIAL.) You, go and take a
look and bring me report. (*The* TF SPECIAL *goes.*) Now we
show them what is popular uprising. (*To the* US DELEGATES.)

Perhaps you see revolution take place in your own super-power country. Yes? Is good for you. Perhaps Bugara take over your capitalist country.

The chant however is clarifying into a chant of 'Out, out, out, Kamini out, out, out, Kamini', interspersed with screams of 'assassin!', 'butcher', 'cannibal', etc., etc. Sirens join in the commotion as police cars screech to a halt.

TF SPECIAL (*rushing in*). Bugaran refugees Your Excellency. They are carrying banners all over the place.

KAMINI. Nonsense. There are no refugees from Bugara. Is propaganda organised by imperialist countries.

TF SPECIAL. I saw some of the banners Your Excellency. One of them read 'BUGARAN EXILES FOR TOTAL LIBERATION'.

KAMINI. Shut up. Is a lie!

Sudden splinter of glass as a heavy object crashes through a window somewhere in the building.

They attacking already?

Another follows, and another. The next crashes through a window up in the balcony, narrowly missing the machine-gunner.

We are surrounded. (*He raises his voice and bellows.*) Fire!

SECRETARY-GENERAL. Your Excellency!

Instantly the guns pointing outwards from the balcony open up. KAMINI strides to the door, flings it open and bellows down the passage.

KAMINI. Fire! Shoot! Shoot!

Guns and rocket launchers open up everywhere. The whine of rockets mingles with the boom of exploding grenades. Screams and panic. The sound of the crowd in panicked retreat. *Instinctively* TUBOUM *and* KASCO *have flung them-selves flat.* TUBOUM *reaches up and pulls* GUNEMA *down with them, pulling out his gun.* KAMINI *swings back into the room, his gun aimed directly at the hostages. Their horror-stricken faces in various postures – freeze. The* SCULPTOR *works on in slow motion. Slow fade.*

FROM ZIA, WITH LOVE

From Zia, With Love was premièred in Sienna, Italy, in June 1992, with the following cast:

COMMANDANT (HYACINTH)	Richard Mofe-Damijo
ADC, SERGEANT, *etc.*	Victor Onyiliagha
DIRECTOR OF SECURITY	Yomi Obileye
MINISTERS OF INFORMATION AND CULTURE/EDUCATION/WATER/ AGRICULTURE/HEALTH/LABOUR/ HOME AFFAIRS	Tunji Oleyana Yewande Johnson Femi Fatoba Lanre Durodola
WING-COMMANDER	Yomi Obileye
NUMBER 2	Wale Ogunyemi/ Femi Fatoba
SEBE	Femi Fatoba/ Tunji Oyelana
STUDENT	Segun Sofowote
MIGUEL DOMINGO	Bankole Olayebi
DETIBA	Fatai Adiyeloja
EMUKE	Wale Ogunyemi
WOMAN SUPPLIANT	Yewande Johnson
SUPERINTENDENT	Ibidun Allison
AREMU/WARDER	Durodola Olanrewaju
FIRST TRUSTY	Yewande Johnson
SECOND TRUSTY	Tunji Oyelana
THIRD TRUSTY	Segun Sofowote
SICK MAN/PRISONER	Bisi Toluwase/ Arthur Aginam
PASSER-BY	Promise Onwudiwe

NOTE

Based on an actual event which took place in Nigeria, in 1984, under the military rule of Generals Buhari and Idiagbon, this play is however an entire product of the imagination, and makes no claim whatever to any correlation with actuality.

A row of cells in a half-arc on one side of the stage. On the other side is one large cell, lit by a kerosene lantern and two or three candles. A burly, scar-faced figure sits on a plastic chair which is mounted on packing cases. He is the CELL COMMANDANT. *His conduct is slightly manic. A naval officer cap is perched jauntily on his head. Behind him stands another inmate 'shouldering arms' with a broomstick, while another stands at the entrance with a piece of plank held like a sub-machine gun. The inmates are a mixed bag – first offenders and hardened convicts, political detainees, 'awaiting-trial', etc. They include some disabled, semi-crazed or eccentric as well as the restless and listless. In a corner is a large metal dustbin which serves the inmates as a latrine. Suspicious stains are clearly visible on the floor and on the walls around the bin; that corner of the floor is also wet. The odd rags, worn towels, enamel and tin mugs and plates, etc. complete the accessories. Against the cell bars hangs a crude board with the sign: 'Abandon Shame All Who Enter Here'.*

A human shape is stretched out on a mat next to the cell door. He coughs and shivers from time to time. A small furtive and obsequious type fusses around with some notepaper and bits of newspapers. He is ADC *to the* COMMANDANT. *In the corner with the bucket,* MIGUEL DOMINGO, DETIBA *and* EMUKE *squat on their haunches, obviously trying to avoid the floor. They stick out from the others. Packing cases, broken stools, chairs, benches, camp beds, pillows, buckets, etc. are used deftly to create sets for the various enactments. The 'Cabinet' is in session.*

COMMANDANT. Minister of Health!

HEALTH (*leaps up, salutes briskly*). Present sah!

COMMANDANT. Make your report.

HEALTH. Seven dead sah!

COMMANDANT. Seven dead? You mean between yesterday and today?

HEALTH. In the last twenty-four hours, Your Excellency.

COMMANDANT. Which local government?

HEALTH. Katanga local government, two; Aburi, one; Soweto, two. And another two in your own constituency, Amorako. Total, seven sir. By tomorrow morning, probably eight. (*Pointing in the direction of the tossing figure on the mat.*) At my recommendation, the Minister of Housing has relocated him to maximum fresh-air security by the door, but I think it's too – late. Unless they take him to hospital.

COMMANDANT. So, we have epidemic.

HEALTH. Permission to speak sah.

COMMANDANT. Permission granted.

HEALTH. Your Excellency, yes sir, we have epidemic.

COMMANDANT. Like last year, no?

HEALTH. Like last year, yessah! Started dead on time, with the first rains.

COMMANDANT. In short, the health situation is stable.

HEALTH. Like a model patient sah, condition critical but stable.

COMMANDANT. Without stability, there can be no development.

NUMBER 2. Well said my Commander. Without stability, there can be no progress.

COMMANDANT. Good. Let's make progress, Security?

ADC. Director of Security Major Awam, by State Command, will once again present his curriculum vitae.

General movement as they all shift to pre-assigned places.

DIRECTOR. Situation report is ready, Commandant sir.

COMMANDANT. Before you begin, let me ask you, are you going to annoy me today?

DIRECTOR. Annoy you sir? Certainly not.

COMMANDANT. Because I warn you, if you do . . .

NUMBER 2. He's assured me he has totally reformed.

COMMANDANT. We'll soon find out. I have yet to hear of the leopard changing his spots.

HEALTH. Let's give him a chance, Your Excellency.

COMMANDANT. All right, proceed. But remember I have my eyes on you!

DIRECTOR (*opens imaginary file, clears his throat*). The natives are restless, sir.

COMMANDANT. I'd be disappointed if they weren't. What next.

DIRECTOR. Sir . . .

COMMANDANT. No! I said, next item. Your job is to take care of restlessness, not bother us with the whys. Move on, Major!

DIRECTOR. Yes sir. Next item is: the religious question.

> *Audible gasp from one or two. Then silence. The* COMMANDANT *sucks in air, expels it, fixes the* DIRECTOR *with a stare.*

COMMANDANT. Major Awam!

DIRECTOR. Yessir.

COMMANDANT. I thought you heard me say . . .

DIRECTOR. It is the next item sir.

COMMANDANT. Don't play your university games with me Major! (*Turning right and left to the others.*) You see? What did I warn you all about? Having university graduates in the army is bad enough, putting them on the Ruling Council . . .

NUMBER 2 (*mildly*). We've been through all that Chief. He is the only senior officer from that part of the country. It's our luck with the geography.

COMMANDANT. The military should have no geography.

NUMBER 2. In an ideal world yes, but – see what a nation we inherited.

COMMANDANT (*gives the* DIRECTOR *a baleful look*). Then we must change his portfolio.

NUMBER 2. Come on Chief, you know he's good. Look at the way he handled the last student riots.

COMMANDANT. Nothing to boast about. He is just another of them after all. He even thinks like a student.

DIRECTOR. But sir, you commended my handling of the workers' demonstration.

COMMANDANT. Yes yes yes, and you don't let us forget it. Maybe you should change Ministries with Danlako. You handle Labour and let him switch to Security.

LABOUR. No no Chief. I'd rather return to the barracks.

COMMANDANT. We'll have to do some reshuffling before long. Or split Security in two. Even three. I'll leave him Military Intelligence and get someone else for National Security. All right, proceed Major. Go straight to the next item.

DIRECTOR. Yes sir. Item Three: food shortage.

COMMANDANT. What about food shortage? Have you taken over the Agriculture portfolio?

DIRECTOR. No sir.

AGRICULTURE. I should hope not indeed!

Guffaws from the Cabinet.

DIRECTOR. Do I have permission to move on sir?

COMMANDANT. Permission granted.

DIRECTOR. The hyacinths are still a hazard to navigation.

COMMANDANT. That's why everybody calls me Hyacinth, so what?

Dutiful laugh from Cabinet.

DIRECTOR. The fishermen can't get at the fish . . .

WATER (*protesting*). My portfolio sir – Water Resources.

AGRICULTURE. No, mine. Agriculture.

COMMANDANT. Silence! Any more of that ancient bickering and I'll merge both Ministries into Agriculture and Water Resources, then abolish both in one stroke instead of two! While you are arguing, this – this busybody is trespassing on your domain yet again. Yes Major, what were you saying? Do carry on. Annoy me.

DIRECTOR. Soon there'll be a serious protein shortage . . .

HEALTH. Health, Health, Major Awam. Keep your paddles out of the stream of Health – if you want to stay healthy.

DIRECTOR. If we lose the fishing it means there'll be a shortage from that food resource. Add that to what the Kwela birds have done to the grain crops this year, and anyone can predict that . . .

CABINET (*derisive chorus*). . . . We are clearly heading for food shortage!

DIRECTOR (*unflapped*). And possible food riots.

COMMANDANT. Have you landed?

DIRECTOR. On this item, yes, Commandant sir!

COMMANDANT. Good. Now let me tell you what you've left out. Would you like to know?

DIRECTOR. Yes. Commandant.

COMMANDANT. You left out what should interest your portfolio – Security. While you were drifting from portfolio to portfolio, minding other people's departments, you missed your boat. And that boat is – Security. With the water hyacinths spreading through the harbours, the nation cannot be invaded by sea. You can't have any secret landings on unguarded beaches. Those sea-borne mercenary and guerrilla incursions have ceased – that is Security for you. Even our waterside prisons have become more secure – Ita Oko Penal island for instance – there has been no escape from there in the past year and a half – that is Security, your portfolio. Cheap, natural, security barrier, what more can you ask for? Gentlemen, I propose three hearty cheers for the water hyacinths – Hip! Hip! Hip!

INMATES. Hurray!.

COMMANDANT. Hip! Hip! Hip!

INMATES. Hurray!

COMMANDANT (*standing*). And make this a truly big one for Commodore Hyacinth himself, the Commander-in-Chief, and your Cell Commandant – Hip! Hip! Hip!

INMATES (*throwing buckets, cups, brooms, etc., in air*). Hurray-ay-ay-ay-ay!!!

COMMANDANT (*waves his arms grandly*). Now that is the sound of stability. And Security. (*Sits.*) Proceed Major, and no more clever-clever circumnavigations or poaching in other people's ponds and fishing in troubled waters. Give us a professional Sit-Rep. (*Looks round.*) Sit-Rep. Situation Report, for you bloody civilians.

DIRECTOR. Thank you, sir. Item Four: Public Transportation.

COMMANDANT (*throws up his arms and rolls his eyes*). Public Transportation. Did I hear the Major say Public Transportation?

DIRECTOR. Yessir. Public Transportation.

COMMANDANT. Major Awam, I know this is only your second session with the new Eternal Ruling Council, but . . .

NUMBER 2. Please sir, let me. Look here Awam, all this should have become clear to you by now. Across this chamber is the Minister of Transportation. He speaks to Public Transportation, Mass Transit, Water Transport, the National Railway, Airways etc., etc. Your territory is National Security. You are embarrassing me, considering how I have just vouched for you.

DIRECTOR. Sir, I *am* speaking on the subject of National Security.

COMMANDANT. See? Will you please tell us what National Security has to do with Public Transportation? Or food supply? Or . . . what else, what else? What were the other fields you've tried to appropriate in the last few minutes? You began with religion I think. Well, maybe you'll excuse yourself there because we don't have a Ministry of Religious Affairs. That last Aafa we had was hanged for ritual murder and we've had no replacement. But we do have a Minister for Transportation, Major! Leave him to address his own portfolio.

DIRECTOR. Sir, intelligence reports . . . the potential flashpoints – have you seen those long queues after work, in the broiling sun? And especially now we've lost the use of the ferries, thanks to . . .

COMMANDANT. Ferries! Transportation! Potential flashpoints! See, grammar! Nothing but grammar. No, wait, it's worse.

He's done it again. I tell you, he's done it again. He's circled back to Health portfolio.

DIRECTOR. Health sir? I'm not sure I understand.

COMMANDANT. Hot sun. Yes, you said they queue in the broiling sun after work. Are you a brain surgeon that you suggest their brains are likely to explode?

DIRECTOR. Well sir, something is likely to explode.

COMMANDANT. And I am even more likely to explode before any of them, Major. Indeed, I think I will now explode! Right this moment!

Cries of alarm pleas. NUMBER 2 *calms down the* COMMANDANT *and turns to the* DIRECTOR.

NUMBER 2. My dear young Major, your problem is lack of experience. You must forget all your funny ideas in here, you understand? On this council, Security means only one thing – counter-subversion, counter-subversive talk. Counter rumour-mongering. Counter incitement to subversion. And you have been given powers to deal with all that. Am I right so far?

DIRECTOR. Quite correct sir.

NUMBER 2. There is no potential flashpoint in your mandate, Major, except this one you create by encroaching on the portfolio of the Minister of Transport. Or Health. Kindly limit yourself to matters of national security.

DIRECTOR. Yessir, yessir. That will be all sir.

Astonished looks are exchanged round the Cabinet.

COMMANDANT. All? What do you mean that will be all?

DIRECTOR. I mean, that's the end of the security report sir.

COMMANDANT. Are you trying to tell me that is the full security report you have brought before this council?

DIRECTOR. Yessir.

NUMBER 2 (*restraining the* COMMANDANT *as he is about to 'explode'*). Major Awam, what the Commander-in-Chief is

trying to say is – where, for example, is the list of the new
detainees? How many organisations have you identified as
fronts for subversive activities? And so on and so forth. We like
to know what's going on in your department. The stability of
the nation requires that the council be kept up to date in these
matters.

DIRECTOR. List, sir? I have no list. There are no new detainees.

Silence: exaggerated stares of horror are exchanged.

HOME. Let me get this right, Major Awam. Are you saying that
you have not detained anyone since you took over the
Department of National Security?

DIRECTOR. Just that, sir.

HOME. You have disbanded your team of agents?

DIRECTOR. No sir. I have dismissed some and recruited others – a
different calibre altogether. The overall strength remains the
same. I think we have a more accurate feel of the national pulse
as a result.

HOME. Maybe you have dismantled your listening posts?

DIRECTOR. Not exactly sir. But they are now diversified. More
flexible than before.

NUMBER 2. Then perhaps the Information Fund has run dry? You
need a new subvention?

DIRECTOR. On the contrary sir, we now disburse only about half
from that fund. But the results remain . . .

COMMANDANT (*exploding*). Unreliable, Major, unreliable! As
proved by your lack of information. Informers must be paid or
they do not inform. And where there is no information, there
cannot be detainees.

DIRECTOR. With all due respect sir, my assessment of the situation
is that we should begin to consider the cases of those presently
in detention. The intelligence I have received is that most of
them need not be there a day longer.

COMMANDANT. Quiet, Director, I have heard enough. I think the entire Council has had enough. Those thieving politicians from whom we saved this nation – is it the heartless prodigals you now propose we should release from detention?

DIRECTOR. If I may sir . . .

COMMANDANT (*increasingly violent. Half-way through, he has risen from his seat*). Or the radicals? Those extremists who open their stinking mouths to demand of us a date for restoration of civil rule? Democracy! Democracy! We have hardly begun our mission of redemption. Where were the bleeding hearts when the nation was being plundered with such unprecedented abandon? Where was their patriotism? Their human rights conscience? Did the very people on whose behalf they now claim to speak – did not those very masses pour out into the streets to celebrate our takeover of government? Who are they to open their mouths now to demand a swift return to civil rule? Just tell us Major, do such people speak for this nation? Or is it the army which has the moral right to speak and act on behalf of the masses? What do they want anyway? Eunuchs! Impotents! Incompetents! Agitators! What the hell do they want? None of us has earned promotion. We have retained our original ranks since we staged this eternal revolution. I could have made myself Admiral both Rear and Front but I remain simple Commodore and Commander-in-Chief. Compare it to the damned universities where they have six professors per department and in some cases there is no teaching because they're all professors and professors only profess, they do not teach. Oh yes Mr Director you are a fifth columnist in our midst, you have been planted here by those bearded bastards and you have been tempting me to explode and geographical spread and quota or no quota I think I am just about ready to explode!

CHORUS. Explode!

COMMANDANT. Shall I explode?

CHORUS. Explode!

COMMANDANT. Am I or am I not overdue for explosion?

A loud explosion follows effected by the SERGEANT-MAJOR *with an inflated paper bag.* COMMANDANT *sinks back in his chair, exhausted. Applause from the* INMATES.

DIRECTOR. Thank you comrades, thank you. And thank you especially, Cell Commandant and Commander-in-Chief of Amaroko for so competently assisting me in the thirty-seventh presentation of my curriculum vitae.

COMMANDANT. My pleasure, my pleasure. My master, the late Maestro Hubert Ogunde himself must be looking down on me from his heavenly abode and applauding with his usual energy.

NUMBER 2. Commandant, I hope he won't discover from which kind of stage you are giving us this performance.

COMMANDANT. Of course he must. He was in and out of prison himself a few times. I am only following in his footsteps.

CHORUS (*groans and moans of disagreement*). 'Oga sah, I beg, no to same thing o.' 'In own different.' 'Baba no dey carry cocaine o.' 'Ogunde na political prisoner,' etc., etc.

COMMANDANT. Shurrup! Shurrup! Prison na prison. (*Pointing rapidly round.*) Political detainee dey here. Manslaughter dey. (*Points upwards.*) Innocents dey over yonder. (*Points to the cell.*) Mistake dey here. Even coup plotter, e dey here, abi I lie, Mr Director?

DIRECTOR. Suspicions. Mere suspicions. I'm just a talker, I enjoy a bit of agitating over matters I really care about. That's all. But they got nervous and decided to get rid of me. You can see how long they've kept me here without trial. The ones who don't talk – they're the ones to look out for. Me, I don't plot coups. I believe in the power of truth.

The COMMANDANT's *expression changes abruptly.*

COMMANDANT. Fe-e-e-e-em!

Instant silence. The COMMANDANT *regains his authoritative posture.*

I'll have to watch out for you Major. See? He believes in the power of truth. No wonder he's here. Major, you are a security risk. A spoilsport. Your CV was most entertaining but – look around. Look at all the faces.

All heads are instantly dropped.

You have depressed everyone. I decree a change of mood.

He is applauded. He makes a move of looking over the agenda.

Call the Minister for Home Affairs.
ADC. Honourable Minister for Home Affairs!
HOME (*rises briskly and salutes*). – Aye aye sir.
COMMANDANT. Make your report.
HOME. Reporting three new refugees delivered to Amaroko local government this afternoon, sir. No notice. I have taken the liberty to allocate them accommodation in the transit quarters.

All eyes turn to the three men squatting near the latrine bucket.

COMMANDANT. I see. Are they present and correct?
HOME. All present and correct, sir.
ADC. Sergeant-Major!

SERGEANT-MAJOR *throws a brisk salute, then yanks up* DETIBA *who is nearest to him and catapults him towards the podium.* MIGUEL DOMINGO *receives the same treatment while* EMUKE, *taking his cue from the others, leaps up and dashes in their direction. The* COMMANDANT *gives a pro-longed stare at the two figures scrambling to their feet and at* EMUKE *who is standing apprehensively, casting desperate looks around him. The* INMATES *watch dispassionately.*

COMMANDANT. Welcoming Committee, step forward.

Flanked by two others, the SERGEANT-MAJOR *strides forward, positions himself behind the group.*

Introduce them to our local government.

A barrage of slaps descend on the men, right and left. They are eventually beaten to their knees.

COMMANDANT (*signals when he thinks they have had enough. Points to* MIGUEL). Beginning with you, give us your curriculum vitae.

MIGUEL. I don't understand. What have we done?

Another slap descends from behind.

SERGEANT-MAJOR. You don't understand, what?

MIGUEL. Please, please, just tell us if we have done something wrong. Why are you attacking us like this? We only came in this afternoon.

SERGEANT-MAJOR. You said, when talking to the Commodore, Commandant and Commander-in-Chief 'I don't understand', I then gave you a chance to correct yourself. Now, try again – You don't understand – what?

MIGUEL *is confused. Looks round the cell for help.*

COMMANDANT (*leans forward. Accommodating manner*). You are uneducated, that is your problem. I will help you, but it will cost.

MIGUEL. Anything, anything you want.

COMMANDANT. You look like a man of resources. And influence. Very likely you will even be taken to a different local government. The doctor will likely prescribe you special diet – bread, omelette, beans with no worms, soft toilet paper, ovaltine, milk, sugar, fresh fish on Fridays, jollof rice with chicken stew on Sundays . . .

PRISONERS (*writhing, salivating noisily*). – Mum-m-m-m, nm-mm . . . Na so, na so.

COMMANDANT. So I will treat you like a man of substance. A man of enviable potential. Even like a tycoon but, lacking education. No culture.

MIGUEL. Thank you, thank you very much.

SERGEANT-MAJOR (*raises his arm again to strike*). Thank you very much – what?

COMMANDANT (*signals restraint*). No, no, he is to be assisted, he and his two friends. And of course he will pay. Won't you, gentlemen?

MIGUEL. Of course. I swear. I have means.

COMMANDANT. Hn-hn. Don't try and be like one businessman politician we once welcomed here. After he transferred to his special hostel he forgot us. In fact, he went and reported us to the prison authorities.

> *Breaks into a prolonged guffaw which is taken up by the* INMATES. *Cuts it off with another gesture.*

Well, he learnt his lesson. That became double education. And he had to pay for that new education from the military hospital where he was sent to recover. And paid for the first also, with interest. So, don't try and disgrace yourself. I am vouching for you personally, on my own personal authority. You understand?

> MIGUEL *nods. So do the other two.*

Good. I think now we can say that we understand each other. Minister of Education!

EDUCATION. Yes. Commandant.

COMMANDANT. Educate these refugees.

EDUCATION. Yes, sir, Commodore and Commander-in-Chief. (*Turns to the kneeling men.*) Now you! You had your ears open just now. I hope you heard me when I addressed the

Commander-in-Chief. Right? What the Sergeant-Major was complaining about was that you addressed your Commander like a common man. When you address the Commodore, you say 'sir'. Is that clear?

MIGUEL/DETIBA/EMUKE. Oh yes, thank you. We're very sorry sir.

EDUCATION. Yesssir. No, sir. I beg your pardon, sir. I understand, sir. Permission to speak, sir. Permission to fall out, sir. And so on and so forth. This is a military regime so don't mess about. Even when we were doing the civilian style – because you see, we try to conform with what is going on in the country outside – so before we changed to military, even then our Commandant was still Commander-in-Chief as well as civilian President. So, no matter what style we are operating, you must address him with due respect and full protocol.

MIGUEL. Yessir. (*Turning to the* COMMANDANT.) I apologise, sir.

COMMANDANT *graciously gestures that all is forgiven.*

EDUCATION. Now, your curriculum vitae – I think an educated man like yourself should know what that means. I am very disappointed and shocked that you can be ignorant on such a simple matter. It means also that you were not paying much attention to what went on just now.

MIGUEL. I'm sorry, sir. I know what it means outside . . .

EDUCATION. Outside or inside, the same thing. You think we don't follow procedure here? Name. Age. Profession. And then, most important of all, wetin bring you here? What crime you commit? How much sentence they give you? If you don't give us your full record, how can the Eternal Ruling Council plan the economy or make the Five-Year Revolving Development Plan?

MIGUEL. True sir, you are quite right.

COMMANDANT. Minister for Information and Culture, take over.

INFORMATION (*steps forward*). Yes, Commandant, sir. Now you, in presenting your curriculum vitae, you can turn it into 'ewi' for us and recite it, or you can sing and dance it – anything – juju, talazo, fuji or disco style – we don't mind. Or you can preach it like a sermon, in which case you can repeat it any Friday or Sunday, depending on which religion you follow. And last but not the least, as you saw just now, you can play it for us. Only, that will take time to prepare. But we are all here to help – you will pay fees to all those you recruit. The play is our favourite of course, especially for the Commodore. He was trained by the late Hubert Ogunde himself, but that was many many years ago.

COMMANDANT. I am still expert, mind you. (*Sharply.*) And I take the first pick of the roles. And more than one if I like. I'm a Master of Disguise.

MIGUEL. Of course sir, I understand.

COMMANDANT. You can depend on me. I learn my parts very quickly. It came in useful in one of my many lines of business. I am very versatile you see.

INMATES (*chant*). Oga Versatility – Versati. Oga Versatility- Versati. Oga Versatility . . .

COMMANDANT. Don't mind them. They are just jealous of my talents. Ask the police – when they booked me for my first impersonation, over thirty years ago, I fooled them into locking up the genuine person in my stead – that's how good I was. Anyway, those were small-time days. Undergraduate times – Shurrup! I know what they were going to chant. But whether you believe am or not, I tell you say I go university. (*He looks round fiercely.*) Education, proceed.

EDUCATION. Yessir Commodore and Commander-in-Chief. E-eh, yes. I think that's all for your first lesson. But of course, you will first give us a shorthand account of your crime. That one is immediate and compulsory. Because you may be transferred from here tomorrow and then we would miss your contribution to our Development Plan. We have to put you on trial, you know. The sentence you get outside, that is their own. In here, we must pass our own judgement, and sentence you.

COMMANDANT. Enough. That is already lessons one and two. Now, you have met the Minister of Education and the Minister of Information and Culture. Between the two of them, they will inform you about all our tradition and customs in this local government. You must learn everybody's rank, because if you make a mistake . . . Look, why don't I simply introduce you to everybody. Would you like that? Get to know your fellow citizens.

MIGUEL. Yessir, that would be kind of you.

COMMANDANT. Good, good. (*Looks round in surprise.*) Look at them, look at them! I say I want to introduce everybody and look at them still standing and sitting all over the place.

SERGEANT-MAJOR (*jumping to action*). Line up, line up! Line up in alphabetical order. (*Shoves and harries them into what is obviously a familiar formation.*)

COMMANDANT (*preening*). We run a democracy here you see, so everything is done by alphabetical order. We begin with 'A', so I come first. May I welcome you formally – Commodore 'Ayacinth at your service.

> INMATES *salute him with the 'Ode to Commodore Hyacinth'. A 'parade-ground dance' accompanies the chorus, while they mark time.*

INMATES.
Behold the lilies of the field
They do not toil, or sow or build

Oh hail the Commander
Rear-Admiral Hyacinth
Cool as salamander
Rigid as a plinth

Ours are the lilies of murky waters

Unsinkable flotsam of rancid gutters

   Legend in their own time
   Legend out of time
   Legend in no time at all
   Overland or maritime

Their roots have dug to bed and sludge
What sprat shall tell the whale to budge?

   Oh hail the Commander (*etc.*)

Oh what a paradox they pose
Rootless, yet they've spread huge toes

   Legend in their own time (*etc.*)

Vast as the kapok's buttress roots
Fretting and squirming in camouflage boots

   Oh hail the Commander (*etc.*)

Bloated from the anorexic flea
To vampire bats on the elephant's ear

   Legend in their own time (*etc.*)

'Well, is it edible?' queried the nutritionist
'No harm in a trial,' offered the abortionist

   Oh hail the Commander (*etc.*)

Sour as the taste of the morning after
A brothel's night of booze and laughter

   Legend in their own time (*etc.*)

Stubbornly green as the bilious memory
You try in vain to cremate or to bury

   Oh hail the Commander (*etc.*)

A godsend, crowed fibre trade
Here floats free raw material aid

   Legend in their own time (*etc.*)

But that machine was not yet invented
To pulp the weeds for the gains they'd scented

   Oh hail the Commander (*etc.*)

Monster from the sea, was another verdict
Feeds on pollution like a heroin addict

   Legend in their own time (*etc.*)

A mammoth dredger ordered from Soughborough
Heaved and strained and cut a furrow

   Oh hail the Commander (*etc.*)

Too soon, we gave a victory cheer
The weeds had closed up in its rear

   Legend in their own time (*etc.*)

Deadly defoliants, left over from Vietnam
Proved sweet as rain, as dew to a river clam

   Oh hail the Commander (*etc.*)

They split like the Red Sea, immune to fear
Of napalm, conqueror of the ozonisphere

   Legend in their own time (*etc.*)

Then, coolly, respread their death-green coverlet
To drown Mr Napalm with a hiss and a whimperlet

   Oh hail the legend (*etc.*)

Saddam was contacted – prime your chemical fuse
The Green Berets are here, masquerading as lettuce

Legend in their own time (*etc.*)

No way, said the terror of mighty petroleum
Wait till I've perfected my bomb plutonium

Oh hail the legend (*etc.*)

Oh hail sweet lilies of our murky grey waters
Midnight guests, eternal squatters
Homely as the gecko, slippery as the eel
Cool as salamander, tempered as steel

Footsteps are heard approaching. A LOOK-OUT *moves closer to the cell door.*

LOOK-OUT. Visitors! Scramble!

COMMANDANT (*his gesture commands instant silence*). Hn, that sounds more than the usual night patrol . . .

A WARDER *dashes in the cell door, panicky.*

What's happening?

WARDER. Scramble! Scramble! The Superintendent himself is here with some people.

Instant activity. The lights are blown out, leaving only the corridor light. Mats and mattresses are rolled back in place and occupied. In a moment there are only audible snores. Enter the SUPERINTENDENT *accompanied by two* OFFICERS.

SUPERINTENDENT. Open up!

A WARDER *unlocks the door.*

Order them out.

AREMU. Mr Domingo. Emuke, Detiba.

Answering sounds from the interior.

Pick up your things and come outside.

Grumbling and curses as they stumble over bodies en route.

SUPERINTENDENT. My sincere apologies Mr Domingo, you should
    never have been brought here. These two occupied a cell
    already and they should have been returned there, together
    with you.

As they turn to leave, voices emerge from the cell's interior.

COMMANDANT. Oga, we dey die here o. We done petition so tey
    we done tire. I tell you say we dey die one by one.

HEALTH. Everybody skin here get craw-craw. The one wey not get
    craw-craw, 'e get beri-beri. De one wey no get beri-beri, 'e get
    kwashi-okor. De one wey no get kwashi-okor, 'e get jedi-jedi.
    De one wey no get jedi-jedi . . .

COMMANDANT (*leaps up and presses his face against the bars*).
    Oga, I hope you dey listen o. Dat na my Minister of Health.
    This man wey dey here dey vomit all in belle night and day.
    Make you come take am for emergency now now or 'e no go
    last till morning.

WARDER. Oh shut up Hyacinth and get back to sleep.

They proceed offstage.

COMMANDANT. Shurrup yourself you common fuckin-rin warder!
    You think I dey talk to the like of you. Oga Superintendent na
    to you a dey make complaint. I tell you dis man dey vomit
    blood and everything wey dey inside am. If you no carry am go
    emergency now now 'e no go last all night.

*As the steps recede further, he grasps the bars of the cell
doors and shakes them violently.*

Oga warder! Oga warder!

*He changes the violent shake to a rhythmic one, and is soon
joined by the other prisoners who bang cups, plates, sticks
and join in the chant.*

PRISONERS.

   Oga warder, oga warder!

   Oga warder, oga warder!

   Craw-craw warder, oga warder

   Sobia warder, oga warder

   Jedi-jedi warder, oga warder

   Gonorrhoea warder, oga warder

   Apollo warder, oga warder

   Syphillis warder, oga warder

   Leprosy warder, oga warder

   Akuse warder, oga warder

   Asinwin warder, oga warder

   Bad-belle warder, oga warder

   Kwashi-okor warder, oga warder

   Epilepsy warder, oga warder

   Oga warder o, oga warder

   Oga warder o, oga warder

   Oga warder o, oga warder . . . (etc., etc.)

Someone begins to stamp to the rhythm. In a few moments the cell is filled with gyrating figures in silhouette, the corridor bulb leaving a pool of light forestage so that the sick man remains visible. He makes a valiant effort to sit up, propping himself on the elbow, a ghost of a grin appearing on his face. As the gyrations reach a crescendo, he collapses suddenly. SERGEANT-MAJOR *is the first to notice that something is amiss. He pulls out of the circle, kneels by the mattress, and quickly raises the head. He closes the staring eyes, lays down the head, gently.*

One by one the others notice, and the dancing comes to a ragged stop. There is total silence as they stare in the direction of the still figure.

COMMANDANT (*violent scream*). Oga warder-er-er!

Lights snaps out.

SUPERINTENDENT *and his group re-enter stage, stop at cell 'C', whose door is already wide open. A naked electric bulb hangs from the ceiling.* EMUKE *and* DETIBA *enter, while* DOMINGO *hesitates, looks back at the* SUPERINTENDENT.

SUPERINTENDENT (*gently*). Yes, you too Mr Domingo. You'll be sharing this cell with your . . . with these two.

DOMINGO *joins the others, walks straight to the sole window and stands with his back to the door, looking out. The door is swung shut.*

SUPERINTENDENT. A warder will be along in the morning with an extra mattress. We are short of beds and other items right now, so you'll have to manage. I don't have to tell you, the prison is overcrowded. But the Military Command and Security send everybody in here as if space is no problem. That's how you got thrown among those others in the first place – I apologise for that mistake by my subordinates. I suppose because we are hemmed in by the lagoon, the regime thinks this is the most secure prison. Well, you two are already at home here, I am sure you will show Mr Domingo the ropes.

Embarrassed silence.

I am sorry about how things turned out for you in court this morning but I hope you didn't take the sentence seriously. This regime wants to put a scare in people, that's all. If there is anything we can do for you – under the circumstances – just summon my immediate assistant. I have instructed him to make you as comfortable as possible. All of you. (*Pause.*) Shall I send you reading material? Or some games? (*Turns to* OFFICER.) Don't we have a spare Scrabble set in the office – the one we confiscated from the political detainees? Yes, they can have that. You could also . . .

Hidden loudspeakers come suddenly to life as a MILITARY VOICE *comes over. The* SUPERINTENDENT *glances instinctively at his watch and, together with the other* OFFICERS, *snaps to attention.* DOMINGO *observes them briefly, turns away.*

MILITARY VOICE. A corrupt nation is a nation without a future. Smuggling is economic sabotage. Smuggling is an unpatriotic act; it is next to treason. Nepotism is a form of corruption. Corruption in all forms has been the bane of our nation. Currency trafficking is economic sabotage; it plays into the hands of foreign powers. It is an act of treason and will be treated as such. So is drug trafficking; the trade of death. Avoid it. Expose any dealers you know. Protect the soul of your fatherland. Make BAI your watchword. Support the Battle Against Indiscipline. Entrol in your local brigade. Be the eye of the nation.

As a click signals the end of the broadcast, the SUPERINTENDENT *signals to the* WARDER *who slams home the bolt and locks the door. They exit. There is silence, except for a soft lapping of water and marsh noises.*

MIGUEL (*quietly*). So the water hyacinths have spread also to this part of the lagoon. I suppose I ought to feel at home.

Turns and walks across to the door and shakes it gently.

Oh yes, I know this is yet another prison cell, but it's that court I am not so sure about. The tribunal where the sentence was passed. Was that part of it for real?

DETIBA. Was our treatment by those hard-core criminals real? You'd think all prisoners would stick together!

EMUKE (*after a pause, bitterly*). You know wetin I think? Even God no fit forgive people like you, Mr Domingo! Some tings dey, wey God no go forgive, and 'e be like your foolishness be one of them.

DETIBA. Emuke, leave the man alone. He took enough punishment among those bastards. Let him have some peace.

EMUKE. No, lef me! I wan' say it one time and then I no go say
anything again. When the man turn up for court today, I no
believe me eyes. I say to myself, abi dis man dey craze?

DETIBA. Well, I said the same thing, didn't I? But – what
happened has happened. We are all in the same boat.

EMUKE. No, we no dey inside de same boat. Even from before, na
inside separate boat we dey. And in own boat better pass we
own. We dey inside custody, so we no get choice. We must
appear before tribunal whether we like am or not. But in own
case, 'e get bail. The court grant am bail. He get high
connection so they gi'am bail. Then he take in own leg walka
inside court – after dey done change decree to capital offence.
Dat one, na in I no understand. What kin' sense be dat?

DETIBA. Well, it wasn't you alone. Or myself, to tell the truth. I
overheard some reporters – even lawyers – saying the same
thing. I don't think I paid much attention to my own case.
(Shrugs.) I already knew the outcome, there was nothing any
lawyer could do for me, unless he could bribe enough members
of the tribunal. So I passed the time asking myself, why did he
come back?

EMUKE. Unless money done pass reach tribunal hand.

DETIBA. Hn-hn. Hn-hn. Either monkey, or connection. I thought
maybe everything had been fixed for him. But when it came to
his turn, and the chairman read out the judgement – 'Miguel
Domingo – guilty as charged' – ah, I tell you, I began to
wonder.

EMUKE. Me too! Na den fear catch me for yansh. I say to myself,
if elephant self fit get craw-craw, wetin common grass-cutter
go get?

MIGUEL (returns to window). It beats me. How could one have
been so completely without any premonition? I have seen this
wall from the outside – I don't know how many times – maybe

over a hundred times. We used to go boating from the family
house in Akoka – quite often we would take this route.
Sometimes we simply came to meet the fishermen in the
evenings as they came in with their catch – over there, in that
direction. The prisoners here would look out from the windows
and wave at us. Sometimes we waved back. At least I did. A
child didn't know better. Maybe I even waved to someone
standing against these same bars. There was nothing like the
water hyacinth then, so the fish market was was a regular
event. (*Pause.*) In all those pleasure rides, I never thought I
would be looking out onto that location from this side. The
thought never crossed my mind.

EMUKE. You can talk all the grammar wey you want. I done been
say am anyway, grammar people no get sense. Chai! Even God
no fit approve dat kin' foolishness. My own condition dey pain
me too, I confess. But as I say before, me and Detiba we no get
choice. Dem refuse us bail, hold us inside twenty-four hour
daily lock-up . . . on top of that, na you make dem go put all of
we inside that palava cell. Before you come na here we dey
jejely. Big tycoon, na 'in dey bring suffer-suffer for petty
criminal.

MIGUEL. I suppose we can't even enjoy that occasional distraction
now. The hyacinths must have stopped the motor-boats.

EMUKE (*hisses*). The man wan' pretend say 'e no hear me.

DETIBA (*joining* MIGUEL *at the window*). Oh yes, the boats have
stopped. Those weeds have made life miserable for everyone.
You can't imagine how it has affected prison life, Mr Domingo.
Before, the canoes – paddles or outboard motors – they'd come
right up to the walls and attend to business. Every morning,
very early. Prisoners would lower messages and money, then
haul up packages or whatever they'd arranged. The prison
officials knew about it but they turned a blind eye. It made life
easier – something to look forward to. Those of us facing the
lagoon acted as go-betweens for others on that side. But,

during the ten months we've been here, the weeds finally gained
the upper hand. First they fouled up the propellers, so only
boats with paddles could come. Then even the paddles couldn't
fight the weeds. For over three months now, not one canoe has
been able to find its way anywhere close to the wall.

EMUKE. What about the Ijaw boy wey drown?

DETIBA. Oh yes, that was a horrible day. Can you imagine, we
actually watched someone drown one morning. No way to
help. Just watch his legs get more and more entangled in those
slimy long roots. It was as if some hidden monster kept
dragging him down.

MIGUEL. You saw him?

DETIBA. Everybody watched, everyone on the water side of the
prison. You see, after the boats gave up, he and two, maybe
three other strong swimmers would find a passage through the
hyacinths with waterproof packs and carry on business. The
scale was reduced of course but, it was still better than this
daily nothing. Then the other swimmers also gave up, leaving
only him. Until one Sunday morning . . .

MIGUEL. This window? You watched him through this window?

EMUKE. Which other window you see inside here?

> DETIBA *gestures to* EMUKE *to ease off, and finds a seat closer
> to him.*

MIGUEL (*softly*). I have never seen death at close quarters, not
even on the roads with all their carnage.

> EMUKE *brushes off* DETIBA's *mimed efforts at restraint.*

EMUKE. Wetin make you come back, Mister? I wan' know. I no
sabbe dat kin' ting at all. Your family get money, dem get
property, dem get plenty influence. You fit dey Russia or
Australia by now and nobody fit catch up. Wetin happen? I just
wan' know. You bribe tribunal and den dey disappoint you?

Hen? For my home town, people for say na your enemy take medicine spoil your mind for dat kin' ting to happen.

DETIBA. Let the man have his peace, Emuke. He'll tell us in his own time. After all we'll have plenty of it on our hands. (*Bitter laugh.*) A whole life sentence of it.

EMUKE. That's if they no fire us tomorrow. These soja people, I no trust them. They fit wake up tomorrow and say – line up everybody awaiting execution. Fire them one time!

DETIBA. No-o-o. Even when that Chairman was passing sentence, I had begun to think how many years we would actually spend in gaol. I agree with that Superintendent.

EMUKE. Wetin you dey talk? You no take your own ear hear sentence? Hey, Mr Domingo, wetin you think?

MIGUEL. What?

EMUKE (*irritably*). The man mind done travel! Detiba and I dey argue about the sentence. You think na 'sakara' den dey make? You tink dey no go put us for firing squad?

MIGUEL. I am afraid they won't; yes, that's what I'm afraid of. Because I can't think of passing twenty years or more behind these walls. Behind any walls. But I fear they will commute it to life. It's obvious.

EMUKE. We go see. All I know is dat dis na wicked country to do something like this. We know some country wey, if you steal they cut off your hand. But everybody know that in advance. So if you steal, na your choice. Every crime get in proper punishment. But if you wait until man commit crime, then you come change the punishment, dat one na foul. Na proper foul. I no know any other country wey dat kin' ting dey happen.

DETIBA. I agree. It's like football. Or any other game. No one changes rules in the middle of a game. Just imagine, half-way through a football game, the referee says the rules have changed. One side has scored a goal but after half-time, he says the net was one inch too wide. Or he says a corner kick which took place ten minutes ago should now be a penalty kick. Can you imagine that? In a mere game it is bad enough, how much more in a matter of life and death.

EMUKE. Only Army mind fit think dat kin' ting.

DETIBA. It's their profession. They don't know the difference between life and death.

EMUKE. Soja man say 'come', soja man say 'go' – everything confuse! You no fit say – A-ah, but na soja man say make I come. The soja man wey tell you 'go' done finish you because you obey soja man 'come'. And if you try Go-come-come-go, both of them go shoot you together. Den leave your body for checkpoint to show example.

DETIBA. It's the training they get.

EMUKE. Chineke! [*God!*] Small crime wey carry only seven years before. Abi? No to seven years maximum before before?

DETIBA. Until three days ago. Anyway, it's all a game of nerves. And the verdict is still subject to appeal. Then the Eternal Ruling Council takes a final decision.

MIGUEL (*quietly, still at the window*). Not another fool surely.

    DETIBA *and* EMUKE *exchange glances.*

There's a canoe trying to break through the hyacinths. I can see its lantern.

    DETIBA *and* EMUKE *dash to the window and press together for a good view.*

DETIBA. Come on, champion, come on!

EMUKE. Na sign, I swear, na sign from heaven.

DETIBA. He's more than half-way through already.

    Excited shouts from the other PRISONERS *urging on the lone paddler.*

MIGUEL (*walks away slowly. Sits on the bed*). What he needs is an assistant wielding a giant pair of water shears, maybe five yards long.

DETIBA. He seems to be doing quite well without it. Come on, dig in man, dig in!

EMUKE. 'E go do am. If not today, then tomorrow. The others go join am try if 'e no manage reach us tonight.

Loud cheers from the entire length of the wall. Then the cheers slow down. Change of tone from optimism to defeat.

DETIBA. He's giving up. He's turning back.

MIGUEL. What did you expect? It was hopeless from the start.

DETIBA. He's rowed through half of it. You'll see, he'll be back tomorrow. With others. They'll finish the job together.

EMUKE (*clasping his hands fervently and looking up in supplication*). Chineke God! Put power for dem shoulder tomorrow. Put plenty power for all dem legs, arms, necks, backside, blockoss self . . .

MIGUEL. No, it won't happen. We are all trapped where it will never happen. And if it does, we won't be here to see it.

The light fades out in their cell as a MILITARY VOICE *comes over speakers. Light on in general cell.*

MILITARY VOICE. What are the watchwords of our national goal? Discipline. Self-Reliance. Self-Sufficiency. Vigilence. A nation which bargains away its integrity through indiscipline loses respect in the eyes of the world. A nation which is slack encourages saboteurs against its very existence. Drugs are the bane of society. Expose the dealers among you. It is the duty . . .

The COMMANDANT *is seen haranguing his* INMATES *in sync. with the words emerging from the loudspeaker.*

COMMANDANT (*his booming voice drowns the speakers*). . . . of every citizen to display his curriculum vitae to justify his right to exist among us because Abandon Shame All Who Enter Here. It's paradise before the apple of knowledge. We run an open government and have nothing to hide, no skeletons in the cupboard, no dirty linen in the wash, no fly in the ointment, no mote in thine own eye, no sand-sand in the gari . . .

ADC. Commandant sir, the student is ready with his curriculum vitae.

COMMANDANT. So am I. And tell him he has to pay extra for that prologue I have just improvised. Or opening glee – that's the term we preferred to use in those days. With chorus-line dancing of course. Hubert Ogunde – God rest his soul – used to drill us to perfection.

Cuts a quick Ogunde* line-up jig with a rendition of 'awa l'ogboju ole, ti nbe l'eti osa'.

NUMBER 2. If we don't start now we won't finish before general inspection. Commandant! Commandant!

COMMANDANT. I've stopped, I've stopped. It's you, Mr Chief-of-Staff, holding up progress.

He surrenders centre-stage to another inmate who is wearing a loose Dansiki over a wrapper. His character is SEBE IRAWE. *Another is seen touching up 'her' eyelashes and stuffing rags into her 'brassière'. Others similarly prepare.*

COMMANDANT (*pointing at the* STUDENT, *he breaks into a chuckle*). Got himself arrested and gaoled for his own protection. I tell you, these students are something else.

His NUMBER 2 *throws him a look of rebuke.*

All right, all right. (*Puts a finger across his lips.*) Fe-e-e-em!

The STUDENT's *curriculum vitae begins:*

SEBE IRAWE *is at his usual seat behind an open window,*

---

* Hubert Ogunde was a famous theatre artiste. In his early days, one of his hallmarks was a 'can-can' style choreography.

keeping an eye on the world, occasionally traversing his teeth with a chewing stick. A placard with the words 'Office Closed' hangs below the window sill. A passing WOMAN *genuflects, moves briskly on her way. A* MAN *half prostrates and* SEBE *gives a condescending nod and wave of the hand. Yet another approaches, sees* SEBE *and spins around, beating a hasty retreat. A* WOMAN *with a tray of goods curtsies, then, as soon as she is out of sight, turns and spits in the direction of the house, muttering under her breath. The* INMATES *supply Muslim and Christian chants, punctuated by some household and other noises to indicate a low-income quarter just waking up. Enter, from a new direction, a neatly dressed* WOMAN. *She consults a piece of paper as if to check directions, appears decided and walks to the window.*

WOMAN. My auntie sends you greetings.

SEBE *studies her slowly, spits.*

SEBE. Don't you people sleep in your house?

WOMAN. When the roof itself is robbed of sleep, how can the house dwellers find rest? When last do you think my eyes have known sleep!

SEBE. All right, all right. Don't give me a sermon so early in the morning. I get enough from all these Lemomu and born-again Kiriyo in this neighbourhood. It is getting so a hard-working man cannot get a good night's sleep in his own house.

WOMAN (*more desperately*). My auntie sends you greetings.

SEBE. I heard you the first time. I'm not deaf.

WOMAN. Then you know why I am here. Answer me in God's name. This is the fifth place I have been in the past week. I said, my auntie . . .

SEBE (*raises his hand to stop her*). My grandfather returns her greetings. (*Ostentatious glance at his non-existent watch.*) It's well before my opening hours, you know. You're making me work overtime before my day has even begun.

WOMAN. She says she lost something in the market place.

SEBE. Right. That will do. I suppose you will like to look at the family album. (*Gets up.*) How long ago did this loss take place?

WOMAN. Two weeks. Exactly two weeks ago.

SEBE (*nods*). All right. Wait here. I'll go get the album.

> The WOMAN *clutches her hands together, obviously under intense emotional stress. Raises her face to the heavens and appears to say a silent prayer. The* STUDENT *approaches. His eyes are bloodshot and his hands twitch.*

STUDENT. Isn't he up yet?

> The WOMAN *is startled. She recovers herself and studies the quivering object before her.*

WOMAN. Who?

> The STUDENT *cranes his neck through the window, as if searching the interior of the house. The* WOMAN *retreats a step or two.*

STUDENT. Baba, Baba o. Sebe Baba.

SEBE (*from inside*). If that voice belongs to the scum I think it does, let its owner not let me set eyes on him when I return.

STUDENT. It's all right Baba, it's all right. I have monkey. I have it right here. (*Starts pulling notes out of his pockets.*)

SEBE (*re-enters with album. Looks the young man up and down*). You have money, you said?

STUDENT. Right here. (*Piles the notes on the window sill.*)

SEBE. I see. And who did you kill to find so much money?

STUDENT (*attempting some measure of dignity*). I am not a murderer. And anyway, since when have you concerned yourself with how people get their money?

SEBE. I'll tell you since when.

> A seemingly disembodied arm makes a swift grab for the young man's head, and yanks it round, drops the album.

SEBE's *other forearm pins the* STUDENT's *neck against the window sill.* SEBE *grabs the monkey and begins to stuff the open mouth with the notes.*

It is since the spoilt, good-for-nothing children of rich socialites like you began to get mixed up in other people's business. You are born with a silver spoon in your mouth, but that is not enough for you. You have to dip it in our own soup-pot, and without first learning our table manners. And then you acquire dirty habits. And that leads to dirty money . . .

STUDENT (*choking*). Sebe Baba . . . please, please . . .

SEBE. Just take a good look of this waterside! The government says it cannot get rid of the weeds. They've tried everything but the stuff keeps growing, growing and spreading all over the place. Do you want to know why?

STUDENT. Please Chief, please . . . I'm choking.

SEBE. He's choking. I tell you the lagoon is choking. And you haven't even asked why. Ask me why, monkey, ask Sebe to tell you why. I said, ask!

STUDENT. Why, Chief, why?

SEBE. That's better. I'll tell you why. It is thanks to excrement like you. Because that is where you end up. With all the other excrement which they flush into the lagoon. As long as the water-weed has plenty of your type to feed on, all those so-and-so marine specialists or whatever they call them, they are wasting their time. There is far too much shit like you, waiting to pass through the sewage pipes and nourish the hyacinths. Have you got that?

STUDENT. Yes, Chief, yes.

SEBE. Chief what? Maybe that's your trouble. Because there are chiefs and chiefs but do you remind yourself which kind of chief you are dealing with? So tell me, what am I called? What is the name that comes after my own Paramount Chiefiness?

STUDENT. I don't get you Chief – please. My throat. I can't breathe . . .

SEBE *relaxes grip but keeps a firm hold on the* STUDENT's *head, shoving it backwards and forwards and sideways, pressing down on his skull as the mood takes him.*

SEBE. Don't understand what? You know my name, don't you? You know what they call me?

STUDENT. Yes Chief, who doesn't?

SEBE. Well, go on. Tell me. What do they call me? How am I known from Badagry to Ilorin and even down eastern-side Cameroon border? Those who seek me out, those people who are sent to me for help, who do they ask for? What name do they whisper?

STUDENT (*hesitant*). Sebe. Chief Sebe.

SEBE (*affably*). No-o-o. Call out the full ting. Give a man his proper name. Sebe wetin.

STUDENT. Se-be Irawe.

SEBE. Louder, louder, use your throat. You think it is a name to be ashamed of? Is that why you are whispering it like a dirty secret? What comes after Irawe? Call it out for the world to hear!

STUDENT. That is . . . that is all I know Chief.

SEBE (*stares at him for a moment, as if he is about to explode, then calms down*). We-e-ell. I suppose I mustn't be too harsh on his ignorance. He can't know everything can he? University is all very well, but they don't teach them about their own heroes over there. (*Chuckles.*) My boy, let me explain something to you – no, first of all, let me make sure you even know the meaning of that name. Go on, tell us. Let's hear if they haven't completely washed your brain clean of your own mother tongue. What is Sebe?

STUDENT. Sebe is a kind of snake, Chief . . .

SEBE. A kind of name, a kind of snake – what is that? What kind of snake? Have you ever seen one?

STUDENT. I only know it's dangerous kind, Chief. Deadly.

SEBE. The pupil knows something. Deadly, that's right. Deadly.
And then – Irawe?

STUDENT. Leaves, Chief. The leaves on the ground.

SEBE. A-ha! That's where you are wrong. Hn-hn. Don't argue
with me. Just listen. Yes, irawe is the leaves on the ground. The
innocent leaves which make sebe even more deadly because it
hides underneath them. It lies in wait. Until you step on it.
Then – you don't even hear the rustle. You don't even know
that something has pinched you. But one minute later
(*Chuckles.*) you no longer know where you are, who you are.
So much for that one. But suppose it is not that kind of irawe?
Suppose the leaves we are talking about, what soja-man calls
camouflage, suppose it is not leaves on the ground at all, but
that other kind which covers up the lagoon? Suppose that is the
kind of irawe under which Sebe is hiding?

STUDENT. I still don't get you Chief.

SEBE (*mimicking*). I don't get you Chief . . . Of course you don't
get me. You can't get me because you don't know my full title.
Sebe Irawe Oju odo, yes. I know you're hearing it for the first
time. My kind of Sebe doesn't wait for you on land. It waits in
the water. Under leaf. Over leaf. Under lake. Over lake. Under
sea. Over sea . . . Over sea . . . overseas. Are you getting me or
am I too deep for you? Can you swim? Are you drowning?

With a sudden motion SEBE *renews his grip on the* STUDENT's
throat.

Now, my package. What did you do with my package?

The STUDENT's *gurgle is inaudible.* SEBE *slackens his grip a
little.*

Speak. I'm listening. The package you say you delivered
overseas. I say what did you do with it?

STUDENT. I delivered . . . I swear . . . I delivered . . .

Stuffing the last note in the STUDENT's *mouth,* SEBE *gives him a powerful shove. The* STUDENT *sprawls on the ground, choking.*

SEBE. They think they are so clever. Because they have been to university, they think they know everything. Listen to me, you leftover of Oro's breakfast – because that is all you are. And less, much much less if that package is not handed back to me within the next seven days. The package, or the money. Now listen! The man to whom you say you delivered the goods in Milan, he was in prison at the time. We have made contact with him. He was arrested the day before your plane touched Rome. We know everything. He managed to arrange for a friend to meet you. That one gave the correct password and you went with him. But you split the package between the two . of you. You conspired to say that your contact was caught *after* you had delivered the goods to him. We know everything, scum.

STUDENT. He's lying. Wherever he is, he's lying!

SEBE. Your partner in crime has confessed his own part. You see, your type is very stupid. That's the difference between you and your accomplice. He was tempted, he fell. Even Adam our forefather was not perfect. But your contact knew it couldn't last forever. He borrowed the stuff, that's what he did. Borrowed it. Made himself some bread. He knew he had to pay it back sooner or later. So when our people over there caught up with him, he tendered. Guilty with reason, he pleaded. But they told him, no, guilty with interest. They calculated the interest. He paid back the capital. And he paid the interest. But you, what did you do with your capital?

The WOMAN *has been watching, fascinated partly by the scene but also by the small album which* SEBE *has left on the window sill.*

STUDENT. Give me time. But please, right now, give me . . . just to keep going. I will find the money and settle everything.

WOMAN. Baba, please my own matter . . .

SEBE. Oh madam, sorry. It's this sort of people who give decent business a bad name. And to come here to pollute my presence first thing in the morning. Take. (*Hands her the album.*) Just go through the photos and see if you find your auntie's missing property in there. As for you, seven days, that's all. Any fool who wants to do business knows that the first law is that you don't eat your capital. You did worse. You sniffed it. Injected it into your bloodstream. That's the way it is with amateurs. Especially when they think they know book.

STUDENT. It's not like that Baba . . .

SEBE. You are dirtying my office you know. Everybody knows I keep regular hours. Seven-thirty sharp and I am open to the public. That's in ten minutes. I've only attended this madam because I felt sorry for her. So I don't want to see your face here when I open up office. Don't give my business a bad reputation.

> *There is a gasp from the* WOMAN *who has been rapidly turning the pages of the album. At the same time she sits down in a heap and takes her head in her hands, swaying.*

SEBE. Ah madam, you have found the missing goods?

> *The* WOMAN *nods, her head still held in her hands.*

God is great. Which one is it? Show us, show us.

> *She gets up slowly. Trembling, she holds out the album at the open page, raises it towards* SEBE.

You! I said take your carcass out of here. Are you deaf? Or shall I feed you to the water-weeds right now?

> *The* STUDENT *stumbles off. He does not go far however.*

WOMAN. The young woman on the right. My youngest sister.

SEBE (*looks at the picture, then at the* WOMAN). It has a cross against it.

WOMAN. What . . . does that mean?

SEBE. I am sorry. You seem a nice person. I feel very sorry for you . . .

WOMAN (*screaming*). What does it mean?

SEBE. Now, now, calm yourself. Remember, this is an office. We don't allow people to shout and scream as if they're in the market.

WOMAN (*with difficulty*). Please . . . what . . . does . . . it . . . mean?

SEBE. And it isn't as if it's the end of the world. I can close this album and that means I have closed your file. Full stop. You came here for information. Whatever you do, remember you always need more information. Even if the goods have been damaged beyond repair, you still need to know where it is kept, don't you? Better bear that in mind.

WOMAN (*nods miserably*). Tell me, I beg you.

SEBE. That's better. We are all human after all. Those who do these things, they have no heart. If they have any, it must be like stone. But they need us, just as you need us. Somebody has to act as go-between, otherwise there won't be a chance for any kind of remedy. This way, they come to us, we put the word out to the next-of-kin and so on. That's all we are – go-betweens. Of course if the police were doing their job properly, we wouldn't be needed. No one would have any use for us. But I don't have to tell you, even the police send people to us. People go to report to the police but the police don't even bother to open a file. They know your best bet is to come to us. We keep proper files.

WOMAN. The cross. Please, the cross. Tell me what it means.

SEBE. Oh, the cross. You know what a cross means – rest in peace. (*Gestures across the throat.*) You people were slow. You should have moved faster. I mean, she was a successful businesswoman.

WOMAN. It was a lot of money they were asking. We tried to borrow. We sold possessions . . .

SEBE. I know, I know. As I said, I feel very sorry for you. But those people, I tell you, sometimes I think they don't even know their own mothers. Well?

WOMAN. Where will I find . . . ?

SEBE. Ah yes of course, you will need to give her a decent burial won't you? Now let's see. Well, shall we say – ten?

WOMAN. Ten thousand?

SEBE. That's the charge. It's a risky business all round, you'll appreciate. Even the police get nasty with us from time to time. You know, somebody high up turns up the heat, and that burns down to our level sooner or later. They have to make a scapegoat here and there. When the oga is appeased, things cool down again and we continue business as usual. (*Looks at his watch.*) Ah, excuse me.

Turns the placard round so it now reads: 'Open For Business'.

WOMAN (*she has taken out five bundles*). That is ten thousand.

SEBE (*scribbles on a scrap of paper*). I won't bother to count it. As I said, I like you as a person. I can tell an honest face when I see one. (*Hands her the paper.*) Go to this address.

WOMAN (*struggling to control herself*). Will I find . . . is that where she's kept?

SEBE. Oh no. Even I don't know that. I don't want to know. I have to protect myself. What you don't know, you can't tell. When you get to that address, someone will take you to her last resting-place.

WOMAN. Who do I ask for? What do I say?

SEBE. No one. No password this time, nothing to say. When you knock on the door, just hand over the piece of paper to whoever opens the door. There will be a driver to take you to the place – that's where all the money goes, you know. So many facilities to provide. Well, goodbye. My condolences. Take it as the will of God. Don't brood too much.

Dragging her feet, the WOMAN *leaves. As soon as the role player is offstage, he begins to unstuff himself. The others slap him on the back to say 'well done'.* SEBE *sighs, begins to count the money. The* COMMANDANT *appears with exagger-ated furtiveness, head down as if to avoid recognition. His voluminous agbada* gives the same suggestion. As soon as* SEBE *catches sight of him, he shuts the window. Opens it again in order to change the placard to 'Office Closed', but leaves the window open.*

'Song of the Social Prophylactic', sung by SEBE. *All* INMATES *join in the chorus 'Man must wack'.*

SEBE.
   Before you start to look at me
   So censorious
   Just remember it's all basic –
      Man must wack

   The issue is quite plain to see
   Nothing mysterious
   The Law of Flesh is not romantic –
      Man must wack

   Some methods may appear to be
   A touch nefarious
   But civilian stooge or soldier's sidekick –
      Man must wack

---

* Agbada: item of clothing worn by the Yoruba.

Rulers are deemed by you and me
Meritorious
They do their job for a safe republic –
   Man must wack

Civil law or stern decree
So imperious
The private sector remains elastic –
   Man must wack

The question to be or not to be
Is precarious
Leave all morals to the cleric –
   Man must wack

Why must we make the obvious plea
Acrimonious
It takes all kinds, both cool and manic –
   Man must wack

Between us we will all agree
On a serious-
Minded approach to the psychopathic –
   Man must wack

My task is thus to oversee
All the worriers
Finding peace in place of heartache –
   Man must wack

And so for a very modest fee
Parsimonious
I act as a social prophylactic –
   Man must wack

Sometimes the case is beyond all plea
So lugubrious
But then isn't life sometimes erratic?
   Man must wack

Let's raise a toast to our control-free
And so glorious.
Never-say-die-till-you're-dead Republic –
  Man must wack!

The stranger hurries past the window which SEBE *again closes.*

During the song, the scene is swiftly altered to indicate the interior of SEBE's *home – a few armchairs, one with an outsize cushion in velvet cover – one of those gaudy covers with a Far-Eastern motif.* SEBE *himself begins to fuss with the cushions half-way through, as if dissatisfied with his furnishing. Finally he leaves everything as it was, with a smug, self-satisfied smile. Rushes forward at the end of the song to usher in his visitor.*

The STUDENT *has been watching his motions. He moves nearer and takes up position near the door after the visitor has entered.*

SEBE. Come in Commander. My dear Wing-Commander, do come in. I didn't know you were back.

WING-COMMANDER (*glances round sharply*). I've told you not to use my rank in public.

SEBE (*calmly*). We're alone. Besides, there are hundreds of Commanders – Air Force, Navy, Civil Defence – name it. Even the Salvation Army. They are outnumbered only by Generals. In any case, no one recognises you people out of uniform. You become mortals, just like the rest of us.

WING-COMMANDER. Just the same, I'd feel better if you learnt to avoid it.

SEBE. Of course, of course. Make yourself at home. When did you return?

WING-COMMANDER. I'm coming straight from the airport.

SEBE. Good God, you must be tired. You'd better have something.
   I know it's never too early for . . .

WING-COMMANDER. I didn't come here for a drink, Chief. I am
   not happy with the situation.

SEBE. Happy? Who is happy, my friend? Who can be happy these
   days when there is so much unhappiness in the world. And the
   economic – ah – situation! If you only knew what suffering
   surrounds one here. There was a woman this morning for
   instance . . .

WING-COMMANDER. I have not come to talk about a woman
   either. I want the latest report. What is going on?

SEBE. Nothing Chief, that's the trouble. Nothing. *There – is – no
   – action*. None whatever.

WING-COMMANDER. That was the same report you sent me in
   Karachi and I'll tell you straight away, I can't accept it.

SEBE (*quiet menace*). You don't believe me, Commander?

WING-COMMANDER (*hastily*). Not you. Don't take everything so
   personally. I'm talking about your boys. Your scouts. Either
   they are imcompetent or they are dishonest. Such a heavy
   consignment cannot simply have vanished into thin air.

SEBE. Of course it cannot my dear friend. It is somewhere on firm
   land. Hidden away. Waiting. It's all a question of how long the
   rogues can wait.

WING-COMMANDER. They don't have to wait! There is no stamp
   on that commodity. You break it up, re-package it and sell it
   off through the usual channels. No one simply sits on stuff like
   that. People get rid of it as fast as they can.

SEBE. No Chief, you've got it wrong. Fifty kilograms! Neatly
   packaged in one fertiliser bag. Just think, if one were able to
   sell such a consignment intact! A one-shot deal. No middlemen.
   No messy distribution. No waste. I think we are dealing with a
   master planner, someone with heavy international contacts.
   Definitely a master planner.

WING-COMMANDER. Someone like you?

SEBE (*pause. Then a big sigh*). Commander, it is the military who produce master planners. You plan all the coups. What time do we others have for planning, we miserable dregs of society who merely try to earn a dishonest living?

WING-COMMANDER (*nervous smile*). Oh come on, I've told you, you're too touchy. That was meant to be a compliment. As a schemer, you can teach even us officers a trick or two. I know you Sebe, don't forget I know you.

SEBE (*rises abruptly*). Let me give you a drink my friend. I don't believe in these overnight flights, even for a seasoned pilot like you. In fact, I don't believe in flights at all, over night or over day. That last flight I took to Jeddah on pilgrimage . . .

WING-COMMANDER. You did? I didn't know you were an Alhaji. So there are things even I don't know about you.

SEBE. Well Chief, I don't use the title . . . Whisky and Campari, right?

WING-COMMANDER. All right. You know the proportions.

SEBE (*setting about the drinks*). There has to be some honesty in the world, whatever people say. How can I call myself Alhaji? It wouldn't be right. I went to Saudi, I went to Jeddah on pilgrimage, but it was strictly a business pilgrimage. I am not a Moslem. Or rather, I am a Moslem. But I am also a Christian, Buddhist, traditionalist worshipper . . . everything you like, and none of them at the same time. How then can I honestly call myself an Alhaji?

WING-COMMANDER. You are impossible.

SEBE. No my friend, you are wrong. I am possible. I am very possible. Perhaps the most possible businessman in this our corner of the world. Here you are. Drink it down and the world will begin to look better.

WING-COMMANDER (*morosely. Sets down the glass without drinking*). I wish it were that easy. There is unprecedented investment on the loose and we don't seem to be able to rope it in.

SEBE. Give it time. This thing is just like pregnancy. After a while there is no wrapper in the world which can hide it.

WING-COMMANDER. I'm losing face. Every day that passes, I lose face. I gave assurances. I assured them in Pakistan that we were in total control over here. Nothing could go wrong. What do you imagine? That fifty kilograms at one go would be shipped out on the personal guarantee of one man?

SEBE. There is always a risk involved.

WING-COMMANDER. Not between governments.

SEBE. Between governments? What are you saying, Commander?

WING-COMMANDER. What? Oh, it's not what you imagine. No, what I mean is ... the people involved over there, my counterparts, they are in government. To deal with them on an equal level, I had to make them believe that it was a government-to-government affair. That there was cooperation here at the very highest level.

SEBE. Well there is. You are still on the Eternal Ruling Council.

WING-COMMANDER. Yes, that was why they approached me in the first place. Even though I went there on one of those courses, almost a student so to speak, the fact that I was on the Ruling Council – well, I had the full VIP treatment. But the real stroke of luck was getting on with the President himself. He took to me, told me to make his palace my second home. I would drop in for a meal or a drink, without notice.

SEBE. This is wonderful! You mean you actually met that tough man Zia?

WING-COMMANDER (*amused, and also a little puzzled*). What do you know about the rulers of countries like Pakistan? (*He starts to sip his drink.*)

SEBE. Only what we read in the papers, Commander, only what we hear on radio or watch on television. I tell you, that Zia man impressed me! The way he ignored everybody's protests and actually hanged a Prime Minister of his own country. This Prime Minister who studied in Oxford – or was it Cambridge? I mean to say, Commander, this Bhutto was even his country's representative to the United Nations. And Mr Zia hanged him – just like that. Hanged him like a common murderer! (*Chuckles to himself.*) I tell you Commander, you soldiers are wonderful people!

WING-COMMANDER. What is so wonderful about that? He broke the laws, and he was given a fair trial . . .

SEBE. Fair trial: Haba, my good friend! According to my lawyer friends . . .

WING-COMMANDER. According to the laws of the land, he was found guilty of murder. He arranged the murder of one of his political opponents. The highest court in the land found him guilty, what more do you want?

SEBE. The laws of the land, Commander? My friend, we know how you people make and unmake laws to suit yourselves. It's our business to know, or we can't be in business. Not that we're complaining but, Commander, look at it from a business-man's point of view. All right? Now let's say I make the same deal in Kótópó as in Kòtòpò.* In Kótópó, the punishment is two years' suspended sentence, while in Kòtòpò – (*Gestures across his throat.*) That's Army government for you, all inside one country like this one. And it doesn't end there. When one started that very business deal, Alhaji Kótópó was in charge, but then, you wake up the next morning and General Kòtòpò has taken over in Pòtòko and the rules are changed overnight. Everything becomes Kótópó-Kòtòpò-Kótópó and you find yourself floundering in pòtòpótó. Well, that's our business life for you but, I mean, it's not fair. It lacks stability and without stability you can't do business.

WING-COMMANDER. Sebe Irawe, I leave business philosophy to you. All I can tell you is that this Bhutto, your so-called civilian

---

* Kótópó/Kòtòpò etc. This is a Yoruba play on words where different accents provide infinite meanings and sometimes no meaning at all. The 'meaning' then is that whatever situation is being described has neither head nor tail.

democrat, was found guilty of abusing his power to commit a capital felony, and he paid the price.

SEBE. But only according to the rules of your man, General Kótópó Zia. One moment, it was one kind of law, then the next day, his people came in . . .

WING-COMMANDER. You are very confused, Sebe. Zia merely applied Islamic Law, and that is constant. Bhutto was free to do the same when he was in charge. Anyway, why go all the way to Pakistan when . . .

SEBE. Commander, I am not the person who went to Pakistan. You did, not me.

WING-COMMANDER. You know what I am talking about! Zia, Zia, Zia! What did Zia do which you bloody civilians haven't done here? I mean, you are beginning to sound like all these university types . . .

SEBE. Is that my fault? They do business with me all the time, they and their tiroro* children. If the leaf sticks too long to the soap, it will soon start to froth on its own.

WING-COMMANDER. Well, the next time one of them comes here, ask him what happened to Diallo Telli. Yes, let your acada† friends tell you what happened to the first-ever Secretary-General of the OAU, the Organisation of African Unity.

SEBE. What happened to him?

WING-COMMANDER. Tortured to death by Sekou Touré's goons. And Sekou Touré was not Army. Or Navy. Or Air Force. He was a civilian.

SEBE. All right all right, I don't know why we dey argue self.

WING-COMMANDER (*flaring up*). We are arguing because I am tired of having everything blamed on us military people. Between Sekou Touré and General Zia or Pinochet or Arap Moi and Houphouet Boigny and other one-party African and Asian dictators, tell me, just what is the difference?

* Tiroro means spoilt, affected and alienated children, usually products of foreign upbringing.
† Acada = academic.

SEBE *shrugs*.

Well, go on, Chief. You know so much of world affairs, so, tell us the difference?

SEBE. When my varsity people come, I will ask them. I can't answer you right now.

WING-COMMANDER. Yes, you do that. Pose that question to your garrulous eggheads!

SEBE (*anxious to mend fences*). Who thought up the fertiliser bags, Commander – as if I need to ask?

WING-COMMANDER (*smiles*). Nothing to it. I said to Zia – why not send us a fraternal gift of a thousand bags of fertiliser – you know, as a gesture of friendship. A contribution to our Operation Feed-the-Nation. Of course he agreed. The rest was easy – special Presidential consignment. Privileged cargo, no question, no inspection. The generals took care of their end. Easy. I was supposed to do the same with ours.

SEBE. God punish those pirates!

WING-COMMANDER. I'm afraid we can't wait on God, Chief. You find them, and I'll guarantee their punishment right here! And fast!

SEBE. God willing, we'll find them. Such beautiful work, so neat my Commander, God won't allow it to go to waste. Or let other people reap where they haven't sown.

WING-COMMANDER. The consignment must be found, Chief. Those pirates have wives. They have girlfriends. They visit bars, brothels. They relax in marijuana dens. They talk. They must talk. This kind of consignment is without precedent in these parts, indeed, anywhere except Colombia. Nobody can sit on it without someone knowing and talking.

SEBE. Chief, you'd be surprised. We'll find it. We'll track it down but, you'd be surprised. An elephant could go to ground in Lagos. It could vanish between Idumota and Iganmu, in full view of everyone, and no one would have seen it happen.

Someone could be sitting on it in Alaba market, or using it for a pillow . . . (*His eyes dart to the outsize cushion, very briefly.*)

WING-COMMANDER. This is different. Nobody can sit on it without burning a hole in his bottom – not in this country!

SEBE. Commander, I must hand it to you. When it comes the Big League, we civilians are simply outclassed. Fifty kilograms at one stroke. Oh, I forgot to thank you for helping out with that affair in Milan. Your minder at the Embassy got through to the courier in prison. We got the full picture. Our own man is back in the country. He has seven days, and then they will pick up his bloated corpse in the lagoon.

The STUDENT reacts. The slight noise is overheard by the two men.

WING-COMMANDER. I thought you said we were alone.

SEBE. Of course we are.

WING-COMMANDER. But the noise. I heard something.

SEBE. Probably some neighbourhood chicken, scratching for its livelihood. Same as me my friend, same as me.

The WING-COMMANDER shakes his head, puts a finger to his lips and begins to tiptoe to the door. He yanks it open, confronting the STUDENT who jumps up but seems too petrified to run.

Well, well, well, if it isn't what the sea washed up on my frontage. You pail of garbage, didn't I warn you to stop polluting my neighbourhood? Vanish!

The STUDENT runs off.

WING-COMMANDER. Who is he? What was he doing here?

SEBE. That's him. That's the scum who tried to double-cross Sebe Irawe.

WING-COMMANDER. You mean your courier? The Milan business?

SEBE. The same. He must have been scared to death when he heard me say . . .

> *Stops dead and stares at his partner. The* WING-COMMANDER *nods slowly.*

The bastard! He was eavesdropping!!

WING-COMMANDER. No doubt about it.

SEBE (*wide-eyed with disbelief*). I thought at first he was simply desperate for a fix – that's why he wouldn't go away. (*Nearly screaming.*) Eavesdropping on me? In my very house? All right, I'll fix him. His seven day reprieve is off! (*His eyes dart to the cushion.*) Spying on me! He had probably been at it before you came in!

WING-COMMANDER. Hey, you look almost scared to death, Chief. What have you been up to?

SEBE. Me scared? What for? It's the principle of the thing. It's indecent. Is a man no longer entitled to some privacy in his own home? I mean, my friend, what is the country coming to?

WING-COMMANDER. Chief, I am more concerned with what he may have overheard since we started talking.

SEBE. So am I, my friend, so am I. But put your mind at rest. Whatever food the frog has eaten, it is still the snake which digests it in the end. Leave it to me.

WING-COMMANDER. But will you find him soon enough, before he does any damage?

SEBE. Will I find him soon enough? (*Laughs.*) Does the snail leave a trail of slime wherever it drags itself? The trail left by a drug addict looking for a fix is wider than the Lagos-Ibadan expressway. My friend, forget that object you saw just now. He is dead. Before you reach your office this morning, he has become part of the ooze of the nearest compost heap. Sebe Irawe does not waste time. Let's talk of better things.

WING-COMMANDER. Well, don't let me regret that I cracked that case for you. If that brat proves to be the knife with which we cut our own throats, it would be a funny way of repaying me.

SEBE (*affably*). Commander, we are all grateful. The way your 'special services' in the Embassies responded – but of course we expected nothing less. You think we can forget the old London exploit?

WING-COMMANDER. What about London?

SEBE. That Scotland Yard affair. Just when it looked as if some top people were in the soup . . . (*He gives a prolonged chuckle.*) We were impressed. Two diplomatic bags full of marijuana, intercepted by Scotland Yard. Scotland Yard swings into action, delivers the bags to our High Commission were they are put in the basement strong room. They thought they were setting a clever trap. Fi-o-o-om! The bags disappear. No trace! An official of the Embassy dies a mysterious death. In his own apartment. Very mysterious. I tell you Commander, we were most impressed. Very impressed. We held a meeting and we decided, these are people with whom we can do business. These are serious people. They know when a bargain is a bargain.

WING-COMMANDER. Then perhaps you understand the gravity of my position.

SEBE. Say no more my Commander, say no more. Even in our modest world, we know. When you promise to deliver, you deliver. And you cover your tracks. Even if it means burning down the Ministry of External Affairs back home.

The WING-COMMANDER *reacts, then shrugs and remains silent.*

Commander, I said, wasn't it a strange coincidence? The timing made one wonder. The papers, even the government confirmed that the crucial report was on its way, from Scotland Yard. It was coming in the diplomatic bag . . .

WING-COMMANDER. So, a fire breaks out? What's so remarkable about that?

SEBE. Quite right Chief, nothing at all remarkable. Naturally, that was the end of the whole matter. Apart from another Nigerian corpse which was fished out of that River Thames of London.

WING-COMMANDER. Who says there was any connection?

SEBE. Not me my friend, not me. The matter died. Even Scotland Yard got the message and retired. I mean, after all, they had done their own part. Our usually noisy journalists got bored – or scared. The comments petered out. I tell you Commander, when you people are involved in our business, we know we are safe.

WING-COMMANDER (*laughing*). No, no, no. Let's give credit where credit is due. Maybe somebody at the London embassy placed an incendiary device in the diplomatic bag, why blame us?

SEBE. Incendiary device – is that what it was?

WING-COMMANDER. I am theorising, like everybody else. If somebody could replace the entire contents of a diplomatic bag with Indian hemp, why couldn't that same someone plant an incendiary device in another bag? You know how it works.

SEBE. No, I don't . . .

WING-COMMANDER (*settling instinctively into professional tone*). There are different kinds. For instance, one method, as soon as the bag is opened to fresh air . . . oh go away! What can you understand about those technical matters!

SEBE. You're right my friend, you are quite right. A diplomatic bag which contrabands, deserves to conflagrate . . .

> SEBE *and the* WING-COMMANDER *sing the* 'Song of the Diplomatic Bag'.

For a diplomatic bag
Is a most elastic bag
It can stretch to hold an elephant
Or a full electric plant
Plenipotentiary pack

It will cover every track
And for any busybody wag
It'll serve as a body bag

The famous Scotland Yard
Its record yet unmarred
Did smell a rat in a diplomat's pouch
Which raised a sleuthly grouch
A crack team did they field
Round the strongroom barred and sealed
But the pouch from the land of the vanishing trick
Had sailed through stone and brick

The Yardmen undeterred
Their detective passion stirred
They followed the trail of a prime suspect
And soon his flat was checked
They found him safe in bed
Diplomatically dead
Of the missing bags no clue nor trace
The Yard had lost the race

This went against the grain
The guilty hand was plain
The dossier went to their distant client
The Yard would not relent
But the show was merely passed
To a different stage and cast
And a different audience now would cheer
The transatlantic fare

So away four thousand miles
Their investigative files
In the Ministry of Foreign Affairs
Went up in glorious flares
In vain the Fire Brigade

Did race to render aid
The steel-lined confidential store
Was razed to the concrete floor

For a diplomatic bag
Is a copious magic bag
It's free from drug-free guarantee
To contraband it's free
Its mouth is open wide
To swallow nation pride
For though it stink in a foreign state
The bag is a sovereign state

> *Cell 'C'.* MIGUEL *speaks as the cell is spotlit.* DETIBA *and* EMUKE *are playing draughts.*

MIGUEL (*violently*). It makes you sick! Any way you look at it, it really is sickening. They're doing it to gain favour with Reagan, that bloody hypocrite! All of them, bloody hypocrites. Do they shoot their own people? No way. They slap them on the wrist with a few years . . .

DETIBA. Which they hardly ever complete.

MIGUEL. Yes, parole takes care of most of it. They do a fraction of the sentence and they get out on parole. But here they shed innocent blood to satisfy the Knight Crusader. Those damned hypocrites know where the stuff is traded like salt, where it changes hands like local currency. The Americans turn a blind eye on the mujahedin in Afghanistan because they're fighting communist rule. In North Pakistan you can buy an armoured tank with a packet of the stuff and collect your change with a mortar or two. So why do we have to shoot one another over here? What the hell are we trying to prove?

DETIBA. And what they call prison life over there – television, outdoor games, well stocked libraries . . . I know about some prisons where you can order food from your favourite restaurant.

EMUKE. You done go prison for America?

DETIBA. Not yet.

EMUKE. Na so you say. How come you know so much about American prisons?

DETIBA. I read, Emuke, I read. Pick up an American newspaper any week and you'll read about a prisoner suing the prison for not providing him a woman for the weekend.

EMUKE. Sho!

DETIBA. It's true. Some prisons actually arrange conjugal visits on a regular basis.

EMUKE. Conju wetin?

DETIBA. Conjugal. Visit by wife or fiancée.

EMUKE. Well, I begin sabbe why one friend wey me and in dey do business, every time, 'e go to pray say, if one day dey must to catch am, make 'e happen for America.

MIGUEL. Don't bet too heavily on America. Some of their prisons make this one look like Sheraton Hotel.

EMUKE. No way!

MIGUEL. It's true just the same. Especially down South. In some places, they say it's foretaste of hell. (*Stops abruptly, staring straight ahead. Speaks more slowly.*) Hell! Just imagine if there actually were such a place!

  EMUKE *and* DETIBA *study* MIGUEL *for some moments, exchange looks.*

EMUKE (*conspiratorially*). 'In mood just change like this. (*Flipping over his hand rapidly.*)

DETIBA. Play.

  They make a few moves on the board. In distant back-ground, the muffled sound of foghorns.

EMUKE. Is as if to say the Harmattan never go away yet. All that mist – na because of am the ship dey blow foghorn.

DETIBA. This morning when I looked out, I couldn't see down to the lagoon. Even the hyacinths had been swallowed up.

EMUKE. Is good to be on board ship when fog dey. Everything around you, 'e dey just like cotton-wool. Sometime you no fit see another man for deck. You are walking like this, and then a body begin commot like ghost. You wake up in the morning and look through porthole, and 'e be like say you dey inside cloud. All the sound for inside ship become soft like dey done wrap every iron with cotton-wool. Even the ship bell . . .

DETIBA. So for how many years were you a sailor?

EMUKE. Nearly fifteen years. And nearly all the time with Nkrumah's Black Star Line. I meet Nkrumah one time. He come inspect ship and we all line up salute am for deck. I done run become deckhand since I be small picken. Long before those foolish generals come take over.

DETIBA. Were you in Ghana at the time?

EMUKE. Na China we dey when 'e happen. The Black Star dey go nearly everywhere. But we return home soon after coup. When I see how things begin spoil, I return here come join Elder Dempster Lines. De thing wey dem general do enh . . .

DETIBA. Their throats were too vast. One of them even swallowed a whole ship.

EMUKE. One whole ship? I never hear dat one.

DETIBA. Well, not altogether. Let's just say, he swallowed its cargo. Took care of the entire load – it was cocoa. You remember what cocoa meant to Ghana? What he did was like sucking all the blood from an infant.

EMUKE. I know. We dey carry cocoa go Sweden, London, Turkey, even Russia self.

DETIBA. Ghana didn't have much else. No petrol, no minerals.

EMUKE. They get small gold. I know, because I dey smuggle am commot for some businesswoman one time.

DETIBA. Ancient history. That's when the country still deserved the name Gold Coast.

EMUKE. Dem still dey dig am for some region o. Upper Volta still produce enough for regular business.

DETIBA. But not enough to matter for the country, that's what I'm telling you. For a few people like your businesswoman, yes, but it just didn't affect the nation's economy. Not like cocoa.

EMUKE. Na true.

DETIBA. Cocoa. Every year. What the government watched was the price of cocoa on the world market. And this general, he sold off nearly one-third of the year's harvest and deposited the money in his overseas account.

EMUKE. Chineke God!

DETIBA. Chineke God indeed. Because Chineke God was waiting for him. Very patiently.

EMUKE. Den catch am?

DETIBA. Oh yes. He was one of those they lined up and shot after the second coup. Or third. Or fourth, I forget which. But the people got their pound of flesh in the end.

EMUKE. Make all of dem dey shoot one another self. When no soja lef' the people go get chance rule demselves without dem wahala.

DETIBA. Well, the way they carry on, maybe they are trying to carry out your wish. Coup today, casualties right and left, executions tomorrow. Then another attempt the day after. And then sometimes, you don't even know who is really guilty of something or whether someone is just trying to settle old scores. That Ghana bloodbath for instance, till today many people say that one general was simply shot out of revenge. He wasn't found guilty of anything.

EMUKE. En-hen! Who beg am go mix himself up with gov'men?

DETIBA. Politicians.

EMUKE. Politicians. Na politicians invite am?

DETIBA. They mess up. That's what leads the army into temptation.

EMUKE. Politicians na civilians. Make soja man change to

civilians if 'e wan do gov'men'. Dem soja too, dey no de mess
up? Dey all wan chop, das all. Anyway, for civilian mess and
soja mess, give me civilian mess any time. At least civilian no fit
do de kin' dabaru nonsense wey put we for dis kin' mess.
(*Pushes the board away.*) I done tire self. (*Walks away from the
board and flings himself on the bed.*)

DETIBA (*approaching footsteps*). Now who was accusing somebody just now of being moody? I think we have company.

EMUKE (*sits up quickly*). Na warder?

DETIBA. Who else? (*Looks through the bars.*) It's a new face.

EMUKE (*to* MIGUEL). Make we try this one?

MIGUEL *hasn't heard.*

Mr Domingo!

MIGUEL. What?

DETIBA. There's a new warder. You want us to try him or not?
Your letter.

MIGUEL. Oh, sure. Why not? Go ahead.

EMUKE *quickly resumes his place at the draughts board. The*
WARDER *strolls in, inspects the* INMATES *and watches the two*
players make a few moves.

WARDER. Good morning. Hm. I see you people sabbe play
draught o.

EMUKE (*without looking up*). I see you get eyes for your head.

WARDER. Haba! Na fight? Man no fit greet you?

DETIBA. Go away. Go and do your spying somewhere else.

WARDER. Me? Spy? To God who make me . . . !

EMUKE. Shurrup! Make you no take God name play for this place
you hear? No to you go report to Security say the Superintendent dey do favouritism for some detainees?

WARDER. I swear, not to me o. Wetin me I get with Security? Who
tell you that kind 'tory?

DETIBA. Word gets around in this place, don't you worry. We were warned against you.

WARDER. Who warn you? You see my face before?

DETIBA. Yes. Someone pointed you out as we passed your morning parade.

WARDER. Anybody wey accuse me for that kind ting, God no go make in own better. I swear . . .

EMUKE. And if na true dem accuse you, wetin make God do you?

WARDER. Make I die for dis useless job! Make all my family no prosper for den life.

> DETIBA *and* EMUKE *look up at each other; they resolve some doubt.*

DETIBA. He'll do, Mr Domingo.

EMUKE. Yes, you fit risk am.

WARDER (*at first puzzled, then a slow grin*). O-oh-oh, na test you dey test me.

DETIBA. What's your name?

WARDER. Amidu.

DETIBA (*offering him a packet*). Do you smoke?

WARDER (*quick look up and down passage*). I go take one for later.

DETIBA. Take more than one.

> DETIBA *shakes several cigarettes into* WARDER's *hand.* WARDER *stuffs them into his pocket.*

WARDER. Thank you, thank you sirs. Ah, you disturb me well well before. Me? Wetin I dey get from government I go spy for them?

DETIBA. We had to be sure. Our friend here needs courier service. He wants to send a letter.

WARDER. Things hard small o. They give us all kind of checks nowadays. Coming in, going out, even spot checks. It's no joke.

DETIBA. He's willing to pay.

MIGUEL. It's just a letter. (*Brings out an envelope.*) The address is on it. Everybody knows the house.

WARDER (*recognising the address, he looks at* DOMINGO *with some awe*). O-oh, na you be the . . .

MIGUEL. Make sure you give it to her, in person. It's my mother.

WARDER. I go bring reply?

MIGUEL. There'll be no need. But hand it to her personally. Don't give it to anyone else.

WARDER. If I no meet her nko?* I fit go back any time you want.

MIGUEL. You'll meet her all right. She doesn't leave the house – except on Saturday mornings. Any other time of day, you'll find her at home. And she'll make it worth your while.

EMUKE. You hear that, Mr Postmaster-General.

WARDER. You sure say you no wan' make she send something? I sure say I can manage bring you anything you want. Anything at all. Whether na food or drink or money, just write am for note.

MIGUEL. No, I'm afraid you can't bring me the only thing I want. But it doesn't matter. Soon we won't be needing anything.

EMUKE *glances at him uneasily.* DETIBA *also, but he shrugs it off.*

WARDER. Look, you people, I no know if you get interest but er . . . (*Nods towards* MIGUEL.) . . . 'e look like say you get the means to do something for yourselves. (*He digs into his pocket and brings out a small, oval object, bound tightly in white leather and black thread.*)

DETIBA. What is that?

WARDER. You hear of bandufu before?

DETIBA. Ban-du . . . Oh yes, bandufu. Is that what that is?

EMUKE. Wetin be bandufu?

WARDER. Some people no believe am but make I tell you, I done see the thing wey bandufu fit do. I take my own very eyes see

---

* 'Nko?' means 'what then?'

am. These oyinbo people can talk any nonsense they want but blackman power dey where 'e day.

EMUKE. Chineke God! You no fit answer simple question? Wetin be bandufu?

DETIBA. I'll tell you. It's supposed to make you invisible. Disappear. Vanish into thin air.

EMUKE. Sho? (*Reaches out his hand through the bars.*)

WARDER. You get interest or not?

DETIBA. Go away, Emuke, don't you fall for that nonsense.

EMUKE. No? Me I get interest, why not?

DETIBA. It's a swindle. These people just use it to make money.

WARDER. I tell you two prisoner vanish before my very eyes. And na dis very bandufu do am.

EMUKE. Tell me how 'e dey work.

WARDER. If you get interest, make we talk business first.

DETIBA. What did I tell you? It's business first and last.

EMUKE. Wait small. Tell me how dis ting dey work.

DETIBA *throws up his hands in despair.*

WARDER. 'E get certain ting wey you go say, that all. You tie the bandufu for your waist, or put am somewhere it must touch your body. Then, you recite the incantation. Very short. You call the name of any ancestor you get wey done die, then your own name – if you get oriki, you call all your oriki. Then finally, the place where you wan' land. Dat one very important because, if you no tell dis medicine where it must take you, 'e fit land you for inside jungle or overseas, or even back inside your enemy hand.

EMUKE. How much 'e go cost?

DETIBA. Emuke!

EMUKE. Look my friend, wetin we go take money do for de place where tribunal wan' send us. Abi bandufu dey work over dere? 'E fit bring me back to this world?

WARDER. Na proper sense you dey talk. But as for cost, you know this kin' medicine must cost. All de ingredients wey dey inside, including the hair from private part of person wey just die. . . .

EMUKE. Why you like dey talk so much? I say how much?

WARDER. Twelve kilos.

DETIBA. What! You bloody fraud!

WARDER. My friend, make a tell you about this very one. The babalawo wey make am, 'e done finish de main ting since three months. But the power no complete because 'e no get that last ingredient wey I mention.

EMUKE. You mean the hair from private part?

WARDER. That's right. Every time prisoner die, I no get lucky to dey for duty, and na me only this babalawo come trust. In any case de other warders, den dey fear de man too much.

DETIBA. Ooh. So the babalawo is inside this prison?

WARDER. Na in a dey tell you! 'E dey for lunatic cell.

EMUKE. Kai. Na crazeman medicine you wan' sell me?

WARDER. No, not to say 'e craze. But the power wey 'e dey take make dis kin' medicine 'e dey turn in head. When dat happen, nobody fit go near am. Na me one den go call.

DETIBA. So where did this vital hair come from?

WARDER (*pointing*). General cell. One prisoner die there day before yesterday. As luck be, na me dey for duty, so I unlock the babalawo make 'e come shave in pubic hair, before I make official report. The hair wey lef', 'e fit make two more, so if all of una want . . .

EMUKE (*eagerly*). You see. De power go still fresh, no be so?

DETIBA. Emuke, don't be such a fool!

WARDER. I'm telling you. Is very lucky. Since that babalawo dey prison, na only four bandufu 'e fit make. And na me dey look for customer for am. I tell you, two prisoner wey use the medicine, dem vanish commot prison. Till today nobody fit find dem. Nobody. One na rapist wey get ten years, de other na counterfeit money maker wey den give fifteen years.

DETIBA. You are worse than a rapist. You are both necrophiliac and grave-robber. But I hope the other one paid you in counterfeit money.

EMUKE (*despondently*). But wissai me a go get twelve thousand, even for counterfeit notes?

WARDER (*gestures to* MIGUEL). 'E fit lend you. If 'e just add small note for this letter, in mama go send de money.

DETIBA. You're betting on the wrong horse. You think someone like him believes in that kind of rubbish?

EMUKE. No to im go use am. Na me wan try de ting.

WARDER. Look, inspection time done near. Make up your mind quick quick or I must go try somebody else.

> EMUKE *hesitates. Then approaches* MIGUEL.

EMUKE. Er . . . Mr Domingo . . . ?

> MIGUEL *turns round slowly, the ghost of a grin on his face. He digs his hand under his trouser waistband and extracts an object identical to the* WARDER's.

MIGUEL. Why don't you try mine Emuke? It's already paid for, and as you see, it has never been used.

DETIBA. You? You mean you . . .

MIGUEL. A family friend slipped it to me on our fateful day in court. (*He takes out a piece of paper, wraps the object in it.*) The incantation is written there.

DETIBA. Did you try it?

MIGUEL. I never would have thought I would. I always laughed at such things but, after that sentencing . . . it's amazing what desperation does to you. (*Throws it to* EMUKE.) Here. Maybe it will work for you.

DETIBA (*breaks into a chuckle*). Better luck elsewhere my friend. Try one of the ex-Ministers . . .

WARDER (*gives a prolonged hiss, then flings* DOMINGO's *letter on the cell floor*). Some people dey, wey even heaven no fit help. Ye-ye people!

The spot traverses stage to reveal the general cell where the STUDENT's *curriculum vitae is still in progress.*

General cell. COMMANDANT HYACINTH's *'Cabinet' surround the* STUDENT *as if he is the centre of an interrogation.*

COMMANDANT. You are sure you are not trying to play tough guy? You actually went back?

STUDENT. I was desperate for a fix. And I thought they would come after me right away. The Wing-Commander carried a gun for all I knew. People get shot all the time in that part of the city, no questions asked.

NUMBER 2. And you sneaked back into the house? Wonderful boy!

STUDENT. It was the safest place to hide and I knew the house inside out. I told you, I was his trusted courier. He would send me to go and take out thousands from under his bed or other hiding-places.

NUMBER 2. Before you caught the habit.

STUDENT. Yes, that was the start of my disaster. He used to fence for us – that's how I got to know him. We stole valuables from our parents' colleagues while our own friends would rob our parents. We left the door open for one another, it was easy. Sebe would buy the goods from us. Stereos, jewellery, even motor tyres and spare parts. Then one day he asked me if I would like to earn some really big money . . . well, from then on, it was one thing leading to another. We got on well. He treated me like a son.

COMMANDANT. Security!

DIRECTOR. Yes Commandant.

COMMANDANT. What do you think?

DIRECTOR. I must confess I am most impressed. The boy thinks like a soldier. First he hides in what seems the most dangerous place. Then he commits a slight misdemeanour to get himself arrested and thrown in gaol – for his own safety.

General nods and noises of approval.

COMMANDANT. Yes, but the question is, what is he worth? How much do you think Sebe will pay if we let him know the boy is here? And that we have people here ready to do the job for him.

HOME. Chief, the young man has thrown himself on our protection.

COMMANDANT. A junkie! Dope addict!

NUMBER 2. Ex.

COMMANDANT. Okay, ex. He had no choice but to kick the habit in here. What you can't maintain indoors you kick out of doors – big deal! The point is, what's the deal? Where does Amaroko come in? If we're going to cross Sebe Irawe over this stray dog, what's in it for us?

HOME. Maybe his CV will tell us.

INFORMATION. Let's vote on it Commandant. I don't like getting on the wrong side of Sebe. We're in here; he is out. He can make things hot for us.

HOME. Not forgetting that he's got the Air Force working for him.

DIRECTOR. I doubt if it will come to the vote, Commandant.

COMMANDANT. No? (*Grins.*) Securico himself! I think the Major has detected something we've all missed.

DIRECTOR. I believe so. Why should he have revealed so much? Why take the risk? (*He walks up to the* STUDENT.) You know where the missing goods are, don't you?

STUDENT (*nods*). Yes, I do. I was watching Sebe very closely.

Excited reactions.

COMMANDANT. See? The boy is devious. Devious! He's been holding out on us.

INFORMATION. You are real sneaky for your age, sonny. Putting us through all those appetisers but you left out the really juicy part.

STUDENT. It's in the final episode.

DIRECTOR. I told you. He's sharp.

COMMANDANT. It's blackmail.

STUDENT. No, it's bargaining. Do we have a deal or not?

INFORMATION. I still say let's vote on it. Sebe . . .

COMMANDANT. Shut up! Who is Sebe? When did his authority extend to Amaroko? I am in command here.

NUMBER 2. Vote, vote, vote! You think we're running a democracy here?

HOME. Those politicians have messed up his brain. I've told the Superintendent he should always put them in a separate cell. They come here and contaminate decent criminals – that's the result.

COMMANDANT. You know what the value of fifty kilos of cocaine comes to? And you start whining about vote or no vote. Nonsense! Take your places for the real thing! Studentco, we talk business later, you and I.

DIRECTOR. Count me in; you'll need my expertise.

COMMANDANT *nods. Signals to the* SERGEANT-MAJOR.

SERGEANT-MAJOR. Places everyone!

They scramble 'offstage', leaving COMMANDANT *and* NUM-BER 2 *in their last positions. They sing the last verse of 'Diplomatic Bag'.*

WING-COMMANDER (*sighs*). Those were kindergarten days, Chief. Peanut pickings. This is our introduction into the Big League, and if we don't act big, we shall lose our membership.

SEBE (*wringing his hands*). I know, I know. It worries me night and day.

WING-COMMANDER. Fifty kilograms of prime grade cocaine is not chicken-feed. Countries have gone to war for less.

SEBE. Don't we know it, Commander, don't we know it? If my

memory serves me right, you soldiers have even declared war against one another over football. Common football!

WING-COMMANDER. Who did?

SEBE. You remember – those a-rhumba-styley countries in Latin America, about the size of my backyard vegetable patch – yes, one of them was Honduras . . .

WING-COMMANDER. And so? What has football got to do with our own matter? I am talking about big league and you start talking football league.

SEBE. Nothing Commander, nothing. I was simply agreeing with you.

A brief silence, during which the WING-COMMANDER *eyes* SEBE *with deep suspicion.*

WING-COMMANDER. You know, Sebe, I get this feeling that you are making fun of me.

SEBE. Me? God forbid! My friend, why should such a thing cross your mind. This is a matter of life and death.

WING-COMMANDER (*with rising fury*). I spend the entire morning telling you that you and your men are slow, and you start talking of some banana republics which begin by shooting football and end up shooting bullets. Are we playing games? Or your men? Somebody is playing games somewhere, and in a matter that touches my honour. My honour is at stake!

SEBE. Cool down Commander . . .

WING-COMMANDER. The operation was master-minded by the very cream of the ruling junta. Nobody knew of the special bag in that shipment in this country except myself – and you.

SEBE (*backing away*). Ah, no, no, not at all, my dear partner. All you told me was to prepare myself for something big, that was all. What it was, when it would come, how it would come . . . Commander, for all I knew it could be guns and ammunition for another coup.

WING-COMMANDER. Don't talk rot!

SEBE. Or for sale or hire to armed robbers. Commander, all I am saying is that I knew nothing. It could have been gold. Or diamonds. Or contraband like ivory tusks – I am just a conduit pipe Commander, I have never pretended to be anything else.

WING-COMMANDER. My arrangements were thorough. I never leave anything to chance – never! I assigned a top officer to clear the consignment and transfer it to the armoury. The formal presentation by the Pakistani ambassador was to await my arrival – I made sure of that. The letter of friendship from President Zia is right here, in my briefcase. Here, take a look at it . . . (*He fumbles with the lock of his attaché-case, opens it and flourishes the letter.*) Take a look! That is the presidential seal . . .

SEBE. Commander, I know, I know . . .

WING-COMMANDER. I just want you to understand that nothing, absolutely nothing was left to chance. Nobody could touch any part of that consignment before I arrived with this letter.

SEBE. The top officer who did the clearing . . . ?

WING-COMMANDER (*irritably*). Except him of course. Naturally. And he knew nothing of the special bag. His job was simply to clear a high-security shipment and store it in the armoury! But the pirates got there before him, the very night the ship berthed.

SEBE. The harm is done Commander. What we must think of is how to undo it.

WING-COMMANDER. Sebe, you hold the key to this entire business. Put pressure on your people!

SEBE. Commander, please. Ask around. I am a middleman. I don't launch pirates against sea-going vessels. Violence is alien to my temperament.

WING-COMMANDER. No one is accusing you, but nearly all the underworld report here, sooner or later.

SEBE. I am only a link in the chain Commander. A small man.

They hold each other's eyes for moments. The WING-

COMMANDER *is barely containing his rage.* SEBE *wears a sardonic smile.*

WING-COMMANDER. Just remember what is at stake. For me. And for you. We military stick together, remember that. We may settle scores among ourselves from time to time, even bloodily, but in the end, we close ranks. When we do . . .

SEBE. . . . we bloody civilians become the scapegoats.

WING-COMMANDER. I'm glad you know that.

SEBE. Or perhaps, to be more accurate, we provide the scapegoats. Expendables. But people like us, Commander, continue with business as usual.

WING-COMMANDER. Not always. Sometimes, the stakes are so big we cannot accept just any scrawny scapegoat. That's when we go for the fatted calf. Then, nobody remains immune. Nobody.

SEBE (*sighs deeply*). I understand, Chief. I understand you only too well.

WING-COMMANDER. I need results Sebe. I need results, fast! My partners are impatient and my standing is at stake. I dare not return without something concrete to report, and of course I cannot remain here for ever. My course still has three months to go – if I stay too long I shall run out of excuses. Once the handing-over ceremony is over . . .

SEBE. You can always amount a coup.

WING-COMMANDER (*looking round wildly*). Don't say that again! I don't find it funny.

SEBE. It's not meant to be funny. It is accepted cover-up practice.

WING-COMMANDER. Not here in Nigeria.

SEBE. Who knows if it may yet happen. But I was thinking of Uganda as a matter of fact. Didn't the one and only Idi Amin stage his coup over his ivory and diamonds smuggling? (*Conspiratorially.*) They say Obote was about to put him on trial when he struck.

WING-COMMANDER (*grimly*). Yes, quite a man of current affairs, we know.

SEBE. Business, my friend, business. We try to keep abreast of world affairs. One doesn't get to know the forest by climbing only the trees in his village. The learning process is what keeps us afloat and alive, Commander.

WING-COMMANDER. Yes, staying alive. That's very important. Let's not forget that, Chief.

SEBE (*casting a furtive look at the* WING-COMMANDER). May I make a suggestion Chief?

WING-COMMANDER. What now?

SEBE. A suggestion. Something I have just thought of.

WING-COMMANDER. Well, let's hear it.

SEBE. You see, it seems to me that you have not really tapped all the resources at your disposal. I mean, you are after all a member of the Ruling Council.

WING-COMMANDER. What are you getting at?

SEBE. Use that resource.

WING-COMMANDER. Of course, I intend to.

SEBE. No, I can tell you haven't thought of this – get the Council to declare a State of Emergency.

WING-COMMANDER. A what?

SEBE. A State of Emergency.

WING-COMMANDER. You must be mad.

SEBE. Am I?

WING-COMMANDER. Declare a State of Emergency! On what grounds?

SEBE. Any excuse will do. Close all the borders. Tighten up Customs. Decree a stop-and-search authorisation for all the uniformed services. Anywhere, any time, night and day or – wait! That's it! Make it a crackdown on drugs, special campaign. Round up all known drug-users and pushers. No exception. Detain suspects without trial. Even the petty ones. When you squeeze the belle tight, the fart go commot.

WING-COMMANDER. You mean, actually admit that a consignment is missing?

SEBE. No, no, no Commander. Simply launch a special campaign – it may even bring you extra aid from World Health Organisation. Make it the next stage of the battle against indiscipline, emphasis on drug abuse. Commander, don't tell me you can't sell such a brilliant, straightforward clean-up exercise to your Ruling Council.

WING-COMMANDER (*gives it serious thought*). It's a sellable idea.

SEBE. More than sellable. It is buyable. We squeeze the users, squeeze the pushers, squeeze the pirates who did the actual hijacking – somewhere along the line someone will break and tell us just who is sitting on a hundred million US dollars. My spies will easily find out who is panicking and then you can pounce!

WING-COMMANDER. It may work. It may work.

SEBE. It will work. It has to. It is a national undertaking, but in true military style. No voice will be raised in opposition.

WING-COMMANDER (*paces thoughtfully*). It should work. I think I know how to present it to the Ruling Council.

SEBE. Sway them Commander, sway them. I know you can do it. Get them to seal up the entire country tighter than a virgin's you-know-what. Give us the old stop-and-search routine. Search, but not destroy!

WING-COMMANDER (*giggling*). After all, the missing item is state property.

SEBE. So it is, so it is.

WING-COMMANDER. Well then, it deserves state mobilisation.

SEBE. That's the spirit, my Commander. It's a state assignment . . .

WING-COMMANDER. For a state consignment.

Together: 'Song of State Assignment'.

State assignment
For state consignment
State machinery

For state chicanery
Scorched earth strategy
Will provoke the allergy
To expose that very hidden
Commodity forbidden

Don't mess with the military
Or we'll write your obituary
Underworld and over-brass
No one dare embarrass
Power, the pure commodity
To which our little ditty
Is for ever consecrated
Don't ignore or underrate it

State machinery
For state chicanery
Let who can resolve the riddle
How we guarantee the fiddle
Mum's the word among the ranks
Mum's the word in foreign banks
When state assignments coincide
With state consigments far and wide

WING-COMMANDER. You know something else?

SEBE. What is that, dear partner?

WING-COMMANDER. We'll make it retroactive.

SEBE. You will make what retroactive?

WING-COMMANDER. The campaign of course. The law, the decree,
the penalties. It will show we mean business. And anyway,
that's our style. That's how people recognise who's in charge.
That's the difference between you and us. Civilians can only
operate in linear time. We go backwards and forwards at will.

SEBE. And in circles. Brilliant! Don't we know it? Your patron
god is Esu. (*Confidentially.*) And let me tell you, we must not
neglect the little fellow.

WING-COMMANDER. Who? What little fellow?

SEBE. Esu. Small but potent. (*Unveils his Esu shrine.*) You know his oriki don't you? He throws a stone today and it kills a man last week. That retroactive twist is just the kind of idea he inspires in men of action.

WING-COMMANDER. Look, Sebe, you stick to your superstitions. I will take care of practical measures.

SEBE. Practical measures, Commander, practical measures? As we are talking here, do you know how many different shrines are receiving sacrifices from our opponents to buy protection for the missing goods? Do you know how many bodies will be found with all their vital organs missing? That missing bag itself is almost a deity that must be propitiated. It has become a god in its own right.

WING-COMMANDER. Sure, sure. As I said, stick to your own plans . . .

SEBE. Commander, I will surely vex with you. You people, you think you know everything. Armed robbers know better. They know what they must do before an operation, and I am telling you Commander, they can proof themselves against your bullets . . .

WING-COMMANDER. We've heard that often enough, but they end up in the morgue just the same.

SEBE. The ones who didn't choose the right experts. There are doctors and doctors Commander, just as there are soldiers and soldiers.

WING-COMMANDER. That's it exactly. Some soldiers believe in all that stuff. I am not one of them.

SEBE. If I could do it all by myself, I wouldn't bother you. But you are the principal. The whole thing began with you. When I visit the major crossroads at midnight to put down the calabash, and Esu asks me, where is the principal petitioner, what will I say? The little man will simply laugh, eat the sacrifice and attend to more serious people.

WING-COMMANDER. You really believe all that rubbish?

SEBE. My friend, do as I say. Come with me. What are we trying
to do if not to seal up all the roads so this juicy mouse does not
escape? We are dealing with the crossroads, so . . . yes, tell me,
doesn't the Bible itself say – render unto Caesar what is
Caesar's and unto God what is God's? It's the same thing. In
any case what is wrong with a little insurance? Commander,
look at me! Just look at me! Moslem, Christian, Animist,
Buddhist, Aborisa – now that combination is what you call –
practical measures. Insurance policies. Maybe if you had
thought of invoking Olokun, guardian of the seas, the pirates
would have been drowned while attempting the hijack. (*He
unveils several shrines while speaking.*)

WING-COMMANDER (*faltering*). This is so much nonsense. . . .

SEBE. Well, humour me. Say you're doing it for Sebe. You are
doing it for your business partner, for your friend, to boost his
confidence. I will even provide you the white cloth to wear, and
black cap . . .

WING-COMMANDER. White cloth! Black cap?

SEBE. Leave the details to me. In one hour, it will all be over. Just
remember that those on the other side are not sitting down idly.
They are mobilising all the powers, and we must neutralise
them. What time do you finish your council meeting?

WING-COMMANDER. Well, sometimes it goes on till midnight. And
if I am to propose these new measures and get them
through . . .

SEBE. Come here straight after the meeting. Four crossroads,
that's more than enough. It won't take more than one hour to
do the rounds. I have my own priest and shrine for every single
deity. I don't broadcast my piety, but I am always prepared.

WING-COMMANDER. This whole thing is crazy.

SEBE. The people who did this thing to us, they want to prosper,
not so? We also want to prosper. Even if I don't know them
yet, I know their habits. I know exactly what they will do, what

they are doing. If I may just adapt our ancient saying to the circumstances – if everybody makes fun of someone, saying that the fellow is acting crazy, and yet we see that fellow prospering, doing well, being successful, then isn't it time we also sipped a little of the potion of insanity?

WING-COMMANDER (*grinning*). You know how to give a twist to everything.

SEBE. I am a practical man, Commander. I keep a toe in every shrine and a finger in every business pie. Your man is Esu, but you are going more modern. Esu only throws stones, you, you fire bullets. But Esu is broadminded, don't worry. He won't be resentful of your prowess – that is, as long as we give him his due. This exercise enh, you'll see, when you fire a bullet today, it will have hit its target long before you ever took over government. Now that is real power for you.

WING-COMMANDER (*rapt in the prospect*). You know, the power to act backwards in time . . .

SEBE. And it was all your own idea! Didn't I say it? You people are trained to think big.

WING-COMMANDER. I shall spin a net with a small mesh. Even the sprats cannot escape it.

SEBE. When you cast that net, Commander, even the fishes that swam through those waters the year before will be snared. There is no escape for anyone, big or small.

WING-COMMANDER. It's the ultimate time-machine. When we launch it . . .

SEBE. All it requires is libation. A little midnight libation, just to be on the good side of the little man.

WING-COMMANDER. Lubrication, not libation. A trusty sub-machine gun well lubricated, that's all it takes to bring things back under control.

SEBE. S.M.G. or S.M.O.G. – the difference is 'O'. (*Shapes his fingers to form an 'O'.*) Zero.

WING-COMMANDER. S.M.O.G.?

SEBE. Save me O God – Libation, prayers, offerings – to whichever powers you choose.

WING-COMMANDER. You are impossible, Sebe.

SEBE. You keep saying that, my friend. Why? I am possible. I am the only possible type of businessman in this country.

WING-COMMANDER. Well, for me, the sub-machine gun guarantees the time-machine. But, all right, I'll humour you.

SEBE. It's ready for launching then. Move it against everything in our way. It's wartime Wing-Commander. It's a moral crusade – slackness, rigidity, forgery, connery, venery, revelry, smuggling, ogling, laziness, eagerness, apathy, telepathy, intolerance, permissiveness, academia, kleptomania, cultism, nepotism, nudity, drunkenness, superstition, godlessness, loitering, muttering, rioting, malingering, rumour-mongering . . .

'Rap of the Military Time-Machine':

The prisoners stomp on stage in a variety of military cast-offs, some with gas masks – half-face with goggles – several with 'Tyson' crew-cuts, cavorting in 'rap' motions. They go through their contortions in precision drill, chanting the chorus in the 'rap-recitativo' mode. WING-COMMANDER *takes the solo, later joined by* SEBE *who hugs himself with delight and dances with approval as the* WING-COMMANDER *develops his campaign of 'reforms'.*

CHORUS.
  I got you in a trap
    on the time-machine
  If you don't take the rap
    I cannot preen
  Myself as Mr Clean
    now that makes me mean
  Too long you've been
    on the money scene
  While the fact of my being

is – my pocket's lean
I ain't worth a bean
   to a sweet sixteen
I ain't been seen
   with no beauty queen
Who says I ain't keen
   on pastures green?
So you've got a trip coming
   on the time-machine
Time you went roaming
   in a change of scene

WING-COMMANDER.
We shan't be confined
   just to future time
Retribution shall fall
   on any previous crime
Of refining, sniffing
   tasting or injecting
Buying, retailing
   distributing, inspecting
(Except of course
   by authorised agents)
Liquid, or solid, or
   powdery hallucinogens
To expedite this mission
   we hereby erect
A military tribunal
   with immediate effect
Its powers shall be subject
   to no confines
No bail shall be granted
   no option of fines
No option of prison
   or community service

No right of appeal
   no delaying device

CHORUS.
   I got you in a trap (*etc.*)

WING-COMMANDER.
   Every offender shall be
      guilty as charged
   Acquittal shall mean
      conditionally discharged
   Surrender of passport
      report every morning
   To the nearest police
      or else keep running
   As for fugitive suspects
      seize every spouse
   And children as hostage
      place a price on the louse
   From the tiniest of doses
      to wholesale vendor
   Habitual user or
      first-time offender
   Laundering of earnings
      from drug operation
   Shall incur something worse
      than life incarceration
   It's forfeit of life
      by firing squad
   And forfeit of property
      at home or abroad
   Be it liquid asset
      or landed estate
   And any other forfeiture
      as decided by the state

CHORUS.

  I got you in a trap (*etc.*)

WING-COMMANDER.

  We're going to clean up
    every damned city
  Without fear or favour
    or any shred of pity
  And those who think
    there's refuge in the village
  Will find we're all set
    for rural life pillage
  So bring out your skeletons
    open up your closets
  Or we'll dig them out
    on the tips of rusty bayonets
  All your dens of decadence
    in affluent suburbs
  Are going to feel the weight
    of military curbs
  So pull up your socks
    the Army's now in charge
  Shape up or ship out
    the drill-major's at large
  We're building a new nation
    cleaning out the rot
  Ending your civilian torpor
    striking while it's hot
  And remember we're the breed
    whose bullets, fired the day before
  Hit their mark the previous year
    and penetrate your door

CHORUS.

  I got you in a trap (*etc.*)

WING-COMMANDER.

> There's too much thinking going on
>> we'll put an end to it
> We've had enough of dissidents
>> they must conform or quit
> We're rooting for the radicals
>> rooting them out
> There ain't room for them and us
>> We're putting them to rout
> Pay attention to my rap
>> or you going to take the rap
> For things you think you never thought
>> but which fit your mental map

CHORUS.

> I got you in a trap (*etc.*)

> *Next to invade the platform is a skimpy figure clad only in*
> *even skimpier underpants, blowing an outsize saxophone.*
> *He is followed by female dancers doing a 'shinamanic' dance*
> *to the tune of 'Zombie'. The earlier group retreat. The* WING-
> COMMANDER *stares aghast, recovers, and breaks into mania-*
> *cal laughter. His voice overwhelms the music of the*
> *intruders, while the first group resume their motions with*
> *greater vigour.*

WING-COMMANDER.

> *Chief Kalakuta priest

---

* Chief Kalakuta priest: This refers to the musician Fela Anikulapo-Kuti, a non-conformist musician who was sentenced to a long term of imprisonment, under the military regime depicted in the play, on trumped-up charges of illegal possession of foreign currency. In an earlier brush with yet another military regime, his commune-style home, with studios, known as the 'Kalakuta Republic', was burnt down in broad daylight by soldiers in uniform, with the connivance of the regime. During that raid, his mother was thrown down two floors; she died not long after. Anikulapo-Kuti led a protest march to the State House where he attempted to deliver a symbolic coffin. The judicial inquiry which was set up to probe the outrage returned the verdict that Kalakuta Republic had been burnt down by 'unknown soldiers'.

we've got him in our sights
The way we deal with mavericks
　he'll scream for human rights
So his club was burnt to cinders
　The culprit was unknown
Accidents do happen
　the affair was overblown
How fairer could we be?
　We set up judicial probes
The learned judge was neutral
　correct in legal robes
This cat's mother fixated
　why the obsessive worry?
She fell out of the window
　soldiers don't say 'sorry'
Does he let her rest in peace?
　He tries to deposit
Her coffin on our doorstep
　– well, that really does it!
Resurrect her if you can
　build another Kalakut
You'll learn the brutal truth
　of power, Mr Cool-and-Cute!

CHORUS.
　You've got a trip coming
　　on the time-machine
　Time you went roaming
　　in a change of scene

WING-COMMANDER.
　He thought we'd chase him smoking pot
　　no, foreign currency
　Was where we chose to nail his arse
　　– no clemency!

CHORUS.

   I got you in a trap (*etc.*)

   As the saxophonist is overwhelmed, manacled and encased
   in prison clothes, his entourage disappear one after the other.

WING-COMMANDER.

   Lock him up! Yap him
      enough years to scare 'im
   Muffle up his Afro-beat and
      scatter wide his harem
   Let him file for bankruptcy
      silence his cacophony
   No air-wave may vibrate
      except to army symphony

CHORUS.

   You've got a trip coming
      on the time-machine
   Time you went roaming
      in a change of scene

WING-COMMANDER.

   This nation is caught
      in a moral crisis
   The road shall be hard
      to dis'plinary bliss
   This new broom's set to sweep
      with all its strands of steel
   No taking 'no' for answer
      all shoulders to the wheel
   All suggestive images are
      banned from stage and journals
   The decadence of modern tastes
      is banished from our portals

It's back to fundamentalism
  strict moralistic values
National flag, national pledge
  public rallies and rulers' statues

CHORUS.
  I've got you in a trap (*etc.*)

  Light comes on in cell 'C'.

LOUDSPEAKER. BAI Culture is for you, and You! Do not exempt
  yourself from the Battle Against Indiscipline. Tighten your belt.
  Redemption may be sooner than you think. No citizen is
  beyond redemption. Cultivate vigilance. Report anything suspicious. Play a role in preserving our sovereign integrity.
  Subversion can sprout in the unlikeliest places – root it out!
  Fight the drug menace. Drug dealers are national saboteurs –
  sniff them out! Root them out! Forward with BAI, the
  vanguard of our national redemption.
MIGUEL (*shakes his head, doleful*). I would have thought that in
  prison at least, one would be spared this obscene litany.
DETIBA. How can? Think of the number of captive audience
  behind bars.
MIGUEL. Do they really believe that any inmate ... I mean, do
  they really think they can make citizens and patriots with such
  banalities?
DETIBA. Think of it this way. It's part of the softening-up process.
  Like being locked up in general cell with those hardened
  sadists.
MIGUEL. What?
DETIBA. The beating-up. Don't tell me you've forgotten ...
MIGUEL. How could I? But ... that was a mistake. The
  Superintendent said so. He apologised.

  EMUKE *breaks into laughter.*

DETIBA. All right, let's give the boss himself the benefit of the doubt. But he is not the one who interacts daily with inmates. Those warders make the rules. Or rather, they break the rules and replace them with a system of their own. It's part of the general extortion racket. The hardcore prisoners soften you up, they rush in and rescue you. You feel eternally grateful.

MIGUEL. Are you saying you've been through it before?

DETIBA. It wasn't as rough as yours but everybody goes through some form of initiation. You see, you are rich, you are well known. You have contacts. You would be expected to know your rights and to stand up for them. So, they had to let you know the rules are different here.

EMUKE. Yeah. You be grammar people. Na you cause the extra sufferment wey me and Detiba suffer. Look, if to say you no came back, they no even go fit sentence we. All the newspaper go cry out say dem sentence small fry while big fish done escape.

MIGUEL. Nonsense! You don't really believe that.

EMUKE. Believe o or no believe o, I still no sabbe why you come back for that court.

MIGUEL. It's nothing you'll understand. Call it fate if you like – I am here, like you, waiting death. (*Bitter laugh.*) Miguel Omowale Domingo, the colonial aristocrat, I think one sneering journalist called me. Business yuppy of the year – that was two years ago I think. But always the favourite media gossip socialite, lionised in any social watering-hole.

EMUKE. Yeah. And now?

MIGUEL. Caged. From all-night dancing to the dance of death.

An uncomfortable pause.

DETIBA. Tell me, that is, if you want to. Emuke and I, well, we were actually caught with the stuff. But you . . . I mean, were you framed?

MIGUEL (*quietly*). In business these days, you walk a tightrope. That's if you really want to make it. Otherwise you're just a

noisy monkey with the rest of the herd. You make enemies and
. . . well, hired assassins or judicial butchers, what's the
difference? Business is just another circus. You have the
clowns, and you have the high-risk performers.

DETIBA. So, returning to face trial when you were free on bail –
was that part of the risk-taking?

MIGUEL. I've told you, there is also that element of fate, or
whatever you choose to call it.

> EMUKE *steps forward impatiently and begins the song
> 'Farewell, Social Lion' with its chorus.* DETIBA *joins in with
> the main verses. He sings with a tinge of pathos while*
> EMUKE'S *chorus is aggressive and impatient.*

EMUKE (*chorus*).
  Yes, yes, talk all the grammar you want
  But you came back like a fool
  Like a pig to the slaughter
DETIBA.
  You're right, it's a circus and you're doing your stunt
  Half-way across the tension wire, the champion starts to drool
  The safety net has vanished; your soul turns to water
EMUKE (*chorus*).
DETIBA.
  Monarch with the coiffured mane, your dreaded claws are
    blunt
  You're a well-trained lion crouching on his stool
  Jumping to the whipcrack of the spangled circus master
EMUKE (*chorus*).
DETIBA.
  Oh brave Mr Lion, welcome from the hunt
  Your poise is so stately, your bearing is so cool
  Is your cage quite cosy or would you like something softer?
EMUKE (*chorus*).

DETIBA.

To turn your back on danger is an option you have shunned
A *preux chevalier*, you never break a rule
Neither in this world, nor in the life hereafter

MIGUEL.

The life hereafter?

EMUKE.

Yes, yes, talk the grammar you want

MIGUEL.

The life hereafter?

EMUKE.

You come back like a fool.

MIGUEL.

The life hereafter?

EMUKE.

Like a pig to de slaughter

DETIBA.

It ends in a staccato, a whimper or a grunt
We'll walk with some bravado, then briefly spurt a pool
Of the purple stuff, and ascend the heavenly rafter

MIGUEL.

Life is a rotter.

DETIBA *and* EMUKE.

Talk the grammar you want

MIGUEL.

Power is even rottener

DETIBA *and* EMUKE.

You come back like a fool

MIGUEL.

But rottener than rottenest

DETIBA *and* EMUKE.

Like a pig to de slaughter

MIGUEL.

Is power that makes the breaks

DETIBA *and* EMUKE.

That makes the breaks

ALL.
The very rule it makes and breaks
It makes and breaks

> *A pause. Then a pair of boots along the corridor. Officer* AREMU *appears and stops at the cell door.*

AREMU. Mr Domingo, the Superintendent wanted you to see this. (*Passes a newspaper to him.*) There is something in there to cheer you up. Everybody is speaking up against the sentence.

> *All three rush to the cell door,* DOMINGO *is handed the paper.*

EMUKE. Wetin den dey talk? Wetin?

DETIBA. Can't you find it? What page is it?

AREMU. It's right there, bottom of the front page. And some other statements inside. One of them is from the former Chief Justice of the Federation. I'll bring the other papers when the boss has finished with them. Everywhere, it's all condemnation, everybody. (*Goes off.*)

MIGUEL (*reading*). 'National Bar Association condemns retroactive laws. The National Bar Association, in a statement issued at its Apapa Secretariat, has condemned the practice of enacting laws to deal with offences committed when such laws did not exist . . .'

EMUKE. Wetin former Chief Justice say, na dat one I wan hear? 'E sentence me one time to four years when 'e still be common magistrate.

MIGUEL. I'm sure they'll say more or less the same thing. Here is one from the Roman Catholic Archbishop. 'No one has a right to take a human life under a law which did not exist at the time of a presumed offence.' Good, 'presumed'. I'm glad somebody is actually mentioning the issue of presumption of guilt. If ever there was a clear case of a verdict dictated from above, against the sheer weight of evidence . . . ah, here's another – it begins to look like a groundswell of protests. Even the editorial – hm. Quite courageous. And the National Students Association . . . Amnesty, national chapter – oh yes, I'm sure Amnesty International will take an interest very soon . . . the Traditional Rulers' Council, they are appealing for clemency. (*Throws the paper away.*) *Clemency!*

DETIBA. Keep cool, Mr Domingo.

MIGUEL. Clemency! Is that the issue!

DETIBA (*picks up the paper*). Does it matter what they call it? They all want the same thing, only they're saying it differently.

MIGUEL. No, it is not the same thing. That is the kind of language that flatters the bestial egos of such a breed of rulers. It makes them feel that the world and every living thing within it is their largesse, from which they dole out crumbs when they are sated. Clemency! Even a retarded child must know that the issue is one of justice.

DETIBA. This would be more to your taste then. I've found the statement of your friend, Emuke.

EMUKE. Wetin 'e talk?

DETIBA (*reading*). 'In his own statement, the former Chief Justice of the Federation, Sir Tolade Akindero warned that if the sentence was carried out, it would amount to judicial murder.' Is that more like it, Mr Domingo?

MIGUEL. Ah, what does it matter anyway? Why do we deceive ourselves? We're living in a lawless time.

DETIBA. Here's one more. The Crusade for National Conscience is organising a continuous vigil outside the prison until the sentence is rescinded.

MIGUEL (*violently*). No!

DETIBA. No? Why not? It all helps to put pressure on the regime.

MIGUEL. Don't you know who they are?

DETIBA. Not much. I've only heard of them once or twice – in the papers.

MIGUEL. They are a religious sect who particularly abhor any form of executions. And they are rather extreme in their methods. If they hold that vigil and they're ordered to disperse, they are just as likely to obey as to disobey, non-violently. This regime will not hesitate to open fire on them. They are desperate to teach a lesson, teach a lesson, teach a bloody lesson wherever and however! I don't want anyone's death on my conscience.

DETIBA. That is really beyond our control, isn't it?

AREMU *returns with a detail of four* OFFICERS, *followed by the* SUPERINTENDENT.

SUPERINTENDENT. Everybody get dressed. Mr Domingo – and you two, same for you. You've been sent for.

MIGUEL. Who by?

SUPERINTENDENT. We don't know. It's the same men from the Special Unit that used to fetch your companions for interrogation. That is, before the trial began.

DETIBA. Interrogation? Are they re-opening the case? Or the Appeal Court? Is the hearing today?

MIGUEL. Today is a Saturday. The courts are not sitting.

They begin dressing, MIGUEL *with deliberate care.*

SUPERINTENDENT. Well, you may be both right and wrong there. You could be appearing before a Review Panel.

MIGUEL. What?

SUPERINTENDENT (*conspiratorial*). I'm not supposed to tell you this, but we received a secret circular yesterday. All offences in your category, including verdicts delivered by the political tribunal, are no longer subject to a decision by the Court of Appeal. The Head of State has taken over their functions. He has created a Review Panel – it's the only kind that would sit on a weekend – I'm only guessing, but I don't see why else they should bother you today.

MIGUEL. Will our lawyers be present? Have they been informed?

SUPERINTENDENT. I'm sorry, I've told you all I know. The usual form for taking you out of prison was brought by the Special Unit. My job is simply to hand you over.

MIGUEL. All right, thank you. (*He looks increasingly thoughtful.*)

SUPERINTENDENT. Actually you don't know how lucky you are to be going away from the premises today. Another set of armed robbers is going to be executed. The stakes are already being set up. Prisoners are confined to their cells – that's the routine – but within an hour the word will go round on the prison grapevine, and then you'd be amazed at the change. The quiet is unearthly, something you feel right under your skin.

MIGUEL. They are shot in the prison yard?

SUPERINTENDENT. No, not inside. On the open grounds outside the prison. The military take charge, so we never know in advance whose turn it is – unless they are our own prisoners of course. They are brought from other prisons mostly, taken directly to the grounds outside. All we get are instructions to prepare so many stakes for such-and-such o'clock one day or the next. Like this morning. You're lucky to be out of it. Well, shall we go?

MIGUEL. I'm ready.

At the last moment MIGUEL *hesitates, then drops on the bed the jacket which he had earlier folded neatly over his arm. The cell door is unlocked. The three file out of the cell.*

SUPERINTENDENT. I am positive there'll be something to celebrate by the time you return. We'll hear about it immediately, you'll see. This junta likes to boast a reputation for quick decisions.

They exit. Faces pressed against the bars on other cell doors watch them go, silently at first. Then they break into the 'Song of Displaced Moralities'.

INMATES.

You thought you packed a hell of clout
Super highflyer, super roustabout
When you could have bailed your carcass out
You went and did a turnabout

Your family contacts in high quarters
Would jump at a fart from your hindquarters
When the moment comes, it's rancid waters
You'll piss like our kind from ghetto quarters

What a waste! Sure, you belonged in the upper class
With plenty of sass, but your thinking was crass
Your ethics at war with the common mass
When you piously tore up your safety pass

All blood tastes alike to the bed-bug
Who grudges the landlord of the prison rug
His tariff? Minions or barons of drug
We bleed alike to the homing slug

A man can only talk so much bull, it
Ends when it's time to bite the bullet
Like a feisty rooster, not a cackling pullet
Stage your bravado and retch in your gullet

Cell 'C'. Enter three TRUSTIES *with spades, buckets and hard scrubbing brushes. They look quickly up and down, enter the vacated cell. One of them lifts his smock and unwinds some tattered pieces of rope which he coils neatly into his bucket. The others are already rummaging through the cell, keeping a watchful eye on the passage.*

FIRST TRUSTY. I don't know why you keep scavenging for those useless bits of rope. Hyacinth will never use them.

SECOND TRUSTY (*testing a piece for strength*). That's only because they don't look reliable. When I find enough of really good pieces . . .

FIRST TRUSTY. Which you know you never will. Bullets have no
    business sense. They rip the ropes to pieces.

THIRD TRUSTY. You think he'll ever try it?

SECOND TRUSTY. He's sawn off two bars. Swears he's only
    waiting for the weeds to thin out, then he'll lower himself down
    and swim across.

FIRST TRUSTY. Weeds my foot! That's only his latest excuse. He
    sawed up those bars a whole year before his namesakes took
    over the lagoon. He's scared to leave, that's all. The world
    outside terrifies him.

THIRD TRUSTY. Not any longer. He is now strongly motivated. He
    is after Sebe's territory, he and that young student. They are
    teaming up together. It's big stuff. The rumour is that there is
    going to be a coup in Lagos underworld. Major Awam is
    masterminding the takeover.

FIRST TRUSTY. Hyacinth is going to feel very sorry for himself
    when he gets to know.

THIRD TRUSTY. What?

FIRST TRUSTY. About those three. If he had known, he wouldn't
    have given them the special reception.

SECOND TRUSTY. Well, he can't blame himself. Who ever heard of
    such cases being put in general cell?

FIRST TRUSTY *goes through the pockets of* MIGUEL's *jacket.
    Runs his fingers along the seams.*

FIRST TRUSTY. This must belong to that socialite. The other two
    never did have more than the clothes on their backs.

SECOND TRUSTY. You think they might get a last-minute reprieve?
    I mean, it may not even be them . . .

FIRST TRUSTY. It's them all right. Three stakes. And all the hush-
    hush. And the rush-rush. I hear someone near the top really has
    it in for them. Or maybe just one of them.

THIRD TRUSTY. Could be woman palava. You never know.

SECOND TRUSTY. Or maybe because of the officer they found

murdered yesterday. These soldier people go mad when any of them is touched.

FIRST TRUSTY. Which officer?

SECOND TRUSTY. I overheard the Superintendent and Aremu talking about it. They say he was found on the road in Agege. At the crossroads. His throat was cut. And his vital organs were missing.

FIRST TRUSTY. Are you sure?

SECOND TRUSTY. It was when you followed the detail warder to collect buckets. I was sitting underneath the window and I heard them discussing the matter. They said his official car was nearby, that was how they could identify him so quickly. Because he wasn't in uniform. He was wearing just a white cloth, a wrapper.

THIRD TRUSTY. A white wrapper?

SECOND TRUSTY. A white wrapper, nothing more. Only it wasn't all that white any more. It was drenched in blood. Oh yes, something also about a black cap.

THIRD TRUSTY. Was it a senior officer?

FIRST TRUSTY. Didn't they mention his name? If he had an official car, he must be very senior.

SECOND TRUSTY. No, they didn't say who it was but it was an Air Force car. Maybe the papers will carry it. Hey, look at this.

He has prised out a twenty-naira note from a shirt collar.

THIRD TRUSTY. That must belong to that Mr Detiba. He and Emuke have been here long enough to know the tricks.

FIRST TRUSTY. There must be more around. Look underneath everything. They may use sellotape to stick it under surfaces.

SECOND TRUSTY. Makes a decent change anyway. When they come from the other prisons, we don't get at the goods until afterwards, and then they are damaged beyond repair.

THIRD TRUSTY. I don't mind the holes so much. Holes can be mended. It's having to clean off all that blood.

FIRST TRUSTY. Stop complaining. You get double rations for a week – that's quite a lot of items to trade with.

THIRD TRUSTY. No it's not. First we set up the stakes, then we take down the bodies and put them in those cheap coffins. After that we still have to take down the stakes again, scrub them down for the next round.

FIRST TRUSTY. Shut up will you! Do you have to make us do it twice over?

THIRD TRUSTY (*giggling*). Look at him. He's squeamish.

FIRST TRUSTY. I don't want to talk about it, that's all. I do what I have to do and that's enough.

> *They look at the small pile of items – cigarette lighter, cigarettes, necktie, handkerchief, a packet of biscuits, half a loaf of bread, and other bits of prison rations.*

SECOND TRUSTY. Not all that much. I hope the warder won't think we have cheated on him.

FIRST TRUSTY. I overheard Aremu say that the socialite wasn't expecting to have his bail revoked. He went to the Tribunal unprepared.

THIRD TRUSTY. Pity. He would have come in loaded with essential commodities.

SECOND TRUSTY. That warder raised our hopes for nothing.

FIRST TRUSTY. Me too. I thought, this time we'd collect some real goodies. (*Retrieving the jacket, wistfully.*) Think we can get away with this?

SECOND TRUSTY (*shrugs*). It will have to go under water.

FIRST TRUSTY (*folds and squeezes it into the bucket*). It will still fetch something. If we don't give that warder something substantial . . .

THIRD TRUSTY. Remember that detainee who used to fly all his clothes to Hong Kong for laundry? I don't know why I suddenly remember him.

FIRST TRUSTY. It's the silk jacket. It should only go to the dry-cleaners.

SECOND TRUSTY. You think he knew? I mean, leaving this behind . . .

Sound of distant machine-gun fire. The TRUSTIES *freeze. A pause, then three spaced-out single shots. The* TRUSTIES *place their loot in the bucket, begin to gather up their spades, scrubbing brushes and buckets.*

In the background, the prisoners' voices rise in a dirge.

A SCOURGE OF HYACINTHS

A Radio Play

A Scourge of Hyacinths was first broadcast on BBC Radio 4 on 8 July 1991, with the following cast:

MIGUEL DOMINGO	Hakeem Kae-Kazim
THE MOTHER	Carmen Monroe
AUGUSTINE EMUKE	Tunde Babs
KOLAWOLE DETIBA	Colin McFarlane
CHIME	Nicholas Monu
SUPERINTENDENT	Louis Mahoney
MILITARY VOICE	Ben Onwukwe
NEWSVENDOR	Clarence Smith
ANNOUNCER	Adjoah Andoh

Directed by Richard Wortley

Tramp of footsteps through echoing corridor – five men in a file, but irregular steps. They come raggedly to a stop. Jangle of a bunch of heavy keys. One is selected, inserted in a lock and turned. A heavy steel door swings open. Two of the men enter.

SUPERINTENDENT (*gently*). Yes, you too Mr Domingo. You'll be sharing this cell with your . . . with these two.

> *The third man enters. The door clangs shut and the key is turned again in the lock. Silence.*

A warder will be along before evening with an extra mattress. We are . . . short of beds and other items right now, so you'll just have to manage. I don't have to tell you, the prison is overcrowded. Both the Military Command and Security send everybody in here as if space is no problem. I suppose because we are hemmed in by the lagoon they think this is the most secure prison. Well, you two are already at home here; I am sure you will show Mr Domingo the ropes.

> *Silence.*

I am sorry about how things turned out for you this morning. But I hope you didn't take that sentence seriously. This regime wants to put a scare in people, that's all. If there is anything we can do for you – under the circumstances – just summon my immediate assistant. I have instructed him to make you as comfortable as possible. All of you. Shall I send you reading material, Mr Domingo?

> *Silence.*

I really am sorry, but you must take your mind off the verdict and try and settle down. Leave the rest to your lawyers. The appeals won't be heard for some time, so there is nothing to do but to put it out of mind. It's hard at first but – we all adjust. Fortunately you are not restricted in any way – well, I mean, not like the politicians. For them it's more and more restrictions every day. No letters, no newspapers, no visitors. In our own case I can use my discretion. You can see I haven't put you in the wing for condemned prisoners – your cell-mates will bear me out – this is the very cell they've occupied while the trial was on. Normally, after a death sentence, we transfer the condemned prisoner to the special wing but, as I said, nobody takes the sentence seriously. Once they've had enough of their little joke, it will be commuted to life. Even less. That's if the Appeal Court doesn't overturn the verdict altogether. Well, I shall drop in on my evening rounds, just to see how you're getting on. Oh yes – Mr Aremu.

WARDER. Yessir.

SUPERINTENDENT. Send them one of the games we seized from the politicians. You see how careful we have to be these days Mr Domingo? Some prison informer sent a report to the secret police that we were giving the politicians preferential treatment. So, orders came that even their pastimes – ludo, cards, draughts and other games – everything was to be withdrawn. The warder will bring you what we have and you can make your choice. (*Pause.*) Try and think of the battle as just beginning, Mr Domingo. Same for you two. I shall call in the evening.

The two officers depart, their footsteps fading down the corridor. Silence, except for a soft lapping of water and lagoon sounds. A bed creaks. Footsteps across a concrete floor. Pause.

MIGUEL DOMINGO (*quietly*). So the water hyacinths have spread also to this part of the lagoon. I suppose I ought to feel at home.

Silence.

Again, footsteps across the floor. Metallic noise as if the door has been gently shaken.

Oh yes; I know this is a prison cell, but it's that court I am not so sure about. The tribunal where the sentence was passed. Was that part of it for real?

Silence.

EMUKE (*bitterly*). You know wetin I think? Even God no fit forgive people like you. Some tings dey, wey God no go forgive, and 'e be like your own be one of them.

DETIBA. Emuke, leave the man alone.

EMUKE. No, lef me! I wan' say it one time and then I no go say anything again. When the man turn up for court today, I no believe my eyes. I say to my self, abi dis man dey craze?

DETIBA. Well, I said the same thing, didn't I? But – what happened has happened. We are all in the same boat.

EMUKE. No, we no dey inside de same boat. Even from before, na inside separate boat we dey. And in own boat better pass we own. We dey inside custody so we no get choice. We must appear before tribunal whether we like am or not. But in own case, 'e get bail. The court grant am bail. He get high connection so they gi'am bail. Then he take in own leg walka inside court – after dey done change degree to capital offence. Dat one, na in I no understand. What kin' sense be dat?

DETIBA. Well, it wasn't we alone. I overheard some reporters – even lawyers – saying the same thing. I don't think I paid much attention to my own case. In any case I already knew the outcome, there was nothing any lawyer could do for me, unless he could bribe enough members of the tribunal. So I passed the time asking myself, why did he come back?

EMUKE. Unless money done pass reach tribunal hand.

DETIBA. Hn-hn. Hn-hn. Either money, or connection. I thought maybe everything had been fixed for him. But when it came to his turn, and the chairman read out the judgement – 'Miguel Domingo – Guilty as charged' – ah, I tell you, I began to wonder.

Silence except for muted lapping of water.

MIGUEL. It beats me. How could one have been so completely
without any premonition? I have seen this wall from the
outside – I don't know how many times – maybe over a
hundred times. We used to go boating from the family house in
Akoka; quite often we would take this route. Sometimes we
simply came to meet the fishermen in the evenings as they came
in with their catch – over there, in that direction. The prisoners
would look out from the windows and wave at us. Sometimes
we waved back. At least I did, as a child anyway. Maybe I even
waved to someone standing against the bars of that very
window. There was nothing like the water hyacinth then, so
the fish market was a regular event. (*Pause.*) In all those
pleasure rides, I never thought I would be looking outwards
from this side. The thought never crossed my mind.

Pause. A wry chuckle.

And Tiatin also, who claims to have visions – well, to be fair,
she certainly makes some accurate predictions, unnervingly
accurate sometimes – but she never foresaw this one, at least
she never told me.

EMUKE. You can talk all the grammar wey you want. I done been
say am anyway, grammar people no get sense. Chai! Even God
no fit approve dat kin' foolishness. My own condition dey pain
me too, I confess. But as I say before, me and Detiba we no get
choice. Dem refuse us bail, hold us inside twenty-four hour
daily lock-up for this cell . . .

MIGUEL. I suppose we can't even enjoy that occasional distraction
now. The hyacinths must have stopped the motor-boats.

EMUKE (*hisses*). The man wan' pretend say 'e no hear me.

DETIBA. They've made life miserable for everyone. You can't
imagine how it has affected prison life, Mr Domingo. Before,
the canoes with outboard motors would come right up to the
walls and attend to business. Every morning, very early.

Prisoners would lower messages and money, then haul up their own mail, or whatever they'd ordered. The prison officials knew about it but they turned a blind eye. It made life easier – something to look forward to. Those facing the canal acted as go-betweens for the others. But, during the ten months we've been here, the weeds finally gained the upper hand. First they fouled up the propellers, so the boats took to paddles. Then even the paddles couldn't fight the weeds. For over three months now, not one canoe has been able to find its way anywhere close to the wall.

EMUKE. What about the Ijaw boy wey drown?

DETIBA. Oh yes, that was a horrible day. Can you imagine, we actually watched someone drown one morning. No way to help. Just watched his legs get more and more entangled in those slimy long roots. It was as if some hidden monster kept dragging him down.

MIGUEL. You saw him?

DETIBA. Everybody watched, all the inmates on the water side of the prison. You see, after the boats gave up, he and two, maybe three other strong swimmers would find a passage through the hyacinths with waterproof packs and carry on business. The scale was reduced of course but it was still better than this present nothing. Then the other swimmers also gave up, leaving only him. Until one Sunday morning . . .

Rapid footsteps across the cell.

MIGUEL. This window? You watched him through this window?

EMUKE. Which other window you see inside here?

Silence.

MIGUEL (*softly*). I have never seen death at close quarters, not even on the roads with all their carnage.

Silence.

EMUKE. Wetin make you come back Mister? I wan' know. I no sabbe dat kin' ting at all. Your family get money, dem get property, dem get plenty influence. You fit dey Russia or Australia by now and nobody fit catch up. Wetin happen? I just wan' know. You bribe tribunal and then dey disappoint you? For my home town, people for say na your enemy take medicine spoil your mind for dat kin' ting to happen.

DETIBA. Let the man have his peace, Emuke. He'll tell us in his own time. After all, we'll have plenty of it on our hands. (*Bitter laugh.*) A whole life sentence of it.

EMUKE. That's if they no fire us tomorrow. These soja people, I no trust them. They fit wake up tomorrow and say – line up everybody awaiting execution. Fire them one time!

DETIBA. No-o-o. Even when sentence was passed, I was already thinking how many years we would actually spend in gaol. I agree with that Superintendent.

EMUKE. Wetin you dey talk? You no take your own ear hear sentence? Hey, Mr Domingo, wetin you think?

MIGUEL. What?

EMUKE (*irritably*). The man mind done travel! Detiba and I dey argue about this sentence. You think na 'shakara' den make? You tink dey no go put us for firing squad?

MIGUEL. I'm afraid they won't, that's what I'm afraid of. Because I can't think of passing twenty years or more behind these walls. Behind any walls. But I fear they will commute it to life. It's obvious.

EMUKE. We go see. All I know is that this na wicked country to do something like this. We know some country wey, if you steal, they cut off your hand. But everybody know that in advance. So if you steal, na your choice. Every crime get in proper punishment. But if wait until man commit crime, then you come change the punishment, dat one na foul. I no know any other country wey dat kin' ting dey happen.

DETIBA. I agree. It's like football. Or any other game. No one changes rules in the middle of a game. Just imagine, half-way through a football game, the referee says the rules have changed. One side has scored a goal but after half-time, he says it is no longer a goal. Or he says a corner kick which took place ten minutes ago should now be a penalty kick. Can you imagine that? In a mere game it is bad enough, how much more in a matter of life and death.

EMUKE. Only army mind fit think dat kin' ting.

DETIBA. It's their profession. They don't know the difference between life and death. Soja man come, soja man go, finish.

EMUKE. Chineke! Small crime wey carry only seven years before. Abi? No to seven years maximum before?

DETIBA. Until three days ago. Anyway, it's all a game of nerves. And the verdict is still subject to appeal, then the Supreme Military Council takes a final decision.

MIGUEL. Hey, come and take a look. There's a canoe trying to break through the hyacinths.

Scramble of feet towards the window. Distant splashes on lagoon.

DETIBA. Come on, champion, come on!

EMUKE. Na sign, I swear, na sign for heaven.

DETIBA. He's more than half-way through already.

Shouts from the other windows along the wall urging on the lone paddler.

MIGUEL. What he needs is an assistant wielding a giant pair of water shears, maybe five yards long.

DETIBA. He seems to be doing quite well without it. Come on, dig in man, dig in!

EMUKE. 'E go do am. If not today, then tomorrow. The others go join am try if 'e no manage reach us today.

Loud cheers from the entire length of the wall. The cheers slow down. Change of tone from optimism to depression.

DETIBA. He's giving up. He's turning back.

Fade in Yoruba-Cuban music, a ceremonial chant for Yemanja. A man's footsteps descend a wooden staircase, slowing down as they get closer to the bottom. Footsteps stop. A pause.

THE MOTHER (*soft intoning*). Oh Yemanja, sister of the clear waters, fill me with wisdom. Find me the path. Cut through the unseen weeds which enfold my house in a fulsome embrace. Save us from this shame hanging over our heads, protectress of the innocent. Let your luminous waters unroll a carpet of light in the direction I must take. Show me a sign. Point your spangled fins in the direction I must proceed. Unveil yourself before me tonight. Let your eyes be the twin stars locked one on each foot. Rescue this house from shame, from the deep shame . . .

MIGUEL. Tiatin. What are you doing up so late?

Footsteps towards the record player. The music is turned down.

Tiatin. It's Miguel.

Pause.

THE MOTHER. Tell me Miguel, why do you think they gave such a lovely name to this infliction? Seaweed is all it appears to be. Parasite. Useless to humans. It chokes the ports. Imperils navigation. Creates hardship for the fishermen – ask your Uncle Demasia, with his fishing trawlers. He has to berth out at sea. The closest he can come is on the salt-water side of Yemanja's island.

MIGUEL. Did you open this window? Oh! You've even left the mosquito netting wide open – what is the matter?

THE MOTHER. Mind you, under the yellow glow of the night sky, one begins to understand why they're here, from where they came. We humans may have no use for the weeds but the gods . . . come closer. Sometimes I think I can sense a pulse in their very stillness, especially at night.

Footsteps in the direction of the woman's voice. A window is opened wider.

THE MOTHER. What do you see Miguel? Do you feel anything about them?

MIGUEL. Nothing new. And I do have an even better view from my window upstairs. A green baize stretching into the horizon, what else? But you are right. It is an infliction. And the government appears helpless. At least, it's done nothing effective.

THE MOTHER. There is nothing that the government – or anyone – can do. It was sent, and it will be removed when SHE is appeased.

MIGUEL. Oh no! Please, Mother!

THE MOTHER. Mother?

MIGUEL. Sorry, Tiatin.

THE MOTHER (*brief chuckle*). You always give yourself away when you disapprove of something I say – or do. Deeply that is, not with anything trivial. When I hear 'Mother' instead of the childhood nickname you gave me, I know I have troubled you.

MIGUEL. No, not really . . .

THE MOTHER. Yes, yes really. But I don't mind, Miguel. I divine the truth and if others do not accept, I am still at peace with what is revealed. But let me ask you something – is this the first time these waters have been blockaded?

MIGUEL. Blockaded? How?

THE MOTHER. Think back, Miguel. Think of the late seventies, at the height of our first grand national madness. Take your mind to the oil boom and all that came in its wake.

MIGUEL (*brief pause*). I can't recall anything. And anyway, I haven't the time. There is a car waiting for me.

THE MOTHER. I know. But you do have the time, I promise you. Surely you remember? The result was not much different then. The scene was different of course. Noisier. Lots of motion. And more colourful, more spectacular. Flags on poles and fairy lights on mastheads stretching into the dark ocean. Every night, the seas lit up for miles. The harbour was one continuous regatta . . .

MIGUEL. Oh, the cement blockade. Good God, what strange recollections you have tonight. I had long forgotten that débâcle. So has the rest of the nation, I am sure.

THE MOTHER. The water hyacinths brought it all back. That is . exactly how it was at the time – a sea blockade. Never mind that the – apparent – causes were different, the result is the same.

MIGUEL. Apparent? The difference was not merely 'apparent' Tiatin. This is a natural infliction. In the other case, the regime licensed importation of cement from all corners of the world. And the world obliged. An armada of ships loaded with billions of tons of cement, sealing up the harbours and even extending beyond our territorial waters. Christ, they certainly made us the laughing stock of the world. The treasury was emptied paying demurrage to ship-owners!

THE MOTHER. You did not find the event – planned? Deliberate.

MIGUEL. Oh I know some claimed it was a conspiracy by foreign powers. Plenty of talk about the western powers conspiring to bring the nation to its knees, strangle its economy, etcetera. That was soon debunked. A simple case of greedy operators, a perfect partnership of business and military.

THE MOTHER. Hm. We are agreed on one thing anyway. The nation was blockaded. As it now is. The army was in power. As it is now.

MIGUEL. Not merely in power. They thought they were the nation.

THE MOTHER. I tell you Miguel, it will prove to have been a thousand times easier to get rid of that fleet of cement-laden ships than it will be to remove these spongy, uninvited guests. Actually they are not unlike the army interlopers. They choke us. Their embrace suffocates the nation. But they are mere mortals, that's the difference. They think they are gods but they are mere men. (*Pause.*) Or lettuce.

MIGUEL. Lettuce, Tiatin?

THE MOTHER. Hasn't it struck you sometimes as you watch them massed on the parade ground? In those olive green fatigues starched and ironed a deadly gloss. That's when they most resemble a field of crisp lettuce. A kind of mutation but still – lettuce.

MIGUEL (*laughing*). Oh Tiatin.

THE MOTHER. But deadly. Poisonous. Nothing I would introduce into a bowl of salad.

MIGUEL. You are impossible tonight.

THE MOTHER. Maybe. But it will be far easier to get rid of this real – though also inedible – lettuce; you'll remind me I said so.

MIGUEL. That's possible. Quite possible. So far it has defeated technicians and scientists – marine biologists and all. They are running around like a rudderless boat, pontificating, doing the old trial-and-error routine . . . damn! What am I doing getting into a discussion with you over water hyacinths at this time of the night!

THE MOTHER. It isn't just the time of the night, is it?

MIGUEL (*soberly*). No it's not. I have to leave. The car is waiting.

A sigh from the MOTHER. *She walks across to a chair. Sound of chair scraping against the floor.*

THE MOTHER. Sit down, Miguel.

MIGUEL. Tiatin . . .

THE MOTHER. Give me fifteen minutes, no, ten. I shall say my piece and then you may leave. Just a small reminder of your family's history, how once it also looked as if we had reached rock bottom.

MIGUEL. You've picked a bad night for family history, Tiatin. The family history is on record, and this son is in one hell of a hurry.

THE MOTHER. We have a name to maintain. Confronted by these barbarians in uniform, that becomes even more important. We have to show them we are from durable stock. We too have fought battles and won. We bear honourable scars.

MIGUEL. I know. But there is more than the family name at stake at this moment. There is the all-important question of my life. No Tiatin, don't say anything. Maybe I am a gambler, like grandfather, but I do not gamble with my life.

THE MOTHER. I am even less of a gambler than you, Miguel. I am also a mother. Your mother. Can you imagine I would gamble with your life?

MIGUEL (*scraping of chair as he rises*). Daybreak mustn't find me in this house. The earlier I leave . . .

THE MOTHER. You don't know when I shall see you again. And you'll be missing next Saturday . . .

MIGUEL. Next Saturday? What about it?

THE MOTHER. It's the Saturday of the Easter weekend, Miguel!

MIGUEL. Our family day? It had escaped my mind.

   Pause.

   Actually it is more *your* day isn't it? Yemanja's Festival Day on the island. That's why you picked it.

THE MOTHER. It's the day the Domingo clan reunites each year – that's what matters. And you'll be missing.

MIGUEL. All right then. Ten minutes, no more.

THE MOTHER. The clock is above my head. You can start counting after you've turned off that music.

Footsteps towards the player.

MIGUEL. I hate to be the one to silence the praise songs of Yemanja . . .

THE MOTHER. Her devotee permits it.

MIGUEL. So, I dare.

Click. Music off.

THE MOTHER. Come and sit here, beside me.

MIGUEL. Ten minutes, you promised.

Footsteps across. Chair against the floor.

THE MOTHER. Thank you. (*Pause.*) There is not much to say. Not now that you have clearly decided. But I must speak with that other Miguel. Not the one who is so brilliant, a little rash and impetuous like his great-grandfather and his father. Not the sensitive one who will yet put into his profession all the music which his mother's life should have been, no, not that Miguel. I want to talk to the Miguel who is much more like his grandfather.

MIGUEL. So now I am the gambler of the family?

THE MOTHER. That's what the family remembers him by. But I think of him more as the careless one. Forgetful. The Domingo who always forgot.

MIGUEL. Forgetful! Grandfather? That's not how I remember him. He was the least forgetful . . .

THE MOTHER. Forgetful of his roots, Miguel. Forgetful of himself. Of the name of the Domingos! No Domingo who takes pride in that name, who remembers what that name means in Lagos, would gamble away the family fortune, the family name.

MIGUEL. I know the story Tiatin. The family fortune was rebuilt. That past is forgotten.

THE MOTHER. And the family name which he also gambled away? Must you in your turn toss it away? Oduaiye Domingo sat at dawn at the gambling table. He had lost all his money, then the

family plantation, the golf course, the stables, this very house –
our ancestral home! Finally there was nothing left to risk –
except the name. (*Bitter laugh.*) You have to hand it to your
grandfather though. No one else I know of has ever gambled
away a name. I mean, to think of that in the dying moments of
the game, just before dawn! He tried to gamble off our other
estates on the island part of Lagos but his gambling partners
knew better. They told him, sorry, all that is already mort-
gaged, for all we know. He tried one business after another but
no one quite knew what the status of the business was, and
gamblers are practical, hard-headed people – your grandfather
being the exception of course. Finally, with nothing left which
anyone would accept, he put his name on the table. There you
are, he said – double or quits. The name of the Domingo
against all my debts. (*Pause.*) At first they laughed, then the
novelty of the idea hit them. So they made him sign a piece of
paper, but there was no need. Oduaiye Domingo was a man of
his word.

MIGUEL. The Domingos appear to wallow in that reputation, I've
noticed. It can be a burden.

THE MOTHER. The man who brought us back – whether as freed
slaves or as seeds in his loins – established that family code.
The family lore is that he flogged his sons with the very whip he
used on his horses – if they made the mistake of breaking their
word. Even in jest. Your great-grandfather burnt the words
which still decorate the lintel on the original bungalow – A
Domingo – Is – His – Word. It is the first thing you were all
taught to read – once you had mastered the alphabet.

MIGUEL. Then great-grandson Miguel Domingo hereby re-inter-
prets that lop-sided lesson to suit the circumstances. I gave no
one my word.

THE MOTHER. But your bail bond Miguel!

MIGUEL. A legal contract only. If I break it, they keep the money.
What more can they demand? This regime changed the rules

after the bond. The entire agreement has been rendered null and void.

THE MOTHER. I have lit sixty candles to Santa Yemanja. I asked for a sign and I received it. You are in no danger whatsoever. I read your innocence in the serenity of her gaze. She takes the innocent under her protection.

MIGUEL. I wish I shared your faith.

THE MOTHER. But you *are* innocent. Miguel, you *are* innocent?

MIGUEL. You see? You still ask me that. If even you can still doubt me . . .

THE MOTHER. No, it's you who doubt yourself. When you say, I wish I shared your faith, what does that mean? My faith is in you. I have faith in your innocence, and that means that I see you in the embrace of Yemanja, protectress of the innocent. Nothing, no one, can harm you.

MIGUEL. I'm sorry but that is one argument I can never win. Not with you. As for the other one, the name of the Domingos, I prefer not to risk it by presenting myself in court tomorrow. Let them try me *in absentia*.

THE MOTHER. Your family has a stake in this matter Miguel. Your bail was given to the family. But for that name, the judge would have refused bail. Do you dispute that?

MIGUEL. Why should I? I know it's true. The other two standing trial with me have spent over nine months in prison custody.

THE MOTHER. Then you know it. You know it is not your affair alone.

MIGUEL. Tiatin, listen please, listen to me very carefully. Tomorrow . . .

THE MOTHER. We have the best lawyer in the country. He has never lost a criminal case. The family will spend its entire fortune if need be. And we have contacts at the very highest level. Your Uncle Demasia . . .

MIGUEL. I am grateful Tiatin. But listen to me. Just listen for a moment. No, PLEASE. (*Pause.*) Try now and grasp the difference. (*He speaks with slow emphasis.*) When I was first arraigned, it was under a civilian government and the crime I am accused of did not carry a capital forfeit. Now it is death by firing squad. You heard it yourself Tiatin.

THE MOTHER. How does that affect you? Your so-called crime and arrest took place before the decree. It can only affect future offenders.

MIGUEL. Did you listen Tiatin? Did you *listen* to that man as he read out the new decree on television? The one with the voice of cold slurry swilling through concrete mixers. The decree affects all those currently standing trial.

THE MOTHER. That was not the way I heard it. And what if it did anyway? You are innocent. Running away will however paint you guilty in the eyes of the world. Miguel, the Domingos do not run. Even your grandfather understood that. He changed his name – yes, he led a wretched existence till he died but he remained here. Disgraced, destitute, despised. But he stayed! But you will let these rootless gangsters chase you out? These – these people without a name?

MIGUEL. Tiatin . . .

THE MOTHER. Look at this quarter. A century ago it was swamp. Nothing but swamp. Not even the water hyacinth thought it worth the trouble of a visitation. Only toads, inedible crabs and mudskippers. A small timberyard was the only sign of life, and a shack with a wooden floor raised on stilts and joined to land by a rickety walkway, where the Cherubim and Seraphim Sect came to dance and pray every evening and on Sundays. Your ancestor roamed the whole of Lagos, found it was the only piece of property he could afford. He bought it and drained it. He turned it into a thriving plantation. The first-ever gold course in Lagos was built here, before even the Europeans built the one at Ikoyi. He was fond of golf. Pa Manuel was an exception that way. The other returnees generally took to racing and polo but, he loved golf. So he built that golf course

here, just for him and his friends. The Europeans and other
aliens used to join him. In those days they were proud to be
seen with the Domingos . . .

MIGUEL. Tiatin . . .

THE MOTHER. Oh Miguel, my Miguel, listen! I am reminding my
forgetful one of his family history. When those lazy, good-for-
nothing Lagosians saw how this fetid, undesired swamp was
being transformed, they turned on him. They tried to force him
out. He fought them in the courts – right up to the Privy
Council in London – and won. Then they tried their strong-arm
stuff, hired the scum of the ghettos, thugs and arsonists,
brought Igun mercenaries from Badagry to invade our home
from the lagoon. In the middle of the night they tried to set the
house on fire! Tried to burn us out!

MIGUEL. I know the entire story Tiatin . . .

THE MOTHER. The Domingos do not run, Miguel. Your ancestors
only ran when they were slaves. Then they ran, and ran, and
ran. They took only their gods with them as they ran from one
island in the Caribbean to another. San Domingo, Haiti, Cuba.
Till they were shipped back to their West African ancestral
lands. But the running is over Miguel, the running is over.
Here! On this earth of Sango, Yemanja, Osun, Ososi! Some of
the returnees chose Abomey, Fernando Po, Douala – some even
went further south to Angola. For your great-grandfather, it
was Lagos. When he disembarked he said to himself – the
running is over. Pa Omowale Manuel unwrapped his most
treasured possession, his iron *ose* of Sango and stuck it into the
ground. May Sango's axe strike me dead, he swore, if I ever
allow any mortal to chase me or my offspring off this land.
When this house was built – only a wooden bungalow at the
time – his wife built a shrine to her own deity Yemanja, on this
very spot. I have kept the flame of that goddess alive, and she
has never failed the Domingo clan.

MIGUEL. Pa Manuel is dead Tiatin. He died over a century ago.

Before this breed of men were born, these ones who burst
through their mothers' wombs with machine guns and hand
grenades.

THE MOTHER. And what breed of men are they? They breathe,
don't they? They fall sick and die. They struggle and sicken
themselves like children over the confection of power . . .

MIGUEL. Ah, you've said it. They do things for power that no one
would ever dream of. But enough. Your time is up Tiatin.

Scrape of chair as MIGUEL *rises.*

We shall talk more of them some other time. Now I must go.

THE MOTHER (*intense plea*). I know you are safe here Miguel. You
are safe! These men cannot harm you, no. They dare not touch
one hair of your head. I have been promised.

MIGUEL. Promised? Who by? Someone in government? In the
army? Someone in the know? In the corridors of power?
Someone right within the very exercise of power? Or – she?
The power which came with the clan from Haiti and from
Cuba and directs the motions of the water hyacinths?

THE MOTHER. Don't blaspheme Miguel. Rein in your tongue and
do not blaspheme!

MIGUEL. Me? Why should I wish to blaspheme against something
that nourishes you so completely? Indeed, you could almost say
I am sometimes envious. I have nothing I believe in.

THE MOTHER (*fiercely*). Last Saturday, as with nearly every
Saturday since your arrest, Iyalorisa went into trance after
trance invoking the goddess over you, Miguel. Oh it has been a
double Passion week for my island people Miguel. We have
fasted as never before in Lent, and our Santa has revealed her
benevolent face to us. So do not ever take that name in vain.

MIGUEL. I do not. You are unjust Tiatin. How many Saturdays
have I risen early just to watch you don your white robes and
blue sash, your face motionless as you lit one candle after the
other in your private shrine, then walk, almost trance-like to

the boathouse. I have followed and watched you untie the chalk-smeared canoe you use for no other journey and row yourself to Yemanja's island. Sure, I stopped accompanying you so many years ago, but do you think I haven't shared in that peace I know it brought you? And not I alone. I tell you Tiatin, it is what compensates for that ... I don't know – because you are a contradiction, Tiatin, that is the truth. One moment you mount your invisible throne and reign over this house like a relic from some foreign aristocracy, the next you are mounted by a goddess just like any of the other village peasants, market women, fishermen's wives and the rest – wallowing in the chalk and sand of that shrine on the island. If I hadn't seen it with my own eyes, I would never have believed it.

Pause.

Yet, when you return from it all, it's as if you bring back with you the flesh of that greeting – Salaam aleikum. A real peace descends on the house, a rare texture of peace you could touch with your hands.

THE MOTHER (*a brief pause, then she sighs*). Yemanja knows our hearts and minds. She is kind, but just.

MIGUEL. It is not your goddess who has pronounced a threat on my life. It is not any maid or mother of the waters but men of studded boots, of whips and batons and guns and mind-numbing propaganda. Why! Even Sango armed with his thunder and lightning would hesitate to take on a sub-machine gun.

THE MOTHER. And is this the first we have seen of them? Is it the last?

MIGUEL. I keep telling you Tiatin, these ones are different. Different! They are out to prove something, I don't know what. But I do not wish to find out – at least, not while I am within their reach. I do not want to be proof of whatever they wish to prove. Tiatin, there is something about these people which robs me of my sleep.

THE MOTHER. And my sleep, Miguel? The sleep of the Domingos, compelled to face the world each day, knowing that one of theirs has fled? Has run off like a coward? Stamped his guilt on the gates, on the walls of their ancestors? And your little sister still in college? Your nephews and nieces. And the rest of the Domingos when they attempt to take their hard-earned pride of place in society? Shall we retire from society, lock up our windows and gates? Shall we change our name like your grandfather did?

MIGUEL. But my LIFE Tiatin, my life! You want me to place my life at risk because of family pride? Because of your place in society? Tiatin, this is a society of short memories – how often have you said it? How often have you complained – oh and with such bitterness! – of the failure of the same society to give the Domingos credit for moulding the being of Lagos out of swamp and sludge! Yes, let's say I run away. Give them three months, even one, and I swear no one will even recall the affair of Miguel Domingo!

THE MOTHER. And we? You think we also have a short memory?

MIGUEL. Enough! Enough, Tiatin, I am leaving. Now, before dawn. I am innocent. But I do not wish to die to prove it to anyone, not even to the Domingo clan!

    MIGUEL's *footsteps going off. Sound of suitcase hitting the floor. A key is turned in the lock. The door creaks open.*

THE MOTHER. Where will you go?

MIGUEL. It's all arranged. I shall stay with a friend – you know him, Chime – tonight. Tomorrow he'll drive me over to the East. Calabar or Port Harcourt. Oron is also likely – it's full of smugglers – their boats are fast and they know the creeks. From there by boat to Fernando Po . . . if the hyacinths have

not yet take over that coastline. In which case we'll head for
Obudu Ranch and cross over from there to the Cameroon.

THE MOTHER. Fernando Po? You've been in touch with Cousin
Vicky?

MIGUEL. Naturally I shall look up our relations but I shan't be
staying with them. I made friends when we went there on
holiday in 'eighty. I've kept in touch with them.

THE MOTHER. Well, thank Yemanja for small mercies. At least
Macias is no longer in charge. That place had become a
cemetery for our countrymen, especially the labour migrants
from the East.

MIGUEL. I wouldn't have dreamt of sharing the same borders with
that madman, not even for a day. No, the situation is much
better now. Even for business. These friends of mine – they're
Easterners – they're really making their millions, and they've
offered me a partnership.

THE MOTHER. Doing what?

MIGUEL. There you go again . . .

THE MOTHER. I have every reason to be cautious. It was also
'friends' who got you, us, into this present mess.

MIGUEL. Believe me Tiatin, their business is completely legitimate.
Totally and lucratively! (*Laughs.*) You should see their factories – plastic and other synthetic products. Their other line is
refining natural oils for export. I have personally inspected
their export ledger. I mean, in hard currency.

   Pause.

THE MOTHER. We shall all pray for you. Go with God –
whichever one you believe in.

MIGUEL. Oh Tiatin . . .

   Rapid strides across the room. Sighs as they hug each other.

THE MOTHER. Yemanja will protect you. Go to Oron. You'll find
no shortage of boats from there.

MIGUEL. I love you, Tiatin.

THE MOTHER. You are my favourite, you know that. A mother
should avoid favourites but I cannot help it. Your siblings knew
it even as children, to my eternal embarrassment. But you are
so much like the image I retain of Omowale Manuel. Stubborn,
strong-willed even when he knew he was wrong.

MIGUEL. Now she wants to start another argument.

THE MOTHER. No. Go. But, wait Miguel. It's so late. You know
the streets are not safe at this hour.

MIGUEL. My friend has been waiting outside while we argued.

THE MOTHER. Oh Miguel, how could you! Why didn't you tell
me? I thought it was your driver.

MIGUEL. You forget I wasn't expecting to find you downstairs.
And then we got talking. He doesn't mind.

THE MOTHER. Where does he live? How far do you have to go at
this time?

MIGUEL. Ikorodu Road. By six in the morning we are through the
toll gates. By the time the Tribunal issues a bench-warrant, I'll
be over the border.

   Pause.

THE MOTHER. Hm. You know what I think is a better idea? The
Tribunal sits at ten, not so?

MIGUEL. When it starts on time, yes.

THE MOTHER. The first flights out of Ikeja begin at half-past five.
It's hardly fifteen minutes to the airport from here, so why
don't you stay the night instead and leave here by four thirty?
You can take your choice – Calabar or Port Harcourt – there
are at least three flights heading east. By seven at the latest
you'll be in . . .

MIGUEL. We need to stay mobile throughout, I must have a car at
my disposal . . .

THE MOTHER. Then head for Port Harcourt. My sister still runs the Palmeria Hotel. She has any number of cars at her beck and call. We can call her right now, yes, that's a good idea.

MIGUEL. Chime has gone to all this trouble . . . no, it's not fair. And it means he would have to drive home by himself.

THE MOTHER. What are we doing with all the guest rooms – invite him to stay the night. I'll prepare a late supper and we'll telephone Matilda.

MIGUEL. There is one more factor you are overlooking . . .

THE MOTHER. What else is there?

MIGUEL. Our famous National Airways – somewhat unpredict-able, wouldn't you agree? We could get to the airport tomorrow and find that all flights have been cancelled. Then what?

THE MOTHER. What a pessimist you are. Everyone knows that the first flights always take off, and on time. At dawn it's quite a display, they take off almost in formation, unleashing them-selves like hungry dogs against all points of the compass. Oh come on Miguel, you have remarked it yourself hundreds of times . . .

MIGUEL. Hm.

THE MOTHER. There is no 'hm' about it. And anyway, if you lose your flight, you can fall back on your original plan. You lose nothing. Agreed? Go and bring in your accomplice. I'll put together one of those night specials you're so fond of.

MIGUEL. All right. I'll call Chime.

He takes a few steps. Stops.

You know Tiatin, you really are amazing. One moment you invoke ancestral ghosts to keep me from fleeing, the next you're actively aiding and abetting . . .

THE MOTHER. Be quiet. You understand nothing. Just bring in your poor abandoned friend so we can all get some sleep before morning.

MIGUEL *chuckles. Footsteps in the direction of the door. Fade in music. Out.*

Back in the prison cell. Fade in MIGUEL *speaking.*

MIGUEL. You know the strangest thing . . . by the time we had finished supper, I was feeling quite secure. Not just cosy with home comforts and all that. Simply secure. In that living-room with its high wooden ceiling, Chime and I relaxed on over-stuffed cushions, sipping sherry sent by our cousins in Fernando Po . . . all the menace I had felt began to vanish. The regime faded into nothing – cheap, cardboard terrors, nothing more. You won't understand unless you knew the house . . .

DETIBA. Is that what happened? You fed well? You felt good? You woke up in your family bed and decided to tempt fate.

Pause.

MIGUEL. I wish it were that simple. It would be easier if I could console myself with the thought that it served me right. But what I felt at night was quite different from what I felt in the morning. True enough, before falling asleep, I kept asking myself – why have I been in such a panic? I was granted bail. My sureties are highly influencial figures in society. We have relations even in the military hierarchy, quite high up – a colonel in fact. I was confident that if I walked into court the following morning, self-assured, ready to clear my name, things would simply take their normal course. The case could go on and on and of course I would return home at the end of each hearing. A verdict of guilty? The possibility of that had vanished completely. Was I not a Domingo?

EMUKE. Sometime, dis ting na fate. Man can't escape his destiny.

MIGUEL. When the prosecution opened the session by applying to withdraw my bail, even before the witness resumed his testimony . . . then, that banished shiver of doubt returned . . .

DETIBA. Me too. That's when I said to myself, this is no longer routine business.

EMUKE. Well, na you give them chance. You chop belleful, you drink, your sense fall asleep. Instead make you go far far as you done plan, you take your own legs walka inside military tribunal wey don change rule for middle of football game.

MIGUEL. No, I did not walk into court of my own free will. (*Quietly.*) I did not.

Pause.

DETIBA. What are you trying to say? We watched you enter, surrounded by your lawyers. They were chatting and laughing with all the confidence in the world. In fact I'll tell you, I felt bitter and resentful. I thought to myself, that's what money and influence can do. We are certain to be convicted but that one will go free.

MIGUEL. No, I did not walk in because I wanted to. I was trying to tell you, or maybe trying to explain something to myself. You see, when my alarm went off, I jumped up a different Miguel from the one who went to sleep – (*Bitter laugh.*) – as our friend said – on a full belly. Oh yes, I did go to the airport as planned . . .

Airport sounds. Jet engines warming up in the background, roar at full throttle, fading off. The somewhat muted motions of an aiport stirring itself awake.

ANNOUNCER. This is to announce the departure of Flight 370 to Yola via Enugu. Intending passengers with boarding passes are invited to proceed to Gate 11 for immediate . . .

A loud click as the microphone is switched off. A clipped military voice takes over.

MILITARY VOICE. A nation without discipline is a nation without a future. The bane of our nation has always been indiscipline. This cancer must be rooted out. Were you at your desk on the dot of the hour for the resumption of duty? Do you put in a full day's work for a full day's pay? Is your favourite pastime malingering? Is your office a private reception room for your friends and relations? Are you the kind of employee who is never on seat? All these symptoms of indiscipline must be rooted out. Monitor your fellow worker. Report any sign of indiscipline to your local BAI. Support the Brigade Against Indiscipline. Long live our glorious Fatherland. (*Click.*)

ANNOUNCER. . . . for passengers on Flight 286 to Kaduna. This flight will now leave from Gate 17 . . . Repeat: Flight 286 to Kaduna will now . . .

STAFF (*shouting over the last words*). Will you please stand in line. Stand in line! It's people like you being preached to by BAI.

PASSENGER. BAI-BAI, Madam. (*Laughter.*)

WOMAN. I want my boarding pass . . .

STAFF. Madam, you can see I am still busy checking in this passenger.

WOMAN. Then give me back my ticket.

STAFF. Which one is it? I have several tickets here . . .

WOMAN. Why? That is how everything gets confused. Why don't you treat one ticket at a time? You too should take lesson from the Brigade . . .

STAFF. Don't teach me my job . . .

ANNOUNCER. Last call for Flight 307 to Abuja and Minna boarding at Gate 15. Final call for Flight 307. All passengers with boarding passes should proceed direct to Gate 15. Final call for Flight 307.

Fade in CHIME's *voice. Sliding doors opening and closing. Both men,* CHIME *and* MIGUEL, *walking rapidly. General airport activity.*

CHIME. Of course I'm coming with you. I am going to deliver you personally to my business partners in Fernando Po.

MIGUEL. Seriously Chime, there's no need. I know this auntie of mine very well. She is most capable. If there is an emergency she will simply hole me up in her hotel and I tell you, all the Security Units can search that place from top to bottom, she won't let them find me.

CHIME. Just the same, I'm coming. You stay right here while I get the tickets.

MIGUEL. You just want a night out in the Garden City, that's all.

CHIME. Sure. It's a long time I've tasted the night pleasures of Port Harcourt.

MIGUEL. En-hen, that's better. I'll go over to the news-stand and see what . . .

MILITARY VOICE. A corrupt nation is a nation without a future. Smuggling is economic sabotage. Smuggling is an unpatriotic act, it is next to treason. Nepotism is a form of corruption. Corruption in all forms has been the bane of our nation. Currency trafficking is economic sabotage. It plays into the hands of foreign powers. It is an act of treason and will be treated as such. All forms of corruption must be rooted out. Your loyalty should be to the nation and the nation only. It is father, mother, brother, sister, mentor and friend. The nation is your first family. Be your family's eyes and ears. Keep watch on those nearest to you. Report any act of corruption to your local BAI. Support the Brigade Against Indiscipline. Long live our glorious Fatherland! (*Click.*)

Silence. Then abrupt resumption of airport activities.

MIGUEL. You mean there is no escape from *that* anywhere?

CHIME. It's improved. They've found someone who can actually string some intelligible words together.

MIGUEL. Go and get those tickets, Chime. Let's get me out of here.

CHIME. Where did you say you were going?

MIGUEL. The news-stand. The papers should have arrived.

CHIME. Okay, I'll meet you there. Best buy all the papers you can lay hands on. You know you'll find only yesterday's editions when we get to the East.

Fade in announcement over last speech.

ANNOUNCER. National Airways regret to announce . . .

MIGUEL. Oh no!

ANNOUNCER. . . . a delay on Flight 107 to Kano due to technical reasons.

MIGUEL *lets out a deep sigh of relief.*

A further announcement on this flight will be made shortly.

MIGUEL. Not today please, no, not today. Clear skies all the way to all Eastern airports, please God, please, whoever, please every single deity Tiatin believes in and I will never never be impatient with her Yemanja again. Lady of the luminous waters, if not for me, then for your faithful one Tiatin, blow away mists and clouds from the skies, reward her fidelity to you . . .

ANNOUNCER. First boarding announcement for Flight 179 to Port Harcourt leaving from Gate 21. Flight 179 to Port Harcourt ready to board from Gate 21. Thank you.

MIGUEL. That's it. That's more like it. Keep the candles burning Tiatin. Don't let even one go out. I can't remember which of them takes care of the skies but please don't ignore him, or her, certainly not today. Tell them to take our wingless airline under their protective wing . . .

NEWS-VENDOR. Beg your pardon, Sir . . .

MIGUEL. What?

NEWS-VENDOR. I thought you asked for papers.

MIGUEL. Did I? Oh yes, which papers have come in? Give me one of each.

NEWS-VENDOR. Sure. We get *Daily Times* ... *Punch* ... *New Nigerian.*

Sound of newspapers being extracted from bundles and slapped down on the counter.

The *Concord* never come in yet ... aha, here is *Vanguard* ... Sir? Wey de man? Oga! Mister man! Mister man! Ah-ah! What kin joke be dis for morning time? Why the man come waste my time so?

Rapid footsteps.

CHIME. Hallo vendor.

NEWS-VENDOR (*half-heartedly*). Good morning.

CHIME. Ah-ah. Hope no problem.

NEWS-VENDOR. No-o, nothing. Is just these foolish people who think it is good to waste a man's time early in the morning. One man come here just now, ask for one of each paper. As I am just putting them together he take off.

CHIME. Maybe they called his flight.

NEWS-VENDOR. Haba! 'E for take only one minute to collect in papers and give me my money.

CHIME. Ah well, never mind. Actually I was looking for a friend of mine. I asked him to wait for me here. Rather tall, he was carrying a brief-case. Blue shirt, yellow tie. Has he been here?

NEWS-VENDOR. Ah? He wear glasses?

CHIME. That's right. Rimless.

NEWS-VENDOR. What?

CHIME. Rimless. You know, the kind without a rim. Just glasses.

NEWS-VENDOR. That's the very man. He order one of every paper and then he just disappear. I bend down – so – to take out the bundle of papers from *Punch*. When I stand up again, he just done disappear.

CHIME. What do you mean? He didn't say anything?

Footsteps approaching.

NEWS-VENDOR. Na in I tell you. I see am one time, next moment I no see am again.

Footsteps come to a stop.

CLEANER. Excuse me Sah, you be Mr Chime?

CHIME (*suspicious*). Who are you?

CLEANER. I just be cleaner. Morning shift. I dey clean toilet when one man come inside. 'E beg me make I come call you. 'E give me one naira, say make I wait for news-vendor if I no find you.

CHIME. Toilet! Which one?

CLEANER. The one downstairs. Stairs wey dey behind Ethiopian Airlines. He say 'e no feel well at all, so 'e run come toilet.

CHIME (*relief in his voice*). Ah, you see Mr News-vendor, that's what happened to him. I'll take the papers – how much?

NEWS-VENDOR. Na two naira fifty for the five. Tell your friend sorry o. No wonder he disappear like that. Perhaps he feel like he wan' vomit, so 'e run go toilet.

CHIME. Yes, I suppose so. (*Rustle of notes.*) Here you are. Keep the change.

Rapid strides over glazed concrete floor. They pass through echoing passage, rapidly down flight of steps, then another brief passage. Swing doors are pushed open. Abrupt stop.

Miguel?

MIGUEL. S-sh. I'm over here.

CHIME. Are you all right?

MIGUEL (*intense whisper*). Over here. Get into the next cubicle. Hurry before someone comes in.

CHIME. What's the matter?

MIGUEL. Get in quickly. There isn't much time.

Rapid steps. Toilet cubicle door is opened, shut and bolted.

CHIME. What's going on? I thought you were ill.

MIGUEL. All is not well Chime. We have to act fast. I saw my
  man.

CHIME. Who?

MIGUEL. The NSO detective who was detailed to my case. I'm not
  sure he saw me – I ducked very fast. He was obviously on the
  watch for someone. He was scanning the lounge like a radar.

CHIME. Oh, he could be on another case. They finished their part
  of the business ages ago. The Investigation Squad take no
  further interest. They don't even follow the prosecution once
  they've finished.

MIGUEL. One can never be sure of anything. Everybody is afraid.
  They'll all be on the alert. What do you think will go through
  his mind when he sees me at the airport? And so early in the
  morning. Anyone can put two and two together. One telephone
  call – even if he has not been detailed here on my account – and
  we'll have a welcoming committee on arrival. That's if we get
  on the flight in the first place.

CHIME. You're right.

MIGUEL. So do we go back to the original plan?

CHIME. We could still get on that flight. I know someone who can
  drive us directly onto the tarmac – one of the maintenance
  engineers. He'll take us in his official van.

MIGUEL. Chime, I am *not* going to try to get on that flight. On any
  flight from here. It would be suicidal. What is my detective
  doing at the airport? Which of his colleagues will come aboard
  to check faces? They've been doing spot checks since the coup,
  remember? Looking for fugitive politicians.

CHIME. Right. Back to the car then. We travel by road.

MILITARY VOICE. No nation survives without vigilance. The price
  of freedom is eternal vigilance. Report anything unusual.
  Report anything suspicious. The enemies of our national
  sovereignty are numerous and tireless. They are both without
  and within our national borders. Play a role in preserving our
  sovereign integrity. Do not sell out your Fatherland. Be the

watchful eyes of the greater family. Lack of vigilance is brother to lack of discipline. A nation without discipline has no future. Assist our BAI with daily vigilance. Support your Brigade Against Indiscipline line. Long live the Fatherland!

Silence.

MIGUEL. When did it start to proliferate to this obscene level?

CHIME. Blow that! Let's think of what we are going to do.

MIGUEL. Oh, but it has everything to do with how we decide to move. Doesn't it give you the feeling of being surrounded? Everywhere you turn – damn it, even in the toilet!

CHIME. Snap out of that mood, Miguel. Let's act!

MIGUEL. Don't worry about me. Actually, I was doing some practical thinking. You see, I don't believe even the roads are safe any more.

CHIME. There is less risk if we leave right away. It's not quite five, do you realise? In another fifteen minutes we can be at the toll-gate. Virtually no traffic.

MIGUEL. And at the toll-gate? At those ubiquitous checkpoints? How soon before an eager cop recognises the face of Miguel Domingo?

CHIME. Well, are we just going to hole up in these cubicles until they find you?

MIGUEL. No. We're leaving now. But I have thought of something else. Much safer. Maybe I should have thought of it sooner – while we were still at home. Never mind, come on. It's time we moved.

Sound of drawn bolts in quick succession. Mild creaks of toilet doors.

CHIME. You can tell me about this master plan on the way. But wait here while I go and see if the coast is clear.

MIGUEL. We'll lose time that way. Every second matters now.

CHIME. How many seconds just to go up and . . . ?

MIGUEL. Let's go together. Don't look right or left, just straight ahead and make for the exit. A flight came in some minutes ago. If our man sees us heading outwards, why shouldn't either of us have been on the flight? Or both.

Swing doors out of the toilet. Up the stairs and on glazed floor, rapid footsteps beneath dialogue. Fade in airport bustle as they walk briskly through the lounge.

I could be rushing back for the trial. You came to meet me at the airport. Or maybe I came to meet you. A new member of my legal team. Or vital defence witness. Maybe both of us just arrived on the flight. The important thing is that we're heading out, not catching a flight. And discussing the celebrated case most animatedly. Most natural thing in the world, don't you agree? Don't look now, but I've just seen my man. Still scanning everyone in the lounge with those mean predatory eyes. I've turned my head to argue intently into your face because he was just swinging his radar in this direction. I'm giving him the back of my head; let him recognise that if he can. Scavengers! Warn me if I seem to be increasing my pace will you? We mustn't appear to be too much in a hurry.

CHIME. No, no, we're doing quite well, Mr Domingo. Just tell me what you'd like me to do or say. And when. Should I gesticulate or something? I feel I'm not contributing.

MIGUEL. A lawyer should also be a good listener. You've been giving me your professional attention. I don't think he's seen me. We're half-way through; another minute and we'll reach the sliding doors and then we head back home again.

CHIME. Where?

MIGUEL. Don't stop Mr Chime. Where else do you expect us to head? If he follows us he'll simply confirm one of our silently transmitted scenarios: the accused dutifully rushing back home for his trial.

CHIME. But home! Yours?

MIGUEL. None other. The boathouse. Only one place remains for
me, that's the island village where my mother goes for her
Saturday worship. I'll borrow her canoe. It's only some twenty-
five minutes paddling – for her, that is. I have done it before in
fifteen but that was years ago. I'm sure I can still manage
twenty. And if you feel like the exercise . . .

CHIME. Of course I'll come with you.

MIGUEL. Then between us we can eat up that distance in twelve or
fifteen. Certainly arrive well before dawn. Uncle Demasia's
fishing trawler can pick me up – Tiatin will arrange it. I'll just
stay put until she can make the contact. May take a day or two
but I'll be safe there. And I don't think they have loudspeakers
there screaming the obscenities of the Brigade.

CHIME. Even if they did . . .

MILITARY VOICE. What are the watchwords of our national goal?
DISCIPLINE. SELF-RELIANCE. SELF-SUFFICIENCY. VIGI-
LANCE. A nation which bargains away its integrity through
indiscipline loses respect in the eyes of the world. A nation
which depends on the hand-outs of other nations loses respect
in the eyes of the world. A nation which does not produce what
it needs to survive loses self-respect. A nation which is slack
encourages saboteurs against its very existence. It is the duty of
every citizen to . . .

*Sliding doors open towards the end of the broadcast, slide
shut and cut off the words. The open-air roar of a plane
about to take off. Sibilant screech as it taxis towards take-
off. Full take-off roar, fading off into distance. Over
vanishing plane, fade in the mournful sound of foghorns,
then a gentle lap of waters.*

*Mix ecstatic section of Yemanja's ceremonial music which
later changes to elegaic. About thirty seconds, gradual fading
out, leaving the sound of water splashing against the sides of
a canoe as two paddles stab into thickly clogged water.*

Occasionally the paddles drag up seeming debris which splash back dully into the lagoon as if it has been dredged up from an unending tangle. Heavy breathing and even groans betray exertion beyond normal paddling.

CHIME. Dawn is breaking, Miguel.

MIGUEL. Worse than dawn will find us if we remain here.

CHIME. What are we going to do?

MIGUEL. Keep trying. Safety is on the other side of that beach-head. Look, I can actually see the prow of the wreck which has lain there half-submerged for half a century.

CHIME. Is that it? That brown wedge just beyond the jutting?

MIGUEL. That's the one. Tiatin swears it was lured there and wrecked by Yemanja to punish the European sailors for encroaching. Her island is forbidden to strangers.

CHIME. She really does believe in that goddess, doesn't she?

MIGUEL. Believe in it? If she had her way Lagos would be renamed Yemanja.

Huge wallop on the water. Heavy breathing of exertion.

Look, just look at that! It's like digging up a network of roots. We'll never get there, Chime. It's over an hour since . . .

CHIME. Keep trying. The water looks freer ahead. Almost clear in fact. Once we get over this section . . .

MIGUEL. You don't think we should go back? At least while the way back is still open?

CHIME. What are you talking about? Let's give forwards one more try.

MIGUEL (*in between exertions*). I don't understand it. She paddles this thing by herself every Saturday to the island – that's where all the devotees from the neighbouring hamlets gather for worship. Last Saturday, she rowed over in this very canoe. I watched her go and return.

CHIME. It is obvious. She knows the passage. We've missed it.

MIGUEL. Impossible. From the boathouse to the tip of that wreck, it's one straight line. Look behind you and see for yourself. We've cut a straight furrow through the weeds.

CHIME (*pause*). Yes, it is pretty straight. Then what? What does it mean?

MIGUEL. It means the weeds have thickened impassably from this point outwards. We have reached dead-end.

CHIME. Since Saturday? Your mother passed through here this last Saturday?

MIGUEL. Even in normal times, she does not miss the weekly worship. Since my arrest, what do you imagine?

CHIME. I wish we had a helicopter.

MIGUEL. Don't make ludicrous wishes, Chime.

CHIME. What else is there to do?

MIGUEL. Go back.

CHIME. Go back?

MIGUEL. Yes, go back. Before these venomous coils close up behind us.

CHIME. Now who is fantasising?

MIGUEL. Fantasising? I am no longer sure of anything Chime. (*With increasing resignation.*) All I know and see is the sun inching up slowly behind that fist of mangrove. It separates our part of the lagoon from the open seas, and we are in this damned canoe with futile paddles battling a malicious tangle of weeds. For all we know these roots may reach right down to seabed. Any moment now the patrols will emerge – they take this route every day on their way to do battle with smugglers – I don't want them to find us here, marooned among the hyacinths. The journals have made my face familiar even to the blindest reader, and a policeman can always do with promotion.

CHIME. Come on Miguel, there's no need to sound so – despondent.

MIGUEL. I must spare our family the humiliation of being dragged out of one set of parasites by another. We'll turn around.

CHIME. As you wish. There is still time to think of something else.

Strike of paddle against the canoe.

MIGUEL. No, no! What are you trying to do?

CHIME. You said to turn around.

MIGUEL. You want us to get stuck? You can't turn the boat around in this tangle. We turn round and face the other way.

Movements within the canoe as they turn round to face the opposite direction. A cry of alarm from CHIME.

Careful, careful, Chime. Keep your hands on the sides and avoid standing straight up. I don't think I could find the strength to pull you out if you fell overboard.

CHIME. You really are one for exaggerating.

MIGUEL. If I fall in, I won't bother to struggle. I'll simply let the tentacles drag me down to their bed of slime.

The sound of water rises to huge splashes. Then tones down to a more rhythmic lapping against a stone wall.

The prison.

DETIBA. She was waiting up when you returned, you said. Didn't she do anything?

MIGUEL. Nothing. And she said nothing at all. Her chair was aligned as if it marked the end of the futile furrow we had just cut through the hyacinths. So was her gaze. Only that had travelled much beyond, perhaps it came to rest on the haven which had eluded us. I stopped by her side, waited briefly, but she remained as she was, immobile. I went up to my room to prepare for the trial.

Pause.
A rattle of the cell door.

WARDER. Mr Domingo, the Superintendent wanted you to see these.

Rustle of newspaper passed through the bars.

There is something in there to cheer you up. Everybody is speaking up against the sentence.

Newspaper noise as the pages are opened.

EMUKE. Wetin den dey talk? Wetin?

DETIBA. Can't you find it? What page is it?

WARDER. It's right there, bottom of the front page. And some other condemnations inside. One of them is from the former Chief Justice of the Federation. I'll come back later for the papers.

Footsteps going off.

MIGUEL (*reading*). 'National Bar Association condemns retro-active laws. The National Bar Association, in a statement issued at its Apapa Secretariat has condemned the practice of enacting laws to deal with offences committed when such laws did not exist . . .'

EMUKE. Wetin former Chief Justice say, na dat one I wan hear. 'E sentence me one time to four years when 'e still be ordinary High Court Judge.

MIGUEL. I'm sure they'll say more or less the same thing.

Newspaper rustle.

Here is one from the Roman Catholic Archbishop. 'No one has a right to take a human life under a law which did not exist at the time of a presumed offence.' Good, I'm glad somebody is actually mentioning the issue of presumption of guilt. If ever there was a clear case of a verdict dictated from above, against the full weight of evidence . . . ah, here's another – it begins to look like a groundswell of protest. Even the editorial – hm,

quite courageous. And the National Students Association . . .
Amnesty, national chapter – oh yes, I'm sure Amnesty
International will take an interest very soon . . . the Traditional
Rulers' Council – they are appealing for clemency. (*Throws
paper away.*) Clemency!

DETIBA. Keep cool, Mr Domingo.

MIGUEL. Clemency! Is that the issue?

DETIBA. Give me the paper. Does it matter what they call it? They
are all saying the same thing, only differently.

MIGUEL. No, it is not the same thing. That is the kind of language
that flatters the bestial egos of such a breed of rulers. It makes
them feel that the world and every living thing within it is their
largesse, from which they dole out crumbs when they are sated.
Clemency! Even a retarded child must know that the issue is
one of justice.

DETIBA. This would be more to your taste then. I've found the
statement of your friend, Emuke.

EMUKE. Wetin 'e talk?

DETIBA (*reading*). 'In his own statement, the former Chief Justice
of the Federation, Sir Tolade Akindero, warned that if the
sentence was carried out, it would amount to judicial murder.'
Is that more like it, Mr Domingo?

MIGUEL. Ah, what does it matter anyway? Why do we deceive
ourselves? We're living in a lawless time.

DETIBA. Here's one more. 'The Crusade for National Conscience
is organising a continuous vigil outside the prison until the
sentence is rescinded.'

MIGUEL (*violently*). No!

DETIBA. No? Why not? It all helps to put pressure on the regime.

MIGUEL. Don't you know who they are?

DETIBA. Not much. I've only heard of them once or twice – in the
papers.

MIGUEL. They are a religious sect who particularly abhor public
executions. And they are rather fanatical in their actions. If

they hold that vigil and they're ordered to disperse, they are just as likely to obey peacefully as to disobey – equally peacefully. This regime will not hesitate to open fire on them. I don't want anyone's death on my conscience.

DETIBA. That is really beyond our control, isn't it?

Four or five pairs of boots marching towards the cell as if in formation. They come to a halt outside the cell.

SUPERINTENDENT. Everybody get dressed. Mr Domingo – and you two, same for you. You've all been sent for.

MIGUEL. Who by?

SUPERINTENDENT. We don't know. The order is from the same Security Unit that used to fetch you for interrogation.

DETIBA. Interrogation? Are they re-opening the case? Or the Appeal Court? Is the hearing today?

MIGUEL. Today is a public holiday. The courts are not sitting.

Bustle in the cell as clothes are changed.

SUPERINTENDENT. Well, you may be both right and wrong there. You could be appearing before a Special Panel.

MIGUEL. What?

SUPERINTENDENT. I'm not supposed to tell you this, but we received a secret circular yesterday. All offences in your category, including verdicts delivered by the political tribunal, are no longer subject to review by the Court of Appeal. The Head of State has taken over their functions. My suspicion is that he has set up his own panel – it's the only kind that would sit on a public holiday. I'm only guessing, but I don't see why else they should bother you.

MIGUEL. Will our lawyers be present? Have they been informed?

SUPERINTENDENT. Mr Domingo, I've told you all I know. The usual form for taking you out of prison was brought by Security. My job is simply to hand you over.

MIGUEL. All right, thank you.

EMUKE. I done ready.

DETIBA. Me too.

MIGUEL. Let's go.

> *Dialogue continues over footsteps through corridors, down flights of stairs until they reach the* SUPERINTENDENT's *office.*

SUPERINTENDENT. Actually you don't know how lucky you are to be away from the premises today. Another set of armed robbers are going to be executed. The stakes are already being set up. Prisoners are confined to their cells – that's the routine – but within an hour the word will go round on the prison grapevine, and then you'd be amazed at the change. The quiet is unearthly, something you feel under your skin.

MIGUEL. They are shot in the prison yard?

SUPERINTENDENT. No, not inside. On the open grounds outside the prison. It's in public, you know. The military are in charge. We never know in advance whose turn it is – unless they are our own prisoners of course. They bring them from other prisons directly to the grounds outside. All we get are instructions to prepare the stakes for such-and-such o'clock on such a day. Like this morning. You're lucky to be out of it. Well, here we are.

> *Door opens into the* SUPERINTENDENT's *office. Men rising to their feet.*

SUPERINTENDENT. Well, gentlemen, all three present for escort. Please sign the receipt forms.

> *Scratch of pen on paper.*

EMUKE (*whisper*). Dese no be our regular escorts.

DETIBA. They change them all the time.

SUPERINTENDENT. Thank you. Well my friends, good luck. See you on my evening rounds.

MIGUEL. Thank you.

Door opens, closes. A short walk by five pairs of feet, two booted.

WARDER. Open the gates.
VOICE. You have the exeat?
WARDER. Here.

Brief rustle of paper.

VOICE. Okay. Open.

Bolts are withdrawn. A wooden bar is raised from its rest against the gate. The wooden gate creaks open. Immediately there is noise from a distanced crowd. Audible moans of 'No', 'No', 'No'. It is a helpless, not aggressive 'No'.

MIGUEL. Who are all this crowd? Oh, of course. The Superintendent said there was . . .
DETIBA. I can't believe people still bring their children to watch this kind of thing.
MIGUEL. Must be one of the really notorious gangs. Just look at the crowd! But, Detiba . . .
DETIBA. Yeah?
MIGUEL. This is not the usual bloodthirsty crowd one sees on television. These ones appear – almost plaintive. Sober.

Four pairs of boots advance, marching crisply, come to a stop. One pair advances two or three more paces.

OFFICER. Identify yourselves as I call out your names. Kolawole Adetiba.

Gates begin to creak shut.

DETIBA. Ye-e-s?
OFFICER. Augustine Emuke.
EMUKE. Present.
OFFICER. Miguel Domingo.
MIGUEL. I am here.

OFFICER. By virtue of warrant signed by the Head of State and Commander of the Armed Forces . . .

Gates slam shut. Bolts are replaced. A lone pair of boots head in the direction of the SUPERINTENDENT'S *office, slowly, as if dragging. Door opens.*

SUPERINTENDENT. Yes, what is it?
WARDER. Did you know, Sir?
SUPERINTENDENT. Did I know what?

A sudden burst of gunfire.

I really must air-condition this office. It's the only thing that will keep out that sound.

Three single pistol shots, one after the other.

Yes, what was your question again?
WARDER. I just wondered if you knew, Sir – the three stakes, who they were for.

Fade in dirge from Yemanja's music.

THE BEATIFICATION
OF AREA BOY

A Lagosian Kaleidoscope

NOTE

Certain Yoruba words which appear in italics in the text are explained in a glossary at the end of the play together with a translation of the song on pages 291–3.

ACKNOWLEDGEMENTS

... to participants in the 'ITI/Sisi Clara' Master Workshop of 1992 where parts of some scenes of *The Beatification of Area Boy* were developed, especially to the old hands from Orisun Theatre – Tunji Oyelana, Yewande Johnson (née Akinbo), Yomi Obileye, Wale Ogunyemi – plus Charles Mike from the Artistes' Collective, Lagos.

The Beatification of Area Boy was premiered at the Courtyard Theatre, West Yorkshire Playhouse, Leeds, on 31 October 1995, with the following cast:

BOKYO	Makinde Adeniran
MAMA PUT	Susan Aderin
MISEYI	Bola Aiyeola
FOREIGNER/FOREIGN DIGNITARY	Stefan Bütschi
TRADER	Femi Elufowoju Jr.
FOREIGNER/FOREIGN DIGNITARY	Lilly Friedrich
BIG SHOPPER/MILITARY GOVERNOR	Ombo Gogo Ombo
SANDA	Tyrone Huggins
MISEYI'S ATTENDANT/MAMA PUT'S DAUGHTER/BAND MEMBER	Miriam Keller
FOREIGNER/FOREIGN DIGNITARY	Roger Nydegger
VENDOR/MC/MOTHER OF THE DAY	Yomi Obileye
PARKING ATTENDANT/MILITARY GOVERNOR'S ADC	Anthony Ofoegbu
BARBER	Olawale Ogunyemi
OFFICER/JUDGE	Wale Ojo
MINSTREL	Tunji Oyelana
ACCUSED/BAND MEMBER	Akinwale Oyewole
CYCLIST/PRISON WARDER	Victor Power
VICTIM/BAND MEMBER	Olabisi Toluwase

Other characters were played by the Cast and Community Company

Directed by Jude Kelly
Designed by Niki Turner
Musical Director Tunji Oyelana
Lighting by Mark Pritchard
Sound by Mic Pool

The broad frontage of an opulent shopping plaza. Early daybreak. As the day becomes brighter, the broad sliding doors of tinted glass will reflect (and distort) traffic scenes from the main street which would seem to run through the rear of the auditorium. This is realised by projections, using the sliding doors as uneven screens. When the doors slide open, the well-stocked interior of consumer items – a three-dimensional projection or photo blow-up will suffice – contrast vividly with the slummy exterior.

Frontstage consists of a broad pavement, with three or four broad steps leading up to it. An alleyway along the right side of the shopping block vanishes into the rear, and is lined by the usual makeshift stalls, vending their assortment of snacks, cigarettes, soft drinks, household goods, wearing apparel, cheap jewellery etc. The closest stall to the street, downstage right corner of the block, belongs to TRADER, *also addressed as* AREA TWO-ONE. *He is busy arranging his stall which soon displays a wide assortment of cheap consumer goods. The barber-stall will be to the left, next to* MAMA PUT's *food corner.*

A partially covered drainage runs in front of the shopping block. Street-level planks laid across the gutter provide a crossing into the alleyway.

A vagrant, called JUDGE, *is perched on a step near the top. His posture suggests some kind of yoga-type body exercise.*

JUDGE. I breathed into the sky before I slept, and – just look at the result.

TRADER. Enh? Oh, good morning, your lordship.

JUDGE. It's a good display, not so? And to think all I did was breathe against the horizon. It was the last exhalation before I lay down – emptying all the secret spaces of my body – (*Gently presses his fingertips against chest, stomach and sides.*) – I had completed my nightly exercises – yoga – do you practise yoga at all?

TRADER. Yo – ga?

JUDGE. I knew it was a good exhalation, deep and purifying. All the day's anxieties and violence — mostly other people's — gathered into one breath. (*Pressing his belly upwards to his chest.*) This is where it gets transformed, and there it all is, spread across the sky. To look at it, you'd never guess what went through my alimentary canal, into the arteries and lungs. But I'm used to it. Even if I sometimes feel like the city's sewage system . . . or its kidneys — most of the purification is done in the kidneys you know . . . the city is all the better for it. Nothing like starting a new day on a clean slate.

TRADER. Oh, that na good idea. That must to feel very good for you, Judge. Na only kind man like you go think of others before you go sleep.

JUDGE. If we don't remit sentences from time to time, the gaols will be full. The entire city, the nation itself, will become one huge prison camp. That is why we have a council for the prerogative of mercy. I have not formally enrolled but . . . (*Points at the sky.*) Isn't it amazing what an individual can do on his own? Have you applied? Of course you'll be on the receiving end.

TRADER (*slight impatience, under his breath*). Other people, when they wake up for morning time just dey pray. Simple prayer, 'e do them. Dis one . . . I done tire!

JUDGE. You musn't tire. Never give up. You apply the first time, they turn you down, you try and try again. I was rejected six times you know. When I was like you, on the receiving end.

TRADER. Na so?

JUDGE. Finally, I wore them down with my petitions. Last night, it was finally granted.

TRADER. Congratulations, your lordship. Congratulations.

JUDGE. I signed the letter myself, for the avoidance of doubt. I know the format. Afterwards you wonder, why hadn't I thought of it all these years? Those who decide Yes or No, they are mere mortals, aren't they? And mostly on an inferior plane of aware- ness, I have written many petitions in my time for clients, and I know the standard responses. One for rejection, the other approval. This time, mine was . . .

TRADER. Approved.

JUDGE. Oh. How did you know?

TRADER. Na you tell me yourself, now now.

JUDGE (*suspicious*). Did you see the letter?

TRADER. Even if to say I did, I fit read. Look, na early morning. I dey prepare for my customers and I wan' think small. We currency done fall again, petrol dey scarcity, which mean to say, transport fare done double. As for foodstuff and other commodity, even gari wey be poor man diet . . . (*Stops as he observes* JUDGE *looking at him with total mystification.*) I just dey explain why I need small time to put new price for all dese goods. (JUDGE *looks even more bewildered.*) Look, no to this time you begin walka for your circuit . . . er . . . circuit court or wetin you dey call am?

JUDGE. The courts will not sit today, so I am master of my time.

TRADER (*groans*). You mean na here you go siddon all day?

JUDGE. No. Today I start on a different journey. I begin the long journey to the kingdom of lost souls. I shall relieve them of their torment.

TRADER (*looks him up and down*). You go need a pair of shoes then.

JUDGE. What?

TRADER. A strong pair of shoes. It sound like long journey. You no fit afford the bus fare.

JUDGE (*at his most supercilious*). I do not recall addressing you. I am not aware that the accused was given leave to address the court.

TRADER. Aha! I done catch you. You no fit start dat one with me today. Who you dey talk to all this time then? Na only two of us dey here.

JUDGE. You see? You should always rely on your counsel. You think you see only two of us but in fact, there are three. Or four. Strictly I should say three but I am giving you the benefit of the doubt. In any case, I was actually addressing my soul, not yours, or you. Ha-ha, any good counsel would have saved you from that trap.

TRADER. Addressing which kin' soul? You no fit use telephone either. And as I see am, the way I bin know you all these years, na long distance call if you want talk to your soul. Expensive.

JUDGE. That's the way it must appear to the soulless.

TRADER. Or inside dustbin. The way you search every morning inside dustbin and refuse dump . . .

JUDGE. For evidence, fool, for vital clues. If the police don't do their work, then the court must search out the truth wherever it may be hidden. I am not one of your sedentary ministers of truth, friend. I did not opt for the circuit courts for nothing, declining even secondment to the Supreme Court. But it's all there in my curriculum vitae – if you care to read it. Or had the ability to read.

TRADER. Thank you. I no fit read, but I sabbe the world pass you. Even Mama Put's small pickin talk sense pass you – make you go preach to am.

> JUDGE rises, stretches himself, then lowers his body and does one or two contortions. Stops. His gaze becomes riveted on the sky.

JUDGE. It is the kind of day when unbelievers are shamed and the faithful exalted. Look at that horizon – there, where the sun is just rising. Have you ever seen a dawn the likes of that? (Grandly.) Do you see how it's opening up the rest of the sky? My work. Pity I slept late, so I could not usher it in with the secret mantras. Still, asleep or awake, that dawn is my handiwork.

TRADER (straining to see). Dawn? Which kin' dawn? I only see the sun wey begin expose all those dirty roofs for Isale-eko. Na so e dey do am every morning. Wetin get special about his one? And wetin concern you sun for sun and sky? The wahala wey you get for this earth no do you?

JUDGE. I am a specialist of sunrise. I have seen more dawns from every vantage point, more dawns than you can count white hairs on my head. I have a proprietary feeling towards dawns you see, not that you can understand but, I have a right to claim that they belong to me. Once, I could only predict what kind of sunrise it would be, yes, I could tell that even before going to sleep. Then I began to pray for the kind of dawn into which I wanted to wake. In detail, you know. Colours. Moods. Shapes. Shades of stillness or motion. It was something to look forward to.

TRADER. It mus' to help take your mind off those mosquitoes. Or rough weather. Person wey go sleep on empty stomach must take sometin' fill in mind. Otherwise, how 'e go fit sleep?

JUDGE. Oh Trader, Trader. Because you see a lifeless form here or in a dark alleyway with ravenous rats for companion, yes, and on the beach sometimes, or in the back of a derelict lorry, a form that wears my face, do you really think my soul will be found within that form?

TRADER. Excuse me o. No vex with me. I think say na you I come dey meet here every morning when I come prepare for the day's business.

JUDGE. You'll never know what it is to wake into day on the rooftops – yes, those rooftops you call dirty – to wake up on the skyline face to face with every day a different face of itself, just as your mind had painted it before you fell asleep. If you prayed hard enough. When I still prayed – and that was a while ago. Because – it's all a matter of self-development, training you know – I began to dispense with prayers. I took charge. I began to make dawns to order.

TRADER. Yeah? You find plenty customer?

JUDGE (*pitying look*). Of course. I forget, you have the mind of a petty commercial.

TRADER. It feeds me you know, it feeds me. I'm not complaining.

JUDGE. How can you complain when you know no better. Nor aspire to something better. (*Looks up sharply in the direction of the sunrise.*) You have wasted enough of my time . . .

TRADER. I have what?!

JUDGE. Wasted too much of my time. By now I should have been foraging in the disposal sector of that new nightclub – yes, The New Lagoon. No matter, when I encounter you again in the morning, you will find I have gone professional.

TRADER. Professional? Doing what?

JUDGE. Doing what I have finally accepted I was meant for. My head is clear on that score. As clear as that sky you see blossoming before my presence . . . yes, my journey to the kingdom of souls begins today. People say the nation has lost its soul but that is nonsense. It's all a matter of finding out where it's hidden. (*Stops, reflects.*) Unless it never had any? Is that possible? No! I have hesitated too long. The route is clearly along the prerogative of mercy. Once I thought it lay along the trail of the majesty of the law but – well, one had to begin somewhere. We grow, we develop . . . (*Goes off, mumbling.*)

TRADER (*shakes his head, sadly*). I go miss am. The day they take am commot here and lock him up, I go miss am too much.

BARBER (*entering*). Who will you miss?

TRADER. Oh. Good morning. You no pass each other?

BARBER. Oh, it's that one. Is he relocating?

TRADER. Who sabbe for am? Today na business of dawn and sunrise. And he say he wan' go professional.

BARBER (*looks up*). Ah, you must admit it's a spectacular one. I noticed it myself as soon as I opened my window.

TRADER. Oh, you too.

BARBER. Me too?

TRADER. All I sabbe na say the morning begin show the pothole and garbage before in normal time. Before before, I no dey see them on my way here. Today 'e get bright so early, I tink say na different street I take reach here.

BARBER. It's still a colourful sky to wake up to. And you can hardly blame it for the refuse dumps, can you? If the town council won't clear them, what can even God do about it?

He sets about preparing his barber-stall. Rolls the plastic cover from the swivel chair. Ties on an off-white apron. Spreads a white cloth over a half-drum on which he then arranges his combs, clippers, scissors, hair lotions etc.

A SHOP WORKER *in the plaza arrives, bids good morning to the two, then looks around, puzzled.*

SHOP WORKER. No one arrive yet? Have you seen Security?

BARBER (*exchanges puzzled looks with* TRADER). But you are early. None of your people ever gets here until at least thirty minutes after I've set up for business. Only Trader gets here before me.

TRADER. You no dey use alarm clock?

SHOP WORKER. Me? I no get watch self.

TRADER. How you dey get to work then? You no dey come late?

SHOP WORKER. Never. As soon as I open my eyes and look outside, I can tell the time.

BARBER (*to* TRADER). You see. Didn't I tell you? That sunrise must have fooled her. I bet it fooled half of Lagos.

TRADER. Abi you wan buy alarm clock? For next time. Make you open the day's palm for me and I go give you good discount.

SHOP WORKER. I beg, leave me. Look how I bin run come work instead of chopping my breakfast jejely. I tink say I done late so much, dem go sack me.

Sits down on pavement in annoyance.

Enter MAMA PUT, *preceded by* BOYKO *carrying all her cooking utensils etc. He assists in setting up her corner. The cooking fires are lit, bowls and plates stacked. He goes off with a pail and returns later with it filled with water. General preparation for business.* BOYKO *alternates between helping her and* TRADER, *practising on a small flute when he is unoccupied with either.* SANDA *corrects his false notes in an indulgent manner.*

TRADER. You late small today, Mama Put.

MAMA PUT. I no feel well at all. But for say I no wan' disappoint my customers, I no for commot house at all.

BARBER. Wes matter?

MAMA PUT. I no know. No to say my body no feel well, na the day inself no look well. I commot for house and I nearly go back and stay inside house. I no like the face of today, dat na God's truth. Make you just look that sky. E dey like animal wey just chop in victim, with blood dripping from in wide open mouth.

TRADER. A be you dream bad dream again last night?

MAMA PUT. Morning na picken of the sleep wey person sleep the night before, not so? Make we jus' lef am so. (*Busies herself with chores.*)

Enter SANDA, *the Security Officer. He has a pile of magazines and a book under his arm.*

SANDA. Good morning, Mama Put!

MAMA PUT. How are you, my son?

SANDA. As you see, Mama, as you see. Morning, Mr Barber.

BARBER. Morning o, Security.

TRADER *has dashed up the steps, righted the stool which was lying on its side, giving it a quick dusting.*

TRADER. You welcome, *oga*.

SANDA. Area Two-One!

TRADER. Na your hand we dey.

SANDA (*sees the* SHOP WORKER). Hey, you're early.

TRADER (*laughing*). 'In bobo trow am commot for house. Na here she sleep all night. E keep Judge warm for night.

SHOP WORKER. God punish your head! (*A car driving past is reflected in the sliding doors. The* SHOP WORKER *springs up.*) Manager done come.

SANDA (*looking up at the sky*). If this doesn't prove a hot day . . .

TRADER. Judge say na in dey make the climate now. E say na in dey tell the sky what to do. De man done craze *patapata*.

SANDA. Why? We do have professional rainmakers, don't we? What they claim to do is the same – tell the sky what to do.

TRADER. Oga self! *Haba!* No to different fancy dey take am every day? Only last week he tell us say 'e done sabbe how to make money. 'E swear say 'e go make all of us rich pass any drug baron.

SANDA. Well, give him time. Maybe he's still working on the magic formula.

TRADER. Wissai? I tell you say na weather and sunshine come interest am now. 'E done forget all about the money business.

SANDA. Genius, friend, genius. Great minds cannot rest content with only one idea at a time. And anyway, how do you know it's not all connected? If he wants to shower us with millions, he must first master the skies. Give him time. When it starts to rain millons, you won't have cause to complain.

TRADER (*amazed*). You tink is really possible, oga? You tink say 'e done find the secret?

SANDA (*taps his head*). Appearances are deceptive. There may be a method in his madness – that's what William Shakespeare says on the subject.

TRADER. Ah, that your friend again.

SANDA. Oh yes, he has an answer for everything.

> *The lights come on in the interior of the store. The door slides open and shut, as if being tested.* SANDA *takes his seat, and opens up one of his magazines.* BOYKO *practises a tune on his flute.*

BARBER. You know, Mr Sanda, to you it may seem a joke, but these things really happen you know.

SANDA. What things?

BARBER. Those who make money with black magic. I mean, there are people who do it. It is bad money. It doesn't always last, and the things people have to do to get such money, it's terrible business. Sometimes they have to sacrifice their near relations, even children. It's a pact with the devil but they do it.

SANDA. It's a pact with the devil all right, but it doesn't produce any money. They just slaughter those poor victims for nothing.

BARBER. Those overnight millionaires then, how do you think they do it?

SANDA. Cocaine. 419 swindle. Godfathering or mothering armed robbers. Or after a career with the police. Or the Army, if you're lucky to grab a political post. Then you retire at forty – as a General who has never fought a war. Or you start your own church, or mosque. That's getting more and more popular.

BARBER. You don't believe anything, that's your problem.

SANDA. There are far too many superstitions suffocating this country. I can't believe all of them, can I?

BARBER. This one is no superstition. Look, Trader, didn't I tell you about the landlord of my sister-in-law?

TRADER. Na true. Ah, oga, make you hear this one o. E take in eye see this one o, no to say den tell am.

SANDA. Don't bother. It's too early in the morning, my stomach won't be able to take it. (*To* BOYKO.) Fe. Fe. Not fa. When will you get that correct?

BARBER. You are the original doubting Thomas. But these things happen, that's all I can tell you. You see all those corpses with their vital organs missing – breasts in the case of women, the entire region of the vagina neatly scooped out. And sometimes just the pubic hair is shaved off for their devilish mixture. And pregnant ones with the foetus ripped out. Male corpses without their genitals or eyes. Sometimes they cut out the liver . . .

TRADER. And what of hunchbacks? Dat na another favourite for making money. They take out the hunch, sometimes while the man self still dey alive.

BARBER. Yes, that's supposed to be most effective, when the hunch is carved out with the owner still breathing. Some people have no hearts. They've sold their souls to the devil! Albinos too – don't forget them. Although I don't know what part of their body they use.

TRADER. No to the skin?

BARBER. No. Can't be. That one they picked up near Ita Faji cemetery had his birthday suit intact. He hadn't been skinned or anything like that. Even the eyes hadn't been touched. You would think it had something to do with the eyes – you know albinos don't like sunlight, maybe they drained the fluid from the eyes . . .

SANDA. Look, I've told you I don't want to hear all that kind of talk on an empty stomach. How soon will that *konkere* be ready, Mama Put?

MAMA PUT. Any time you people can take your minds off the satanic work of these get-rich-quick swine.

Enter BLIND MINSTREL *with his box-guitar, singing 'Lagos is the place for me'. Stops when he reaches the food-stall. Greetings are exchanged and he fumbles in his pocket for money.* MAMA PUT *ladles out some bean pottage and fried stew.*

MAMA PUT. With or without?

MINSTREL (*brief hesitation*). With.

She sprinkles some gari *over the pottage.*

SANDA. How are you this morning, Troubadour?

MINSTREL. As you see me, Bro., as you see me. Five naira *ewa* no fit fill picken belle these days, how much more grown man like me?

SANDA. A-ah. But the soldiers say life has improved since they took over.

MINSTREL. Perhaps for inside dere barracks. Not for my side of the street!

SANDA. Well, those who get, get. And they know how to spend it. Our banqueting-hall is booked for tonight. Plus the entire courtyard of the plaza. Big wedding ceremony. Broad Street is closed to traffic – from seven o'clock – all the way from the junction of Balogun Street to that flyover. Never happened before. The Military Governor himself signed the permit.

MINSTREL. Thank you, sir. I shall ensure my presence here in the evening.

SANDA. Don't even wait till then. Stay around the neighbourhood today. The relations will be coming and going all day, to oversee the arrangements. They are bound to be in a generous mood.

MINSTREL. I'll hang around then. Mama, I think I'll have some *sawa-sawa* with this *ewa* after all. Two naira. (*Flashing the money.*)

MAMA PUT. Keep counting your chickens before they're hatched.

MINSTREL. Mama Put, I can already hear the rustle of fat naira notes. My voice needs lubricating. So bring that other stuff you keep for special customers. Give me one shot with the change.

MAMA PUT. See what you've done? You've turned the poor beggar's head and he has not even earned the money he's spending. (*From the recesses of her cupboard, she brings out a bottle and pours him a shot.*) Here. Fortunately your voice can't be any more jarring than it is already.

SANDA. He'll earn it. There'll be plenty of bread to go round today. Even the prisoners won't be left out. A batch of them are already detailed to clean up the neighbourhood. They should get here in the afternoon. (*Chuckles.*) I suppose they'll expect me to give them an advance on their expectations.

MINSTREL (*gargles with the liquor and swallows. Beams*). We no go let you go back to your Rivers town, Mama Put. The way you sabbe brew this *kain-kain*, 'e no get competition for Lagos.

MAMA PUT (*brandishes what looks like a bayonet*). When I'm ready to move back, let's see who will try and stop me. (*Begins to cut up meat with the knife.*) It's bad enough that I've had to live in Lagos all these years; do you think I also want to die in it?

MINSTREL. You can't escape Lagos. Even for your Ikot Ekpene, you go find Lagos.

MAMA PUT. Yes, but not in such a strong dose. Lagos na overdose.

MINSTREL. True word, Mama Put, true word.

He laughs and plucks at his box-guitar. BOYKO, *as usual
whenever there is any singing, manfully tries to accompany
him.*

MINSTREL (*sings*).

> I love dis Lagos, I no go lie
> Na inside am I go live and die
> I know my city, I no go lie
> E fit in nation like coat and tie
> When Lagos belch, the nations swell
> When the nation shit, na Lagos dey smell.
> The river wey flow for Makurdi market
> You go find in deposit for Lagos bucket.

MAMA PUT. Hey, not that one near my food-stall, you hear?

MINSTREL. No blame me, blame Oga Sanda, na in teach me all the
bad songs. Anyway, wait small. I nearly reach the part wey
celebrate the Civil War wey drive you commot for Ikot Ekpene. I
know na that part you like to hear. But first, make I salute we
famous Lagosian landscape.

> The Russian astronauts flying in space
> Radioed a puzzle to their Moscow base
> They said, we're flying over Nigeria
> And we see high mountains in built-up area
> Right in the middle of heavy traffic
> Is this space madness, tell us quick?
> The strange report was fed to computers
> Which soon analysed the ponderous beauties
> The computer replied, don't be snobbish
> You know it's a load of their national rubbish.

They respond with laugher. Even MAMA PUT *allows herself a
chuckle.*

> But make I return to history
> Dat war we fight in recent memory

When music wey come from barrel of gun
Was – we must keep the nation one.
Me I tink I get problem for me eye
I dey see double, thas the reason why
When I look, na two I see,
Make I explain, I tink you go gree.

MAMA PUT's *customers begin to drift in. They join in the chorus: 'I love this Lagos'.*

Make you no worry, both nations be friends
When they fight, they soon make amends
When one back de itch, de other go scratch
One go lay eggs, de other go hatch
Eggs are eggs, and plenty done rotten
But make I tell you, some are golden
I tell you my country no be one
I mean, no to yesterday I born.
    I love this Lagos *etc.*

One twin go slap, the other go turn cheek
And soon they're playing Hide-and-Seek
Sixteen billion dollars or more
Wey be windfall from Saddam's war
Vanish for air like harmattan dust
Twin Seek cry, *Haba*, this country go bust
Brother Hide stay cool, he set up commission
Of enquiry with prompt decision
Seek from Turkey to China Sea
The more you look, the less you see.
    I love this Lagos *etc.*

The other day, I lie for my bed
And the radio suggest say I sick for my head
Cause the government say e get no option
But to wage war against corruption
I pinch myself to be sure I awake

Then I laugh so tey, my body ache
Pot tell calabash your belle de show
Snail tell tortoise, how come you so slow
Monkey go market, baboon dey cook
You tink one chop, de other siddon look?
Before battle start, the war done lost
Plus billions den go say the battle cost
    I love this Lagos *etc.*

Enter, during the singing a young GIRL, *in school uniform. She helps* MAMA PUT *in serving the customers, then spruces up to go to school, picks up her satchel.*

GIRL. Morning, Mr Sanda.

SANDA. Morning, sight for sore eyes. Now this boastful sunrise has some decent competition.

MAMA PUT (*gives her a quick once-over*). You have the new books? (*The* GIRL *pats her satchel.*) Don't lose them. It's all I can afford for now. Tell your teacher we'll get the rest next month. Or next term. Whenever God chooses to increase my profit. (*Hesitates. Looks up at* SANDA.) You know, I don't really want her to go to school today.

SANDA. Because of the missing textbooks? Come on.

MAMA PUT. No, it's that same dream . . . it came back again last night. I really think she should stay home today.

GIRL. Dreams can't take care of my schooling, Mama.

MAMA PUT. If I thought they could, I wouldn't be out here every morning sweating over these pots to pay for your school fees. And anyway, who was talking to you?

SANDA. Forget the bad dreams, Mama. Everyone has them from time to time. Believe it or not I dreamt only last week that I got married. But I still had to put on my uniform and come to work. All I wanted to do was to lock up the windows and doors, stuff up the cracks in the walls and hide under my bed.

MAMA PUT. Oh you! You make fun of everything. All right girl, off you go. Here, don't forget the money for your school lunch. And

make sure you return here directly after school. Tell your teacher
I don't want you on any after-school assignment. Not this week
anyway.

GIRL. All right, Mother. Bye-bye Mr Sanda. (*She runs off.*)

SANDA (*shakes his head, smiling*). You really are some kind of
Mother Courage, you know. Even right down to the super-
stitious bit.

MAMA PUT. There are dreams and dreams. This one . . .

SANDA. . . . is exactly like the one you had before the last excite-
ment on our street. What was it now? Oh yes, something terrible
had happened to Lagos. You woke up one day and there wasn't
any Lagos anywhere. No warning, no nothing, just – pouff! –
Lagos was gone. Disappeared into thin air. And you thought
that was a calamity!

MAMA PUT. Nobody cares to listen to me . . .

SANDA. You know we do. Someone has to do the worrying on the
street after all, so we leave all that to you and carry on with
normal life. It works perfectly, believe me.

MAMA PUT (*sighs. Stirs the pot, then looks up*). I don't remember
waking up to a morning this bright. Not a blemish. There isn't
even a speck of cloud in the sky.

SANDA. I'm glad you've noticed. Dark dreams at night, then
daylight comes and banishes all the misgivings they sneak into
the heart.

MAMA PUT. You are wrong, son. Woefully wrong. A sky such as
this brings no good with it. The clouds have vanished from the
sky but, where are they? (*Jabs the tip of the bayonet against her
breast.*) In the hearts of those below. In the rafters. Over the
hearth. Blighting the vegetable patch. Slinking through the
orange grove. Rustling the plantain leaves and withering them –
oh I heard them again last night – and poisoning the fish-pond.
When the gods mean to be kind to us, they draw up the gloom to
themselves – yes, a cloud is a good sign, only, not many people
know that. Even a wisp, a mere shred of cloud over my roof
would bring me comfort, but not this stark, cruel brightness. It's

not natural. It's a deceit. You watch out. We'd better all watch out.

BOYKO *looks upstage at some distraction, gets up and runs off.*

SANDA (*softly*). You'll never get over that war. Not ever. Nobody does. It would be abnormal. But you must forget the fish-ponds, Mama. And the orange groves. This is Lagos, city of chrome and violence. Noise and stench. Lust and sterility. But it was here you chose to rebuild your life. You've done better than most, made a new home for your children. Sent them all to school and to university, just from frying and selling *akara* and concocting superlative bean pottage, not to mention the popular brew. You deserve a medal.

MAMA PUT. Medal! And what would I do with that? Keep your medals and give me back — yes, even the mangrove swamps. (*Sudden harshness. She waves the bayonet violently around.*) And don't remind me of medals! They all got medals. Those who did this thing to us, those who turned our fields of garden eggs and prize tomatoes into mush, pulp and putrid flesh — that's what they got — medals! They plundered the livestock, uprooted yams and cassava and what did they plant in their place? The warm bodies of our loved ones. My husband among them. My brothers. One of them they stabbed to death with this! And all for trying to save the family honour. Yes, and children too. Shells have no names on them. And the pilots didn't care where they dropped their bombs. But that proved only the beginning of the seven plagues. After the massacre of our youth came the plague of oil rigs and the new death of farmland, shrines and fish sanctuaries, and the eternal flares that turn night into day and blanket the land with globules of soot . . . I suppose those oilmen will also earn medals?

Enter BIG MAN SHOPPPER, *pursued by* BOYKO.

BIG MAN SHOPPER. Go away! I tell you I have no car for you to look after. Go and find yourself another customer.

BOYKO. Oga, this place no good. Anything can happen to your car. But if you lef' am to Boyko, na one hundred per cent guarantee.

BIG MAN SHOPPER (*stops and faces him squarely*). I think something is wrong with your ears.

BOYKO. Na all this traffic noise, oga, 'e fit make man so deaf 'e no go hear en'ting, even thunder self. Even if dem dey break windscreen for Mercedes in broad daylight for in very front, person no fit hear.

BIG MAN SHOPPER. Is that so?

BOYKO. To God who made me!

BIG MAN SHOPPER. Well, young man, you'd better pray for a miracle from the same God who made you so you can hear me when I say (*Bellows.*) Get off me! Scram! I have no Mercedes whose windscreen you and your gang can break.

> *He breaks off and walks down briskly, turns the corner and mounts the steps. The boy slouches after him.*

SANDA (*looks up lazily from his journal*). Has that boy been annoying you, sir?

BIG MAN SHOPPER. Don't mind him. He thinks people aren't wise to their tricks. I no longer park where vandals and extortionists like him operate.

SANDA. Very sensible. That space just under the flyover — where the fish trucks supply the market women — that's one of the safest places. I always recommend it. Nothing can touch your car there.

BIG MAN SHOPPER. Oh no, it's much better behind the old UAC building. The gang doesn't operate in that area at all; it's too close to the military pay office.

SANDA. You're right. They daren't mess about near those soldiers. Enjoy your shopping, sir.

> BIG MAN SHOPPER *enters the store.* SANDA *resumes his reading.* BOYKO *remains near* TRADER'S *stall, below* SANDA, *who*

has picked up another journal and appears to be checking a list within it. He speaks without taking his face off the magazine.

Yeah. Just wanted to make sure, but it's the same old Toyota Crown, at least when owner was last registered. (*Runs his finger down the journal.*) LA 6161 OD – Tell Area Two-Four to take care of it, then return here so you can take him warning when our Big Man has finished his shopping. (BOYKO *sets off.*) Wait! Warn Two-Four he shouldn't be fooled by the car's ancient appearance – it's brand-new inside. Tell him to tackle the boot – that's where he keeps his briefcase. If it's not there, take the radio and the seat-covers – it's all high-class stuff. Go!

BOYKO *runs off.* SANDA *sighs, shakes his head dolefully. He speaks as if to no one in particular.*

If there's one thing I hate, it's disloyalty. People should be loyal. We used to look after that man, never any complaint. If he wished, he could leave all the doors of his car open and there'd be nothing missing on his return. Heaven knows what gets into all of them these days. All kinds of duplicity from those who should set an example. Why dent the sides of a custom-built Toyota, just to make it look like a botched-up panel-beater job. And then the paint! Looks more like surface primer blended with rust. But just you take a look inside – drinks cabinet, a dainty little refrigerator – very cute – I wouldn't mind something like that myself, only, where does it go on a motorbike? The chamois leather seats – well now, a strip of that will have no problem on the seat of the motorbike. No, the interior of that car is something else – polished oak panelling on the doors, electronic dashboard, rugs so deep your feet don't notice the pot-holes. You'd never suspect any of that. You'll walk past that beat-up Toyota, wondering why such junk should be licensed to ply the motor road. But we got the inside picture all right. (*Chuckles.*) Two-One!

TRADER. I dey here, oga.

SANDA. I say do you remember that camouflage man?

TRADER. No to him pass enter shop just now? We no see am since last year riot.

SANDA. Yeah. If he had not taken one of our – er – pilots on board, for safe passage, we'd never have known what the interior of his Toyota really looked like.

TRADER. The pilot charge him double after he see all dat super fancy interior. In fact, I remember, he even wan' cancel his safe conduct altogether.

SANDA. No, we couldn't allow that. A deal is a deal. (*Sighs.*) We had such a nice community here – we still do. Once you're registered, that's it for life. Now he goes and hides his car outside our area. It hurts one's pride. (*Shakes his head reprovingly.*) People should support their community. (*He resumes his reading.*)

TRADER. True talk. Even oyinbo man 'in say, charity begin for home.

> A CYCLIST *has slowed down in front of his stall.* TRADER *appears mesmerised by this visitation. The* CYCLIST *inspects the goods, but* TRADER's *attention is focused entirely on the bicycle.*

CYCLIST. How much this tie, oga?

TRADER. Oga Sanda, you see wetin I take my eye see?

CYCLIST. What? I say this tie. Wetin be last price?

> TRADER *gets up slowly, as if in a trance. He circles the bicycle, warily.*

TRADER. Oga Sanda, make you look this ting wey I dey look so o. Mama Put, Mr Barber, all of una, make you come look o. Because I no believe this thing at all at all, even though my eye tell me say no to dream I dey dream am.

NEWSVENDOR (*enters, pressing his bullhorn*). City News. Daily

Courier. National . . . (*Stops dead, transfixed in turn by the contraption.*) Sho!

BARBER (*also approaching. Looks from the bicycle to the* CYCLIST). Maybe there is a circus in town.

NEWSVENDOR. No, no news of circus for any of my newspaper.

MAMA PUT. I feel homesick. Oh, the sight of this thing, it makes me feel homesick.

TRADER. But you mean say na true? Na true true this machine here, or na magic?

CYCLIST. Wes matter with all of una? I say I wan' price this tie.

BARBER. Was he the one? Did you bring this contraption here?

CYCLIST. Wetin be contraption? Why you all dey take eye look me as if to say I be one *saka-jojo*?

MAMA PUT. It makes me homesick, that's all I can say. It just makes me feel so homesick I want to pack up and go home. Today. (*Returns to her corner.*)

NEWSVENDOR. Wey all these reporters self? Man no dey see them when something extra dey happen. O-oh, if to say I just get camera.

CYCLIST (*bristling*). Camera! For what? I be freak show? I get two head or you see tail commot from my yansh? Look, if you try . . . !

BARBER. No, no, please. Please don't take offence. We are all naturally curious, you see. Did you actually bring this thing into town. I mean, ride it into town?

CYCLIST. How you think say I get here? Of course na ride I ride am. All the way from new Ajegunle settlement. You wan' make I carry am instead?

TRADER. I fit touch am? You no go vex? I just wan' touch am small.

NEWSVENDOR. Me too.

CYCLIST. Wetin come dey worry all you people? All this *wahala* just beause I wan' buy tie? Na trade you come trade or na decorate you just dey decorate street?

BARBER. You know, if a submarine were to surface here, it could not cause a greater sensation. Even a spaceship from outer space.

That reminds me, Mr Sanda, I have still to take you to that preacher who was abducted by spacemen in their flying saucer . . .

SANDA. Sure, sure . . .

BARBER. Seven months and seven days he spent with them. They landed the saucer in his front garden you know. All silver and blue, about the size of a football field . . .

SANDA. And it landed in his front garden.

BARBER. It could contract and expand, like an accordion. It expanded to its full size as it took off . . .

CYCLIST (*drops the tie*). All of una, I tink you dey take me play. I go take my business go somewhere else.

SANDA. You don't understand, my friend. Even I, I don't recall when I last I saw one of those in the streets of Lagos. It is quite a sight, I promise.

TRADER. I tell you this na wonderful. Wonderful! A real bicycle inside Lagos. Which place you find am?

BARBER. He must be part of a circus. You know, those cycling acrobats. The Chinese were at the National Theatre last week, remember?

SANDA. Don't be daft. Does he look Chinese to you?

BARBER. They did magic too, you forget, very good magic. Disappearing and cutting themselves in two and so on. You think they can't turn themselves into Lagosians like you and me?

SANDA. Your mind and magic and all kinds of superstition! Where are you from, my friend?

CYCLIST. Ajegunle new settlement. And na tie I wan buy, that's all. But e be say dat one done become commotion. Who get this stall? E wan' sell tie abi 'e no dey sell?

TRADER (*rushing back behind his stall*). Ah, sorry, sorry. I sorry too much. No vex, my friend. Na de ting wey bring you come cause all the wonderment. Wetin you wan' buy? Take your time, I beg. Everyting na reduce price, specially for you. You go see, I go give you special reduction. (*His attention is still partially on the bicycle.*) You say you like the tie? How much you wan' pay? Ah, but this is wonderful. The last time I see bicycle for this Lagos na before the oil boom. Enh? You mean to say somebody still dey, wey no troway in bicycle inside lagoon? (*Rakes down a whole row of ties and hands them over.*) Make you look am proper. Choose the one wey fit gentleman like yourself. (*Sneaks back to the bicycle. Spins the pedals.*) No vex for me o, I just wan' . . . (*Rings the bell. Rings it again, delightedly.*) Na original oga. Na genuine pedal locomotion, the kind my great, great grandpa dem call iron horse when oyinbo missionary first ride one for Lagos last century. (*Looks wistfully at* CYCLIST.) You no mind, my friend? I just wan' see if I still fit balance.

CYCLIST (*gives up*). Do anything wey you want. Make you no wreck am, thas all. Because na borrow I borrow am.

NEWSVENDOR. Me too, my brother. Make I ride am small, I beg. Ha, if to say I be reporter, na scoop of the year 'e for be. If only man fit get photographer . . .

TRADER. Na waya for me today. (*Jumps on it and rides, barely able to balance.*) Common bicycle. Inside this very Lagos of oil-boom and daily millionaire. I tink say everyone done smash in bicycle or sell 'am for scrap iron.

CYCLIST (*trying on the ties*). You wait small. As our people say, na cudgel go teach crazeman sense; na hunger go reform labourer picken wey dream say in papa be millionaire. When the time come, na *omolanke*, common push-cart, na 'in even senior service go take go work. Na *omolanke* go full expressway inself.

TRADER (*chuckling as he wobbles from side to side*). True word, my brother. Before before, for early morning, na bicycle dey jam-pack Carter Bridge as people dey ride go begin work or return go home. Den, oil boom come. Government dash everybody salary increase, salary advance, salary arrears, motor car advance, motor car incentive, motorcycle advance, all kind vehicle allow-ance, any kind incentive.

CYCLIST. My friend, make we forget better time. No to that time de Minister of Finance inself boast for budget speech say, any increment wey no dey, we go increment am?

TRADER. Any allowance wey no dey, we go allow. (*Both burst into laughter.*)

BARBER (*from across*). No forget the other one — any incentive wey no dey for worker, we go incent! (*They roar with laughter.*)

CYCLIST. That man make the whole country tink say money just dey fall from sky.

TRADER. Why not? Wetin you wan' make common Minister make 'e say when in own Head of State done announce to the world dat — de problem we get for de nation no be money, but how to spend 'am. Abi na my memory dey lie?

CYCLIST (*reproachful annoyance*). Oh look, why you come now dey remember better time? E be like say man wey go sleep wit' empty belle come begin dream say 'e dey inside wedding feast. When 'e wake up, in suffer-suffer go double.

MINSTREL *begins the song: 'Alaaru T'o Nje Buredi'. Gets up after a verse or two, crosses the stage, still singing, his voice remaining audible in the neighbourhood for some time. The* NEWSVENDOR *takes over the bicycle for a while.*

TRADER. No mind me, I beg. Na this sight of your bicycle come begin remind me. Sai! Dat time, money dey walka street and buka, supermarket and corner shop like 'e no get tomorrow. Everybody just dey blow money as if Father Christmas siddon inside aeroplane, begin scatter manna from heaven . . . Even schoolchildren, 'e be like say den begin shit money.

SANDA. Do you never tire of all that good-old-days belly-aching? My friend, pay no attention to him. Tell him to migrate to the Republic of China where everybody rides bicycles. Then ask him if he himself didn't profiteer plenty from that Udoji oil bonanza.

TRADER. If not why not? I be trader, not so? I think say market be like prostitute — money for hand, open ya leg. I sell stereo . . . everything from video to electric toothbrush. Automatic become de national craze — because why? Because nobody wan use in own power again. But time done change. Austerity done catch monkey. Ah, na special tie dat one o, my customer.

CYCLIST. Hn-hn. How much?

TRADER. Ninety naira, my brother, and only because you be my first customer.

CYCLIST. Ninety nai . . . ! *Haba*, my friend, oil boom done finish now.

TRADER. But devaluation never stop. Remember say ninety naira today na only one dollar. So, make you tell me, you fit buy that kin' tie for America for one dollar? Na dat kind eye make you take look am. Look the label . . . look am, look am . . . Made in Florida, USA. You tink na one dollar 'e cost for USA?

CYCLIST. Even so . . .

TRADER. Na first-class tie. Proper bargain. If to say we government dey give American people visa as dem dey want am, na for dis very place Americans go come do them shopping. Den own goods cheap here pass the very place where den dey manufacture am.

CYCLIST. You sure say dis no to Made in Taiwan?

TRADER. Look label now. You tink say na me put label dere?

CYCLIST. But you sabbe say those Taiwanese can put Made in Paris, or London, even Made on the Moon for anything they make for dem backyard.

TRADER. Come on my friend. I can see say you no sabbe trade at all. Taiwanese no dey bring ties here, na only motor spare part. If na spare parts you talk, en-hen, I no go argue with you, but as for ties . . . Believe me, Made in Florida na Made in USA – make we no waste any more time. Eighty naira – dat na my very last price. You fit go try somewhere else if you no believe me.

> CYCLIST *takes one more look at the effect of the tie against his shirt, using one of the small mirrors also on sale. He nods. Begins to give it a fat knot around his neck. Then moves on to the sunglasses, trying them on, one after the other.* BOYKO *returns, squats down by* TRADER's *stall.*

CYCLIST. OK. You catch me cheap cheap because I get appointment with one sisi for later. Na in make I go borrow my brother's bicycle self because man no fit trust public transport again. You wait for bus all day and then, when one *molue* finally arrive enh, then Somalia war go begin. Shirt and trouser wey you done wash and iron to blow employer mind or scatter girlfriend in sense — (*Hisses.*) — e become like rag for second-hand *bosikona* market . . .

TRADER. Oh, na me you dey tell tory? Na drama for that bus-stop — (*Points.*) — every day, every morning going for work or evening time after work. Everyone for inself, man or woman, old or young — nobody care. One third body inside, one leg outside, remainder under luggage and other people's body. I done see big man — e fat plenty — dem squeeze am so hard, 'e shit inside in trousers.

CYCLIST. Ugh! I beg, make we talk better ting for early morning time. (*He appears to have made up his mind about the glasses, a psychedelic styled model.*) This one, how much?

TRADER. Take am one-twenty last. Honest, me I no dey like haggle for early morning.

CYCLIST. Hundred.

TRADER (*heatedly*). Look, you no hear me talk say . . . ?

CYCLIST. Hundred. Is all for this interview wey I get tomorrow, and na my brother borrow me de money. Na two thing I dey buy from you now. Haba, you no go give me special discount? Even for sake of good luck for my interview. If I get the job, you go know say na you help me.

TRADER (*makes as if outraged, then simmers down*). All right. Put five on top hundred — for sake of good luck. And after all, you give me my bicycle ride for first time in twenty years.

CYCLIST (*beams with satisfaction as he takes out the money*). Tomorrow na tomorrow. Since all dis time wey I dey write application — more than two hundred application for three years, no only now den give me chance for interview.

SANDA. If you don't get the job, ride your bicycle this way again. Sometimes, I get to know about vacancies you know — all the big people who come here, when they need driver or steward or this and that, they come and ask me to help them.

CYCLIST. God bless you, sir. God bless una both.

He jumps on his bicycle. Before he is even balanced however, the BARBER *clicks his clippers at him and points to the placard displaying his range of styles. The* CYCLIST *hesitates.*

BARBER. For that interview, I would recommend the Lumumba Slide-Back.

CYCLIST. I don't have the time.

BARBER. Your interview is not till tomorrow.

CYCLIST. Yes, but right now, I have an appointment with one . . .

BARBER. I heard. The more reason to knock her out with a brand-new haircut. Don't worry, I don't waste time. And it's fifty per cent discount since you are my first customer.

CYCLIST (*attracted by the model on the placard*). You really think . . . ?

BARBER. Definitely the Lumumba Slide-Back for you. It would clinch the job. And the girl.

CYCLIST *gets down and begins to prop up his bicycle.*

CYCLIST. All right. If you're sure it won't take long.

BARBER. I am known for my lightning clippers. Even the soldiers know me. I can shave the head of an entire batallion between one coup and the next. Sit down and relax your back. Cycling is not easy when you've abandoned it for some time. I made that mistake once, many years ago. I couldn't get up for days afterwards.

TRADER (*rushes to relieve him of the bicycle*). Make a warm am for you while Barber dey do your hair.

BARBER. Warm what up? It hasn't got an engine. (*Starts preparing his client for the haircut.*)

TRADER. You know sabbe anything about bicycle. If the pedal get too cold, the wheel no go turn properly. Even handle, 'e go become stiff. (*Rides off.*)

BARBER. All the street mongrels are going to snap at your heels,
you'll see. Area Boy on bicycle! The police will use it as an excuse
to lock you up, mark my words. Mr Sanda, you'd better get
ready to go and bail him.

SANDA. It's a free country.

BARBER. Is it? I'm sure this fellow got so far on his machine because
people were taken by surprise. And he is a stranger around here.
Otherwise, it could easily have caused a riot.

TRADER (*rides in, singing*).

I thought it was a case of an optical illusion
I don't recall a journey in a time-machine
Damn it! This is Lagos, not a rural seclusion
And nineteen ninety-four, far from colonial mission
No one worth his mettle goes pedalling a bike
Not even with petroleum on an astronomic hike
There's something fishy here, or else a miracle
To see a Lagos body on a bicycle
Chorus:
There's something fishy here, or else a miracle
    To see a Lagos body on a bicycle

Rides off again during the chorus.

BARBER.

The city's gone to pieces if this can really happen
They're trying to pull us back to some prehistoric age
Evil is on the loose; we've got our wits to sharpen
Supernatural forces are out to dent our image
Not even children ride a bike to school – it's indecent
It shames the home, embarrasses the status-conscious parent
Even a messenger would go on strike for an official vehicle
Than be caught dead delivering letters on a bicycle.
    Even a messenger *etc.*

MAMA PUT.

Once the palm-wine tapper's trade was a performance test
How he kept his balance was a sight for jaded eyes

With frothing gourds on either side, his cradle round his chest
The cycle was his camel, a most practical device
For navigating bush paths, then rolling into town
To quench the burning fire of thirst beneath the worker's
frown
But now the tapper thinks himself a butt of ridicule
To enter the big city on a bicycle.
        But now the tapper *etc.*

SANDA.

A motorcycle is the lowest Lagos can accomodate
And preferably nothing less than a five-hundred c.c.
State of the art, aerodynamic, not a detail out of date
With a fierce accelerating roar, or else you're just a cissy.
But the car is really it – Japan, US or Scandinavia
Before it's unveiled at source, it's cruising in Nigeria
Transfer of technology? We've passed that obstacle.
It's Benz, Rolls-Royce or Lexus – don't prescribe a bicycle!
        Transfer of technology *etc.*

BARBER.

Oh, a sight like this is a portent to be exorcised
The devil's at his dirty work, it's pure satanism
We've private gyms if flabby muscles must be exercised
And jogging's the in-thing for those free of rheumatism
So the roads are pot-holed, and public transportation
Dead? There's foreign exchange for private car importation.
This is boom-town, where heretics of the Mammon oracle
Are run out frontier-style, tied backwards to a bicycle.
        This is boom-town *etc.*

Re-enter the BIG MAN SHOPPER.

SANDA. Would you like me to get you some help for that, sir?
Where are all these small boys . . . ?
BIG MAN SHOPPER. No thank you. That's how the no-good vandals

get to know where one parks his car. I can manage by myself.
Much safer that way.

SANDA. Very sensible, sir, very sensible.

> *The* MINSTREL*'s song has changed to: 'Adelebo T'o Nwoko'.*
> *The song weaves in and out of hearing until the entry of*
> MISEYI.
> *The* NEWSVENDOR *accosts* BIG MAN SHOPPER *as he reaches*
> *street level, following him into the alleyway.*

NEWSVENDOR. *Business Times*, Sir? Or *City Gent*? I get latest
Expose and *Newswrite*. Comrade Ugo Bassa done explode for
Update! Sensational interview, sir, sensational! Look am sah,
make you just look de cover. Den say Minister of Commerce
may resign because of drug scandal. Only twenty-five naira!
Copies nearly finish. (*Switches to a low singsong voice, as he
quickly dips in a pouch and fishes out a different batch of
magazines and video casettes.*) Hot, hot, hot . . . Adult magazines sir . . . Hot, hot, hot . . . Sexy videos . . . Hot, hot, hot . . .
Secret Nights in the Bishop's Vestry . . . Hot, hot, hot . . .
Madonna Meets the Prince of Darkness – Sai! – Sizzling hot, hot,
hot – the very latest, not yet officially released . . . Sex Slaves in
Saudi Arabia – Hot, hot, hot – na we own pilgrims just smuggle
am commot for Jeddah. You not fit get copy anywhere else . . .

BIG MAN SHOPPER. Will you take your dirty merchandise elsewhere
before I set the police on you?

NEWSVENDOR. Sorry sir, make you no vex. But I also get the latest
releases from Hollywood. Even self, dey no release them yet for
anywhere. I get *Terminator IV* and *V* – half price. And all the
films wey den nominate for Oscar, everything reach here even
before the Oscar and Academy people begin see the film . . .

> *Disappears with him through the rear.*

BARBER. . . . with these my very eyes, I tell you, with these my very
eyes. I went to visit them one day, you know, the sister-in-law I
was telling you about. Their landlord was this chief, he lived

upstairs in his own apartment, all by himself. Apartment? More like a palace.

CYCLIST. Oh yes, I sabbe de kind. Na penthouse den dey call am. Proper luxury.

BARBER. Wait till you see this one. It had a covered roof garden into the bargain. And that roof garden had a small hut in a corner. So — here, take the mirror. How does that look from this side? Shall I take a little bit more off? It's my own original variation on the popular Lumumba cut, but you can tell me how you yourself want it.

CYCLIST. It's er . . . yes, it's fine on that side. Go on with your story.

BARBER. Ay yes. You won't believe it but . . . anyway, the husband said, let's go and pay a courtesy visit to the Chief . . .

CYCLIST. The landlord?

BARBER. Thank you, the landlord. Let's go and visit the landlord, he said, he always likes to meet my relations. So, up we went. Did I tell you it was evening, quite dark?

CYCLIST. You had finished dinner, you said.

BARBER. And finished watching the nine o'clock news. I was about to take my leave in fact but my in-law said, let's go and say Hallo to the Chief. So, up we went. But you know what? We couldn't find the Chief. The door was open, we went in, we called out several times, but there was no answer from the Chief. Shall I trim it all the way down to the neckline?

CYCLIST. Yes, yes, go on.

BARBER. I told you this wouldn't take long. It's all practice, you know. I can do almost any style even while sleeping.

CYCLIST. The landlord, where was he?

BARBER. I told you, there was no sign of him. So, my in-law said, well, I shall tell him we did call on him. And we decided to turn back. That was the moment we first heard the noise.

TRADER (*dissatisfied with listening from a distance, he has been moving steadily nearer*). Tell him what kin' noise. No forget that detail.

BARBER. A choking noise.

CYCLIST. Someone was trying to choke him?

BARBER. No, not that kind of choking. I can't really describe it. As
if someone was vomiting and cursing at the same time. That kind
of choking. We rushed there, thinking the Chief might be in pain
or was taken ill, might even be dying. That's what we were
thinking. So we rushed to the room but the door was locked.
What to do? It was my in-law who noticed that the window was
opened, so we rushed there – that was when we saw what we
saw.

CYCLIST. What? What?

BARBER. Keep still, my friend. I don't want anyone to accuse my
hands of being unsteady.

TRADER. You can't blame him. Didn't I nearly fall into the gutter
myself when you first told me what happened?

CYCLIST. Well, go on. What happened? What did you see?

BARBER. A human head! No, before that, we saw the landlord. He
was lying face down naked, prostrated on the floor, stark-naked
I tell you. Not a piece of cloth on him.

CYCLIST. Stark-naked? And the head. What about the head?

BARBER. Ah yes, that was on a white table – no, I lie – a table
covered in white cloth, like an altar, covered all the way to the
ground. And that human head was sitting on the table, yes,
sitting squarely on its neck, neatly sliced off – here!

CYCLIST (flinches as the BARBER draws a finger across his neck). Oh
my god! Was it freshly cut?

BARBER. Not a drop of blood. But . . .

TRADER. Now you'll hear it for yourself. My oga doesn't believe in
it but you'll hear it for yourself.

BARBER. A book was opened in front of the head . . .

CYCLIST. Hen? You mean that head dey read?

BARBER. The book was open, that's all I say. I never claim beyond
what my eyes clearly saw. The book – was – open. My in-law
says it must have been the Sixth and Seventh Book of Moses, you
know, the missing ones, well known for conjuring. But we didn't
enter. I didn't have the courage to enter and check for myself.

Who wants to run mad seeing what human eyes are not meant to see?

CYCLIST. So then what? The head, what about the head?

BARBER. The mouth of that head was wide open, just like the eyes. And it was vomiting – notes! Crisp naira notes. Fifty-naira denomination.

CYCLIST. Na so! Na so den dey do 'am. Na so my brother tell me before.

BARBER. In neat bundles. With the paper band around each neat package. As if it was coming straight from Central Bank.

TRADER. Na from dere. Na from dere 'e take magic conjurate am fly commot.

BARBER. Or the mint itself.

TRADER. Or the mint.

SANDA. Or your head, you foolish barber. You think I haven't been listening?

BARBER. You listen but you don't learn. Look, my friend, don't you mind that unbeliever. I saw it with my very eyes. The whole floor was covered, nearly up to the window level. That landlord was already buried in it – in fact, we just managed to see him.

SANDA. I thought you saw him stark naked from top to toe.

BARBER (*heatedly*). With all that money pouring down in bundles and falling off his body, anyone could see he was stark-naked.

SANDA. And to think you all say the Judge is mad. If your story is not rank lunacy on the loose . . .

> A FOREIGNER *moves onto the frontage from the direction of the parking lot, accompanied by the* PARKING ATTENDANT, *with whom he is arguing furiously.*

FOREIGNER. I already paid once. I'm damned if I'm going to pay a second time.

PARKING ATTENDANT. Then show me your receipt, sir. It's very simple what I'm asking – your receipt.

FOREIGNER. And I keep telling you I was not given one. I do not have a receipt to show you.

PARKING ATTENDANT. In that case, sir, you cannot leave your car in the parking lot. You must return and remove it at once.

FOREIGNER. What sort of a swindle is this? It's a bloody racket and you're all in on it. I'm damned if I let you play me for a sucker.

PARKING ATTENDANT. You can't leave your car in the car park without paying, those are the rules. I have the receipt book here – in your own interest, pay me, sir. If you don't, your car will be towed by the time you return.

SANDA. Is there some problem? Can I be of help, sir?

FOREIGNER (*suspiciously*). Who are you?

SANDA. Store Security personnel, sir. Maybe I can help.

FOREIGNER. I hope you can, my friend, because I'm getting damned near tired of being ripped off everywhere I go in this damned country. I pay to have my car garaged . . .

PARKING ATTENDANT. Which kin' pay? Show me your receipt.

SANDA. Let the man talk. You'll have your turn in a moment.

FOREIGNER. Thank you, sir. But look, let me first ask you, is that parking lot over there not an official one?

SANDA. It is, sir.

FOREIGNER. Good. Now, do you have more than one set of people collecting parking fees?

SANDA. A-ah, I see what the problem is. Yes, yes, I think I can see what happened. You must have fallen into the hands of the Insurance people.

FOREIGNER. Insurance? It's a hired car. Fully insured.

SANDA. No, I'm afraid you don't understand. Er, let me see, were you offered a choice at all?

FOREIGNER. A choice of what? What are you talking about?

SANDA. Ah, of course not, I forgot. You being a foreigner, you'd probably just have been charged the standard rate. How much did you pay?

FOREIGNER. Seven naira fifty. They asked for ten, but I beat it down. I'm only three months old in the country but I'm not totally green you know. I'm quite dry behind the ears – I haggled and beat them down to seven naira fifty kobo.

SANDA. Hm. You were given the discounted rate for foreigners. Normally it's ten naira for comprehensive insurance, five for third party.

FOREIGNER. Sorry, I don't think I get you. Are we talking about the same thing?

SANDA. Well, you do know what insurance is, I expect. The same principle operates with these . . . oh, it's embarrassing, I mean . . . you're right, it's extortion but, I'm afraid that's what goes on here. Everybody puts up with it, and the police condone it.

FOREIGNER. Could you explain please? I haven't quite caught on.

SANDA. I am sorry; I thought it would be quite clear by now. Comprehensive is always advisable because, then, the safety of your car is absolutely guaranteed. You see, sometimes, you have more than one gang operating. So, if you took Third Party, it exposes you to third party risks. Another gang could come and 'do' your car, and you see, the first gang wouldn't interfere. It's the code they have among themselves. Once a gang leaves a sign on your car which says 'Comprehensive', that's it. All other gangs keep off. Third Party buys you immunity only from the party to whom you paid.

FOREIGNER. I . . . I'm trying not to understand what you're telling me.

PARKING ATTENDANT (*disgustedly*). What is there left to understand? The man has taken the trouble to explain to you that you've paid your money to the wrong people. (*Laughs.*) And you don't even know if you have comprehensive or third party . . .

SANDA. Oh no, I'm sure it's comprehensive. They must have been teasing you with that haggling act – that was all pretence. The seven naira fifty is the foreigner's special rate – I hear them discussing these things all the time, though I pretend not to listen.

FOREIGNER. This is outrageous. How come they're allowed to get away with it?

PARKING ATTENDANT. The police station is over there – go and report if you like. But if I leave here without collecting your parking fee and giving you a receipt, I'm sending for a towing vehicle. Two naira fifty please, if you'll be so obliging.

FOREIGNER. You know what this bloody well does, don't you. It gives a very bad impression of you people to foreigners. You're driving people away from your country. Airport, the same grab. Customs ditto. Dash, kola, bread, wetin-you-carry, donation, gift, sweet-belle . . . I love that one – oga, make you pass me some sweet-belle now – very poetic – I thought I had mastered all the extortion rackets going on – two dozen at least – and now you tell me there's another one called Insurance.

TRADER. Wetin dis man dey talk about? You no get protection racket for your country? Abi no to your Europe dem place, and America dey come perfect protection and Mafia and wetin else? De Nigerians wey dem kill for America dis last year alone, e pass twelve, all because they refuse pay protection money. Some na simple taxi driver, one wey dem report for paper only last week, 'e just dey push ice-cream bicycle. Den shoot am to death because 'e refuse to pay . . .

SANDA. Pay no attention to my friend. He's a firebrand. He is planning to go into politics. Very nationalist. But he's right, you know . . .

FOREIGNER (*weakly*). It's the principle of the thing . . .

TRADER. Which kin' principle? You fall victim to common *wayo* people, and you begin cry like woman. For your country, if you make correct payment, you no go ask for receipt? Commot my friend!

SANDA (*at his smoothest*). Now, now, that's not the way to speak to our foreign guests. The man has had a bad experience, and it should make us feel ashamed. Our visitors should feel protected. I tell you what, sir, you leave the park attendant and me to sort this out . . .

FOREIGNER. No, no, it's all right. I'll pay.

SANDA. No, sir, I insist. I apologise for my countrymen. Please, go in and enjoy your shopping. I'll settle with the attendant and he will personally see that your car is given full protection.

FOREIGNER. I really hate to . . .

SANDA. It's perfectly all right, sir. I'm sure you would do the same for me if I happened to be in your country and the same thing happened to me. I'll get you a small boy to help you carry your purchases when you've finished.

FOREIGNER (*going*). This is really most decent of you, I must say . . . (*Enters shop.*)

BIG MAN SHOPPER *erupts from the rear end of the alleyway, his fingers firmly attached to* BOYKO's *ear as he drags him along.*

BIG MAN SHOPPER. You don't fool me one bit. You're part of the gang and I am taking you to the police. When they give you the proper treatment you'll confess who your real bosses are. An honest, hardworking citizen can't even go about his normal business, thanks to street garbage like you. You think I don't know you're the lookout? That's the way you all begin and you end up armed robbers . . .

SANDA *casts one brief look at them as they come round the corner, calmly puts his book down and awaits them.*

SANDA. What's the matter, sir? Can I help?

BIG MAN SHOPPER. Oh yes, Security, I've got one of them. They burglarised my car. They broke into the boot and stole my briefcase, tore out the radio . . .

SANDA. Impossible! In our parking lot?

BIG MAN SHOPPER. No, it was parked . . . I told you where it was parked. This young robber must have been watching me. He didn't fool me with his eye-service, dashing towards me and offering to carry my shopping. He was coming straight from where my Toyota was parked. I saw him.

BOYKO. That's what he keeps saying. Just because I see a big man and I go and help him carry his bags. He doesn't want to give me a tip, that's all.

BIG MAN SHOPPER. Shut up! You're one of them. Your gang vandalised my car and took my briefcase.

BOYKO. If you don't want to tip me, just say so. Don't use the problem of your car as an excuse. A big man like you, trying to cheat a small boy . . .

SANDA. Quiet! Don't mind him, sir. Honestly, I don't know what kind of children the country is producing these days. Someone old enough to be your father is talking and you keep putting your mouth in his. Don't mind him, sir.

BIG MAN SHOPPER. I'll teach him manners today – at the police station. Just take care of him for me while I get the police. In fact, I should have taken him to the Army barracks and let the soldiers deal with him.

SANDA. The Army, sir? Sure, they might give him some lashes and lock him in their guardroom but, they don't run things around here. They themselves find it convenient – sometimes – to pay protection money. After all, they understand what it's all about – that's why they keep seizing power. They're past masters of extortion – oh, pay me no attention, I get carried away sometimes. Now let's see. The problem is that place where you parked – it is actually outside our supermarket area. I can't very well lock him up in our detention room . . .

BIG MAN SHOPPER. Please, don't create unnecessary problems. Security is security. Lock him in your toilet if you like. If we don't keep him we'll never catch the rest of the gang.

SANDA. Well, sir, you know. Management is very careful about this sort of thing. If it had taken place within our jurisdiction, you understand, by now we would know what to do. But to involve Management, especially if it turns out that we've gone and locked up an innocent boy . . .

BIG MAN SHOPPER. Innocent! Are you telling me he's innocent when I tell you I saw him coming from the car. He was beside the car, then he started racing towards me, doing eye-service. There was a man at the same time . . .

SANDA (*turns fiercely on the boy*). Aha, what have you to say to that? Did you or did you not have an accomplice.

A crowd begins to gather.

BOYKO. Nobody, I never see anybody. Just the normal people coming and going.

BIG MAN SHOPPER. Let's get him to a police station. That's the only answer.

SANDA. Wait, sir. I have an idea. (*Turns to the* TRADER.) My friend, I beg, come.

TRADER. Me? Ah, who will look after my stall?

SANDA (*fakes impatience*). Come, my friend! Which kin' stall? No to me dey look after 'am when you go chop or follow woman? Come! As for all you people, scram! Go about your business. Who invited you come watch cinema show? Mr Trader . . .

TRADER. All right, all right. I dey come. E just be like man no fit trust anyone any more these days. Imagine small boy like this . . .

SANDA. Keep your eye on this rascal for me while I have a word with oga here. He's a regular customer, even though we haven't seen him for some time. But you know, once a neighbourhood member, always a member. We must do our bit for him. The matter is actually outside my jurisdiction but . . . Come, sir. I have an idea. (*He takes* BIG MAN SHOPPER *aside.*) Yes, sir, you are right, we could go to the police.

BIG MAN SHOPPER. Let's do that rightaway. We've lost too much time already.

SANDA. But then again, sir, you know what the police are like. (BIG MAN SHOPPER *becomes instantly crestfallen.*) Yes, sir, I am glad to see you do. He's only small fry, and his real bosses will simply come and bail him out, and that's the last you will see of him, and your missing valuables. The police will take their money and forget you.

BIG MAN SHOPPER (*sighs*). I have documents in that suitcase. Even my passport. The money doesn't matter so much, but I have important business papers . . .

SANDA. That's the way it usually goes. Now, I don't have to tell you, in this job, one must have one's ear to the ground, know all kinds of people.

BIG MAN SHOPPER (*sudden optimism*). You think you may be able to . . . pass the word? Sniff around and things like that?

SANDA. I can give it a try. The people in this neighbourhood, I understand their psychology. I know them, and they happen to show me some respect . . .

BIG MAN SHOPPER. Yes, yes, it's something I've noticed myself. For someone doing security job, you seem very well educated. One of my business partners said the same thing when she came shopping here last week.

SANDA. Thank you, sir. Well, if you're willing to have me try . . .

BIG MAN SHOPPER. We could do both. What about that? The police also have their sources you know . . .

SANDA (*shakes his head firmly*). The police know only what they want to know. They find out only what they want to find out . . . And they remember only what they find convenient to remember. We security people know them, that's why we operate separately. If you want me to handle this with our own people, we must do it our own way and that means – no police.

BIG MAN SHOPPER. All right, all right. I leave it to you. Do what you can. You will not complain of my gratitude.

SANDA. Ah yes, I was coming to that, sir. Things may move faster if we had a bit of . . . er . . . manure to spread along the ground. We'll plant the seed at once but, it would germinate much faster if . . . you understand?

BIG MAN SHOPPER. Of course, of course. (*He takes out a wallet and peels out several notes.*)

SANDA (*stopping him as he increases the amount*). No, no, this is more than enough. Good God, we're not the police. In fact . . . (*He returns a few notes.*) . . . yes, this will do very well – for preliminaries.

BIG MAN SHOPPER. No, take it. It's better you have more than enough. I don't want you being held back because of lack of . . .

SANDA. It's better this way. Just enough for expenses as we proceed. If we run against a brick wall and we have to abandon the search, then we wouldn't have wasted your money. Even my own contacts are not perfect; if I give them too much to begin with, they will think the bread is without limit. When it's over, I'll leave it entirely to you to — make them all right.

BIG MAN SHOPPER. You won't be disappointed, I promise you. Oh, let me give you my card. That way you can find me if you need further expenses . . .

SANDA. But, sir, everyone knows you here. Who doesn't know the offices of such a big man as yourself. Don't worry, sir, I know how to find you. (*Turns to the captive.*) Hey, you juvenile delinquent! Follow oga with his shopping back to his car and report here afterwards . . .

BIG MAN SHOPPER. Hen? You think that is wise? Suppose he runs away?

SANDA. Who? That one — run away? Where to? I know his mother's house — if you can call it that. More like a shack for storing firewood but — that's the way life is for many around Ita Balogun. Where is he going to run to?

Still dubious about the wisdom of such a decision, BIG MAN SHOPPER *lets* BOYKO *precede him, and watches him closely all the way through the alley.*

BIG MAN SHOPPER. I'll expect to hear soon from you?

SANDA. Trust me, oga. (*He watches them go, then shouts after him.*) And don't give him any tip. Just send him back to come and face his music. We'll get the truth out of him.

TRADER (*silent chuckle*). Oga Security, shay a fit go back to my station?

SANDA. Go 'way!

Trader scampers down, chuckling. SANDA *resumes his place, and reading. A few moments pass, then* AREA TWO-FOUR *enters, carrying a small shopping bag. He takes it to* SANDA, *opens it so he can see its contents.*

TWO-FOUR. Bread no plenty; na so-so paper dey inside. Passport, passbook, files and so on and so forth. (SANDA *flicks a most cursory glance over the contents, not even taking the bag.*) Make we throway the case inside lagoon?

SANDA (*thinks for a moment*). It's good quality leather.

TWO-FOUR. Na good quality evidence – should in case the police follow the case.

SANDA. No-o. This one na *so-o-say*. No *wahala*. In any case, we musn't waste the case. We shall proceed to – find it. He's promised a large reward. Put it inside safe.

TWO-FOUR. As you like, oga.

SANDA. Right. And, from now on, see that that area around the military pay office is patrolled. Some of these car-owners think they're very smart.

> *Exit* TWO-FOUR. SANDA *picks up a journal, makes some notes inside, and ticks off a column with a flourish. He resumes his reading. Enter* MISEYI, *accompanied by her housemaid, heading for the store entrance.* SANDA *does not look up. Instead, he focuses on the high heels, then slowly raises his gaze as their owner climbs the steps, so that his eyes become level with her head as she reaches the entrance, by which time her back is turned towards him. Suddenly, he freezes. At the same moment, the woman stops, then turns round. Their eyes meet.*

SANDA (*a slow smile breaks over his face*). I was sure there was no duplicating that walk, even going up the steps, or the carriage side-view. Then of course the head profile, especially where the neck bridges it with the shoulder . . .

MISEYI. And I thought there was also no mistaking the habit of the head when hunched over a book or anything in print. But then I grew doubtful, seeing that it was hidden under a ludicrous storefront security cap – Sanda! What on earth are you doing in that outfit?

SANDA. What else? Earning a living of course.

MISEYI. This is one of your jokes? Wait a minute – no. Today is not Students' Rag Day or we'd have seen them all over the place rattling their beggars' tins for one charity or the other. So, it has to be some other kind of stunt – let's see now, what's today?

SANDA. Stunt? Students' Rag Day? What's the matter with you? Don't tell me time has stood still for you these past four years. Four? Or is it five? Yes, five years since we last spoke to each other, and you look every mature day of that passage of time.

MISEYI. You are still your unflattering old self I see, but . . .

SANDA. No. I meant that most sincerely. Time has done some lovely toning on your face, on your skin. You have bloomed beyond my wildest hopes for you – I did say, mature, didn't I? Yes, you do look mature, in the most delectable way.

MISEYI. Don't expect any grateful response from me – if what I am looking at is for real.

SANDA. This? It's real enough.

MISEYI. No, it's not.

SANDA. Yes, it is.

MISEYI. No way. It cannot be.

SANDA. Oh yes it is.

MISEYI. Sanda, ple-e-ease, explain this joke. You saw me coming, didn't you? You came shopping just like me and then you saw me from a distance. You borrowed the cap and the jacket . . .

SANDA. And the trousers? I changed from whatever I was wearing into this outfit just to tease an old friend?

Pause. They confront each other, he light-hearted, she increasingly tight-lipped as she realises that this is for real.

MISEYI. I wish I could be struck blind, suddenly, no, even before now. Or that my feet had taken me any other way but this.

SANDA (*sadly*). I can see your mind has not kept pace with the rest of you – that's a great pity.

MISEYI (*heatedly*). And your mind has stood still, Sanda! Still, still, stagnant. You are still the way you *talked*! The eternal student at heart. People grow. They develop. You . . . you . . . Christ, it

makes one weep inside to look at you! Did you abandon your
degree programme, one year to graduation – for this? A *megadi*
uniform for what should have been . . .

SANDA. . . . an academic gown? (*Laughs.*) Now who is out of
touch with change? Me or you? Do you know how many
hundreds of PhDs are roaming the streets, jobless. Me, I have a
full-time job. And even compared to those with jobs – my take-
home pay is twice theirs any week. And when I make up my
mind and decide to earn good tips, I can take home six times
that pay.

MISEYI. And you're proud of that? You wear that *megadi* uniform,
hold the door open for people . . .

SANDA. It's a sliding door, haven't you noticed? Automatic. It
opens by itself.

MISEYI. Don't try to be funny. I'm looking at you helping big men
and their women with their shopping bags, holding open their
car doors while they roll in their fat bodies, and there you *are*
funny, ludicrous.

SANDA. Oh no, I'm not allowed to leave my post. A simple whistle
from me – (*Whistles. Three or four small boys dash in from all
corners.*) – See? I try to be fair, make sure they all get a fair share
of the porterage. Let's see now – you and you – (*He makes a
selection.*) – Just two will do. As you see, Madame has brought
her own maid, so your job is to follow her and make sure no one
tries to snatch her purse. And of course you carry anything she
or her maid wants you to carry, and you see her to the car – oh, I
take it your car is being – er – looked after? Oh, but of course
you would have come with a driv – beg pardon, ma'am –
chauffeur. Well, there it is in action. No sweat at all. And
naturally, as you're leaving, you'll sidle towards Oga Security,
slip a ten or twenty-naira in his hand. And you'll be interested to
know – or wouldn't you? – it isn't a naira note that some
madams slip into my hand, even married ones, but a card, a slip
of paper with a telephone number, and a whisper . . .

MISEYI (*turns to the maid, head flung high*). Let's go. You need a
psychiatrist, Sanda. You need a good session on the couch.

SANDA. That's just what those madams whisper when they come up to me. Couldn't you have been more original?

MISEYI. Oh you're lost. You've become decadent.

SANDA. And you are — beautiful my dear. And hopelessly anti-quated.

MISEYI (*stung, she spins round*). Well, instruct me then, Mr Clever! Introduce us into this . . . these — lower depths — into which you have chosen to sink. Mr Slum Artist, Street Sociologist. We shared classes, so I think we do speak the same language. I say you're nothing but a sham, a poseur, masquerading among a class to which you don't belong. You're a cheat even, you know that? Others need those tips more desperately than you, because they have no other way of earning a living. But you scrounge for the same scraps with them, don't you? So who are you to preach anything when all you do is waste the training you were given? Go on, I'm listening. You were trained at some-body's expense you know. So give us more of that old student gibberish. You think there is some nobility in this way of living, something that makes you superior to the rest of us?

They confront each other, one furious, the other smiling.

SANDA. Who said anything of nobility? Or superiority? I've merely chosen the way I want to live, what's wrong with that? I decided to return home, to where I was born. And if you knew the rest of it, oh-oh, if you only knew the rest of it, you wouldn't dream of accusing me of acting superior. (*Sighs, and turns away.*) Oh, Miseyi, go your way, as we both did five years ago. We've met by chance. I would have loved it if you had offered me a drink although, come to think of it, I should offer you hospitality, since this is my territory, my constituency. However, since things have to be this way . . . (*He doffs his cap.*) . . . enjoy your shopping, madam.

MISEYI. You failed, is that it? What you set out to do when you dropped out. You failed. You were whipped. You were to make your first million within six months — where is it?

SANDA. The waters were too murky. I couldn't swim in them.

MISEYI. Not even for the revolution? The millions were to go into the struggle, that was the whole purpose, wasn't it? Couldn't you stand a little dirt for Utopia?

SANDA (*smiling*). A little dirt. Oh, the little you know. Go, go. Go before you learn more than what your mind can take.

> MISEYI *flounces off, angry.* SANDA *returns to his bench and resumes his reading.* TRADER *watches him for some moments, fiddles around his wares in some embarrassment.*

TRADER. Hm-hm, oga, make you take time. Take time for that woman o. I no like de ting she talk at all. I no like am at all at all.

SANDA. What did she say that you don't like?

TRADER. No, not the actual ting wey she talk, na the way she talk 'am. When woman talk like that enh, make man get ready to dodge.

SANDA. We're old friends. That's the way we used to shout at each other in the university. (*Shakes his head, bewildered.*) It's amazing how we fell smoothly into the old routine, as if we parted only yesterday.

TRADER. Hn-hn. Hn-hn. As if to say I know all dat before. Still and yet, make all dat be as 'e be. Me, I just say, standby to dodge o!

> Enter a POLICEMAN, *dragging a bleeding, badly damaged man by his trouser waistband. A small crowd follows. A missile is hurled at the* VICTIM *just missing him and landing near* SANDA's *feet. One of the crowd carries a worn car tyre. The crowd is rather unusual in that each of the men has at least one hand over his crotch, while the women cover their breasts with their hands, or use one arm across both.*

SANDA. What the . . . !

> The POLICEMAN *sees possible assistance in a man in security uniform and runs towards him with his captive.*

POLICEMAN. Can you help, sir? Is there somewhere we can keep this man away from the crowd. They're determined to lynch him, although, why I should bother . . .

SANDA. What's the matter?

POLICEMAN. Missing genitals.

SANDA (*groans*). Oh, not again!

> Shouts of 'Hand him over!' 'Let's roast him here before he roasts in hell.' 'They don't deserve police protection.' 'Tyre done ready, kerosene dey plenty.'

SANDA. Stand by, Area Two-One. Send Boyko for some of ours. (*To the* POLICEMAN.) Which of them claims to be the victim?

VICTIM (*steps forward*). It's me, brother. He touched me, and it was gone.

SANDA. You are sure.

VICTIM. Am I sure? Don't I know what I left home with? And now there's absolutely nothing there. Nothing. He touched me and I felt it disappear. (*Starts crying.*)

POLICEMAN. Stop crying like a child. Stand up and behave like a man.

VICTIM. Behave like a man? Like a man? But that's the core of my problem. How do you expect me to behave like a man without it.

SANDA. And it happened after he touched you. You're sure it was this man?

VICTIM. I have witnesses. (*Approaches one of the crowd.*) That gentleman . . .

WITNESS. Hey, keep your distance.

VICTIM. What? Are you denying you . . . ?

WITNESS. I'm not denying anything. I saw it with my own eyes and I am ready to testify in court. But you don't have to touch me, do you? Just point at me from a distance.

VICTIM. Hey, what's this? (*Turns to the next person.*) What's the matter with him?

WOMAN. You heard him. Keep your distance. We all feel sorry for you, and we want to see justice done. But don't spread it around.

VICTIM. Don't spread . . . It is not an infectious disease! I've lost my manhood, that's all. What is infectious about that?

WITNESS. You never know. That's how AIDS began you know. Before you knew it, it was spreading like wildfire.

VICTIM. AIDS! The whole world has gone mad. I tell you I'm just a victim of vanishing organs. My genitals have disappeared — what has that to do with AIDS?

WOMAN (*stubbornly*). That's how AIDS began. First we didn't even have it here, in Africa. Then they said it started here. With monkeys.

WITNESS. Yeah. Green monkeys.

VICTIM. Oh my manhood! My manhood!

BARBER. It's probably making millions for his syndicate somewhere in Lagos. They work in syndicates you know. It's funny, we were just talking about it.

SANDA. Don't add fuel to this dirty fire, Mr Barber.

BARBER. You never believed me, but there it is, before your very eyes.

VICTIM. My manhood!

POLICEMAN. Look, my friend, just restore his genitals and I promise you full protection.

SANDA. Cut it out, officer! Is that the kind of example expected of you?

WITNESS. The policeman is right. We can't let even the victim loose. Suppose he touches someone else, how do we know that person's own won't also disappear?

BARBER. They're right, you know. It's a good thing you kept them both. Instead of the hard work of going round touching likely victims, you touch only one. It saves the labour. That one doesn't know he's become a carrier, so he touches another, and so on. Soon you have a hundred people running loose with no genitals, causing others to lose theirs. And meanwhile somebody sits in his mansion, spiriting millions from the Central Bank.

SANDA. You either shut up, Barber, or I terminate your occupation rights. I think you've all gone mad.

WOMAN. Have we? What of the government role in all this? Have you thought of that?

SANDA. The government. What about the government?

WOMAN. Suppose they're behind it all. It's a military government and they've been preaching population control. It's just the kind of wicked tactics they would think of.

WITNESS. They want to rule forever, don't they? What better way to do that than to emasculate all of us?

ANOTHER WITNESS. Hey! You've said something, believe me, you have said something! Since this thing started, have you seen it affect any of them? I bet they give them an injection against it before they leave their barracks. My God!

WITNESS. Don't forget the police. Look at that one. He's not afraid to touch that devil. I bet he's also innoculated. It's a plot against the civilian population.

SANDA. There's one way to stop all this nonsense. (*Approaches* VICTIM.) Watch me shake hands with him. I'll even embrace him.

VICTIM (*retreating*). Don't come near me.

SANDA. What?

VICTIM. Don't come near me. How do I know you're not one of them? After all, you're in uniform.

SANDA. Oh my God, it's an asylum!

VICTIM. I don't want you to prove anything with me.

SANDA. Well, there's nothing there, you said, so what do you stand to lose?

VICTIM. What of the other organs? I don't want them to disappear. I don't trust anyone. Just make him undo his handiwork or else leave me alone.

SANDA. All right. That's it. Take down your trousers.

VICTIM. You said what?

SANDA. I said, Take – down – your – trousers!

VICTIM. You want me to . . . before all these people?

SANDA. Why not? There is nothing there, so there is nothing to be coy about.

POLICEMAN. That's a good idea. Take them off!

WOMAN. Why didn't we think of that? Let's prove it to these unbelievers once for all. Take off your trousers and shut up their mouths.

VICTIM. You're all making fun of me. You want to expose my nakedness to all these people? (*Waves his arm around the audience.*)

WITNESS. You'll have to do it in court anyway.

VICTIM. That brother is right. This is a lunatic asylum. You actually want me to strip in public?

WITNESS. We can go inside if you like. Let's find a secluded place inside the plaza.

SANDA. Enough! That's more than enough. No one is coming in here except the policeman and the genital brothers. Everybody else, back! Go home. That's quite enough idiocy for one morning.

ACCUSED. God knows I didn't do anything.

POLICEMAN. You didn't touch him?

ACCUSED. At a crowded bus-stop? Everybody touches everybody. Everyone is squeezing everyone else to death.

SANDA (*to* TRADER). Get one of the girls. Pick one with . . . er . . . you know. I'm going to lock this one in a room with her and we'll see if the right stimulus doesn't give us results.

TRADER. I think I sabbe the very one wey fit defeat any kind *juju* attack. If she get customer. I go wait make in finish.

SANDA. And tell the boys to clear this rabble. I don't want to see any of them around when I get back. As for you, Barber, you can go with them if you want to continue spreading around that rubbish.

BARBER. Did you hear me say anything?

SANDA. You've said more than enough. It's people like you who turn the most docile crowd into mindless beasts. (*Goes in with the trio.*)

TRADER. Move, you lot. You done hear, oga. Or you want make I set the boys on you? This no be your territory, you know. Vamoose!

The crowd melts away, grumbling.

BARBER. The world is filled with too many unbelievers.

TRADER. Make we no quarrel o. You know say meself I believe say something dey for dis business, but oga done say make we no talk am again. So, no talk am again.

BARBER. All right, all right. (*Whispers to the* CYCLIST.) You see? As if we knew this was going to happen when I began telling you about that severed head . . .

MAMA PUT (*scoops up some steaming bean pottage with a ladle and rounds on* BARBER, *pulling his trousers outwards by the waistband with the other hand.*) You want me to scald your own manhood with this hot stuff?

BARBER (*clutches his crotch*). I beg, I beg, I done shut up.

MINSTREL *crosses the stage, singing: 'Iy a Meji Eyi J'okobo O'.*

The FOREIGNER *emerges from the store, followed at a short distance by* SANDA. SANDA *is reading a newspaper as he walks back.* FOREIGNER *sees him, stops and slips a twenty-naira note in his hand.*

FOREIGNER. Just a small token of appreciation. Oh – and let me leave you my card. In case you ever decide you want to change jobs – ours is a new firm – you strike me as the kind of person we could use.

SANDA. That is kind of you, sir.

FOREIGNER. Not at all. Be seeing you.

As he reaches the bottom of the steps, a rickety bus is heard roaring to a stop. Instantly, a huge commotion begins as a long-suffering crowd struggles to climb on board. The FOREIGNER *watches, reacting to the scene. Then he unslings his camera and begins to take pictures. The chaotic scene is partially reflected in the sliding doors. Shouts, curses, groans, with the* CONDUCTOR's *voice raised above the din to which he adds by banging on the side of the bus.*

SANDA (*eyes glued to the paper*). So they did it after all. They wiped Maroko settlement off the surface of the earth.

MAMA PUT. Maroko? What now? Can't they ever leave those people alone?

SANDA. They will after this. There is no more Maroko. It's in this evening paper.

TRADER. Oga, you mean they chase the people commot?

SANDA. According to this, they weren't just chased out, Trader. The entire place was flattened. Here. There are even photos. (TRADER *takes the paper.* MAMA PUT *goes across to read over his shoulder.*) Now where do a million people go to find a home?

BARBER. But they took the government to court. They won. The court ordered government to leave them alone.

MAMA PUT (*tight-lipped, walks back to her station*). It's a military government, isn't it? That means they can defy even God's commandments.

CONDUCTOR. Marine Road Apapa. Marine Road last stop. Next stop Iganmu. Four place on board. I say only four place on board . . . Iganmu next stop . . . We no fit take more than four . . . Hey! You people dey craze? I say only four place dey inside . . . Hey, mind that woman. Mind that woman! No, no load at all. We no fit take load inside. Driver, make we move. Go next stop. Move, I beg, move on! Anybody wey no commot for step, na your palava o. (*Bangs on the bus.*) Move on driver, go, go! No more space!

Re-enter MISEYI. *She hesitates, then takes a decision and goes to* SANDA, *who is still distracted by the commotion from across the road.*

MISEYI. I'm sorry. That was all very childish. I think I was shocked, that's all. We didn't have to quarrel.

SANDA (*his attention is still fixed in the direction of the bus-stop*).
Old habits die hard.

MISEYI. I'm getting married.

SANDA (*that does get his attention*). What?

MISEYI. Getting married. That's why I came here. To check the arrangements in the plaza.

SANDA. Oh. You mean it's you? The booking. I hadn't linked . . .

MISEYI. For tonight? Yes. Everything is tonight – the asking ceremony, the formal engagement and the traditional wedding. I didn't want an elaborate affair.

SANDA. You didn't want an elaborate . . . The street is being closed from seven. And you say that is not an elaborate affair?

MISEYI. If you knew what both parties wanted! My parents. And my fiancé himself. He has a rather ostentatious side to him. Exhibitionist even, but he manages to be sweet with it.

SANDA. Oh, it's not my business. I just never thought . . . there are three music bands in attendance, right? Good God!

MISEYI. What's the matter?

SANDA. Talking of bands suddenly reminded me – do you still play the xylophone?

MISEYI (*laughing*). Hardly ever. Not since I left college. And you? How is the bass guitar?

SANDA. Off and on, off and on. I still jam with the odd group after work.

MISEYI. You still write songs? *That* kind?

SANDA. What kind do we live? (*Waves his arms around.*) What other kind is there?

The brief silence is awkward for both.

MISEYI (*wistfully*). We did have some good times.

SANDA. Life beckons, we respond. You cross another bridge tonight.

MISEYI. Yes, tonight. Everything will be over tonight, thank goodness. I put my foot down over that. Those wedding events that drag on for ever . . .

SANDA. Not even the usual follow-up church wedding?

MISEYI. Me? A white wedding? Come on, we've talked about such things often enough. You know my views.

SANDA. People change.

MISEYI. But not you. Not the immovable Sanda.

SANDA. Oh, don't be so sure. Well, who is the lucky man?

MISEYI. Why? Don't you know?

SANDA. For me, it was just another big do. I didn't bother to check. Most people just book the space anyway. My job is to look after peace and order. People make their own arrangements. So who is he?

MISEYI. You won't approve of him – he's rich. And likes to show it. But he works hard for his money. Here. (*Thrusts an envelope at him.*) That's your invitation, if you feel like coming to lend moral support. I mean it, you'll be more than welcome – for old times' sake.

SANDA. Thanks. But I'll be here anyway. I'm on duty. I work overtime any time there's a function in the plaza. I enjoy them. The tips are overwhelming.

> *Increased commotion as the bus takes off.* SANDA *is just easing the card out of the envelope when a* PASSENGER's *scream rips through the scene. Dropping the card,* SANDA *races out in the direction of the scream.*

PASSENGER'S VOICE. Dey done kill me. Dey done kill me. Dey done take the only thing I get for this world. Wicked people, dey done take my life. I get nothing left, nothing in the world. No, lef' me, lef' me make I die. Dey done kill me, dey done finish my life. (*Violent scream.*) No touch am! Take your hand commot, I say make nobody touch am! I go curse anybody wey touch am. In hand go wither for in body, in hand no go do better thing for the world. I say make you commot your hand . . . !

> *The sound ceases abruptly.* MISEYI *descends a step or two, so that she is standing by the* FOREIGNER *as, a few moments later,* SANDA *re-enters, carrying the limp body of a* PASSENGER *in his*

arms. He climbs the steps and enters the store, TRADER
following with a small bundle wrapped in a shawl. MAMA PUT
moves rapidly towards him.

MISEYI. Sanda! (*He does not respond.*)

FOREIGNER. What happened?

TRADER (*lifts the bundle towards him, without stopping*). This
used to be dat woman pikin. They done trample am to death.

MAMA PUT *makes to take the bundle from him but* MISEYI *gets
to it first. They follow* SANDA *into the store.*

MISEYI (*to Maid*). No, you get the driver. Meet me at the back of
the plaza.

TRADER *sits on the step, holding his head. Enter* MINSTREL.

MINSTREL. Wey Oga Security? I hear all dat noise. Wetin happen?

TRADER. Oga dey inside.

MINSTREL. Me, I tire small. (*Sits on the step and unslings his
kanango.*)

TRADER. Now wetin dat woman go tell in husband when she reach
home?

MINSTREL (*disturbed. Appears to be listening hard*). What's the
matter? Everything seems suddenly quiet. Did something bad
happen? What was the woman screaming about? I was too far
off to make it all out but . . . there was so much pain in the air.

BARBER. Nothing much happened, my friend, nothing unusual. Go
on, sing that old favourite you sang for us the day Mama Put's
daughter took her communion. Do you remember the party we
had here? Three full pots of beans and plantain Mama Put
cooked for the neighbourhood, with solid chunks of fried pork.
And was she raging when Sanda tried to pay for everything?

TRADER (*cheering up a little*). Yeah. Dat Mama Put, she sure get
temper.

MINSTREL *begins to sing: 'Omo L'aso'. Towards the end of the
song,* SANDA *returns and resumes his seat on the stool.* MAMA

PUT *follows moments after. He picks up a magazine and tries to concentrate on it. Puts it down after some moments. Enter the* GIRL, *back from school.*

MAMA PUT. You're back early. Weren't you given any after-school assignment?

GIRL. But Mama, you said I was to return right away.

MAMA PUT (*for a moment, she is puzzled*). Oh yes. That dream of mine, I suppose. Dreams make me nervous, that's true. But the grief belonged to someone else. I was smothered by its approach, but the grief was elsewhere. Are you hungry?

The GIRL *nods. She serves her food from the pot.* SANDA *watches both.*

It's a hard school we attend here, girl, so be sure to enjoy yours. Work hard at your books, but also enjoy what fun is still left in your schools. Here, don't use your hand. Use the fork and knife like you do at school. Oh, I know. I snatch the knife from you sometimes and prefer to eat from a clay bowl, but that is only when I remember . . . I even prefer clay pots for cooking. But it's not that I refuse to touch metal. After all, I prepare the meat with this heirloom. I use it to cut up vegetables. (*She grips the bayonet hard.*) And I keep it handy. It's a hard school we go to, a hard school in a heartless city, and today one child didn't even get to enjoy her childhood.

SANDA. Where is Boyko?

BOYKO. I dey here, oga.

SANDA (*after what appears to be a thoughtful inspection*). Hm. Look at him after a mere three years. When he came, he was no bigger than the bundle Miseyi has just managed to restore to that despairing woman. But he was actually seven years old, only, there was nothing on him you could call flesh. Wasn't it you who first spotted him, Trader, rooting in this very gutter for something to eat. You remember what he looked like?

TRADER. Na Barber first see am. But like you said, oga, in bone no get flesh.

SANDA. I vomited, just to watch him pick that thing out of that gutter. I had no idea he would actually put it in his mouth. But he did. Wiped it against his thigh, then stuck it in his mouth, and chewed away. By the time Barber screamed out loud it was too late to stop him. I threw up.

BARBER. You did, I remember.

SANDA. You do, do you? You see, I wonder sometimes, maybe I should have turned my back on that sight. We save some, yes, but others kill them anyway. They kill them before, or they kill them afterwards. It doesn't seem to make much difference, because we all join hands to kill them anyway. In other places, they do it differently of course. Bogota. Or Rio de Janeiro, where our businessmen make an annual date with the carnival, Boyko would be dead in one of those places. They have death squads over there for people like him. For picking up food from the gutter, he'd be marked down for death. Class sanitation, right from infancy. (*He looks increasingly troubled.*) Mama Put is right. We live in a cruel land. A cruel time in a cruel land. To breathe at all is to breed cruelty, to scatter the spores of hardcore, unsullied cruelty. Hardcore as in pornography. Innocence means death.

BOYKO. You get assignment for me, oga?

SANDA. What? Oh no, sorry. Oh yes, I want you to give more time to that flute. If you practise less than four hours a day, I'll crack your head. Now go and give Ma Put a hand. Everyone must pack up earlier than usual. (BOYKO *crosses over to* MAMA PUT's *stall*.) The police and soldiers will be here soon to seal up the streets. And the prison detail to clean up. The affluent are about to take over the neighbourhood, then they'll restore it to us again.

> Enter JUDGE, *but startlingly transformed. His long hair has been permed and curled so it actually looks like a judicial wig. He also has on the semblance of a purple robe, certainly much the worse for wear. The* BARBER *looks the most shocked and displeased, and is first to recover his voice.*

BARBER. Mama Put . . . Oga Security . . . do you people see what I'm looking at? Do you see how Judge has slighted me?

TRADER. You? Wetin be your own for this *alawada* man?

BARBER. Haven't you got eyes in your head? Where did he get that hair treatment? Where? Did you see him get up from my chair? Has he not bypassed my own salon and taken his custom to some total stranger? Security, is this how we are supposed to help one another here? Where did you go anyway? Look at what they did to your head? And you sat down and let some amateur . . .

JUDGE. Where are your curlers?

BARBER. What?

JUDGE. Curlers. Rollers. Hot comb. Relaxers etcetera. The trouble with the world is that everyone refuses to accept their limitations. You think a high court judge goes to some wayside barber's shack to perfect the presence that may pass sentence of life and death? In derelict spaces and makeshift hovels?

BARBER. My salon! Do you all hear him? He's calling my salon a hovel.

JUDGE. Don't be so parochial, man! The majesty of the law discriminates, but is impartial. It recognises neither friend nor foe, stranger or relations. Majesty! Ma — jes — ty. (*Beatific smile.*) Can you conceive it? The ma-jes-ty of the law. I told Trader I was set on the journey to souls' kingdom — he should have passed the word round, then you would have been forewarned. Still, I shall not distance myself altogether, have no fears on that score. And I shall prove it to you. You see — (*Wagging his finger.*) — I thought of you all the time. Sitting under the dryer, my scalp massaged by trained fingers, I thought of you.

> Goes to the BARBER's chair and faces the CYCLIST. He scampers up and JUDGE takes his place. CYCLIST moves into MAMA PUT's corner. From the recesses of his robe, JUDGE produces a small plastic pouch.

Here. Sprinkle this on. I saved the final treatment for you.

BARBER (*suspiciously*). What is it?

JUDGE. You can see there is something missing up there, can't you? (*Pointing at his head.*)

BARBER. Oh yeah, we all know that.

JUDGE. Naturally, a professional like you would spot it right away. Yes, the judicial wig must undergo some ageing process. Use that!

> BARBER *unties the pouch, sniffs, then takes some of the powdery content between his fingers.*

BARBER. This feels like ashes.

JUDGE. The finest and the best. (*Points.*) Scooped it up from Mama Put's ash mound before I set off. Spent all morning sifting out the cinders and grosser particles. What you have there is fire in absolute purity, purged of passion, divorced of its past. It is the pure element that is fire, but without the heat, its destructive career subsumed in serenity. Sprinkle it on. Spread it evenly from strand to strand.

BARBER. Look, I'll use the aftershave talcum powder. It's free of charge, in case it's the money you are worried about. (*About to throw it away.*)

JUDGE. Don't! Don't you dare!

BARBER. How can I use this stuff? It's against all my professional instinct. I am still hurt, I can't deny that. But, anyway you look at it, this is a work of art. Maybe I would need time to master the technique to produce something like this but, no, I can't do it. It's desecration.

JUDGE. You're a fool. No, you're blind. Blinder than that singing beggar over there. Give it back. (*Snatches it from him.*) Security.

SANDA. Yes, Judge.

JUDGE. May I ask the favour of the loan of your young jack-of-all-trades for a short spell.

SANDA. Boyko, attend to the Judge. But you can't keep him too long. He's helping with the packing up.

JUDGE. I thank you. Here, boy.

BARBER. Not in my chair!

TRADER. Come on, make you humour the man now.

BARBER. I have my professional pride. I can't allow him to desecrate my salon.

MAMA PUT. You know he won't give us any peace of mind; let him have his fun. If a customer comes, I promise I'll make him give way.

SANDA. Do us all a favour, Barber.

BARBER (*grudgingly*). All right, all right. Let's get it done with and get him off my chair.

JUDGE. You will be proud to remember this moment, my friend. You have all, in many ways, contributed to this last act of my transfiguration. Here, boy. Sprinkle it gently, then use this comb to distribute the fire dust evenly along the strands of majesty. (*Produces a tiny comb from his pocket and hands it over. Leans his head back on the head rest, closes his eyes and sighs with content.*)

TRADER. The only thing wey I no understand be, how 'e get money for pay dat kind hairdresser. Only proper saloon fit do that kind hairstyle.

SANDA. Does anything about the Judge still surprise you?

TRADER. Oga, you think say he be actually judge before. He siddon court dey pass judgement?

SANDA. No-o. I thought you all knew all about him.

TRADER. No. Na so 'e dey here like everybody else. Just as you come meet all of we. Nobody dey ask questions but, this time, I jus' wan' know.

SANDA. He was never a judge. But he was a lawyer. And he got debarred.

TRADER. De-wetin?

SANDA. Debarred. Struck off the roll of lawyers. Not allowed to practise.

TRADER. Ah! Wetin 'e do?

SANDA. I've forgotten. It was a long time ago. I was just a schoolboy at the time.

TRADER (*chuckling*). You self, oga? Is so difficult to see you inside school uniform, dey carry books go school, den come home do homework like Mama Put in daughter.

SANDA. Why? Why is that so difficult to believe?

TRADER. E be like say na for dat stool you dey since de day den born you, just siddon dere dey read book and magazine. And even yet, all the time person tink you dey read, your eyes dey look everything going on around here.

SANDA (*thoughtfully*). Me too. There are days when I feel I have never been anywhere else but here. But then, I was born and raised here. I only turned expatriate through boarding-school, then college . . .

TRADER. The neighbourhood owe you plenty. Until you come here begin organise everybody, we just dey run about like chicken wey no get head.

SANDA (*his eyes on* BOYKO). I wonder sometimes, Trader. I wonder sometimes if I'm in the right place or doing the right thing.

> TRADER *looks worried, gives him a searching look. Turns away slowly and begins to fiddle with his wares.*
>
> *Approaching, the prison detail. The* WARDER's *voice is heard keeping the group in order: 'Left – Right – Left – Right – Left – Right – Single File – Left – No lagging. No hanging back! You there – Left – Right . . . ' Soon, they are reflected in the doors.*

SANDA. Here they come. Better get the welfare package ready for them to take back.

TRADER. Anytin special you want make I put?

SANDA. Just make sure there's plenty of their local currency.

TRADER (*chuckles*). Independent Republic of Kirikiri Maximum: hard currency, Sirocco High Filter; local, Elephant tusk. Black market – raw tobacco leaf.

WARDER'S VOICE. Left – Right – Left – Right –

PRISONERS (*singsong*).

Lefu – Rete – Lefu. Lefu – Rete – Lefu.

Ati warder, at'elewon

Ikan na ni wa
Ati soja, at'olopa
Ole paraku
Eni a ri mu la l'edi mo
Ole mbe l'ode
Jaguda nwo khaki
Olosa General
Major adana
A gba'ni lo ju gba'ya al'aya
A lo ni l'owo, gba'le on'ile
Riba l'otun, egunje l'osi
Aiye yin mbe ni bi o
Aiye yin mbe l'ewon
Lefu – Rete – Lefu. Lefu – Rete – Lefu.

WARDER. Left – Right – Left – Right – Mind your tongues. You're in public. Careless talk or careless singing, it's a crime of treason. Sorry, sedition – well, one of them anyway, the SSS will find something to hang on you. Left – Right – Don't look for trouble. Left – Right – Don't get me in trouble. Left – Right. I don't want companionship in misery – certainly not yours! And don't forget your remission. Don't sing yourselves out of possible remission. This is a no-nonsense government, don't fool around with military feeling – if they have any.

PRISONERS:

Lefu – Rete – Lefu. Lefu – Rete – Lefu
Eru o b'odo. Lefu – Rete. Mo ti w'ewon
Lefu – Rete. Moti g'oke, mo ti so
Faka-fiki faka fi
Aginju o joju, papa o ya'nu
Se b'afoda nti gada?
Afoda l'ejo elewon
Mo ti w'ole na, mo ti gba number
Sapagiri nbe n'ikun
A t'odo Oya, a t'ibu osa
Afoda nt'afefe lele

Railway nsere ni, ko s'ohun t'oju o riri
Wole-wole nparo ni
Atan l'atan nje.
Tanwiji mbe n'isale amu
O ba a se ju t'esi
Lefu – Rete – Lefu. Lefu – Rete – Lefu.
Soja oselu, jaguda paali
Baba bilisi. Oo gbe'bon mo
Oo ja'gun la, kontirakiti lo nle kiri.

WARDER. Stand at ease! Stand easy! Trouble makers I don't want.
Trouble makers I don't like. Watch your tongues. Even the
potholes have ears. Don't provoke the khaki boys. Warm up and
get going. Songido, get them started!

PRISONERS (gyrating into a single file, rap-style chant).
So we'll do the army conga
To make the work go faster
Prison is the land of free speech
Dungeon inmates are out of reach
Except for experts sworn to teach
And do-good preachers come to preach
Co-co-co-conga Co-co-co-conga

So knack us the rulers' conga rap
Give us the good old military crap
Don't look too far for the credibility gap
It's the hole beneath the General's cap.
Songido, lead off man, we're waiting
Sing us that one with an X-rating.
Co-co-co-conga Co-co-co-conga.

PRISONER I (looks in the direction of SANDA). Make I ask permission from Oga Security first. Na in get de copyright after all.
(SANDA waves them to go ahead.) OK, OK, make you give man
some solid funky conga beat.

They set up a beat with cutlasses, iron files and dustbin
covers.

My friends, come gather round
And dig the latest sound
It's a universal drumbeat
In tune with every heartbeat
    My friends, come gather round
    And dig the latest sound

Invented by a soldier
In a land where flows the Niger
It's the ideology conga
That makes a nation stronger
    Invented by a soldier
    In a land that flows the Niger.

A little to the Left – shake!
A little to the Right – shake!
Red Flag or Imperial Purple
All you need is a waist that's supple
    A little to the Left – shake!
    A little to the Right – shake!

Learn from the Soviet Union
Don't stick to doomed opinion
You must swim with the tide
And take your people for the ride
    A little to the Left – Right
    A little to the Right – Left

The conga law of equity
Yields economic parity
You squeeze the left and waste
Its resources on the right caste
    A little to the Left *etc*.

It's revolutionary
For minds that are visionary
Who needs the aid of opium

Until the next millenium?
 A little to the Left *etc*.

The conga shuns restraint
No room for the plaster saint
Be you National Exchequer,
Or a budding nation wrecker
 A little to the Left *etc*.

The Naira's doing Right
It's floating out of sight
There's virtue in thrift
No purchasing power Left
 A little to the Left – Right.

Drugs have fled the clinic
Hospitals ain't no picnic
But fortunes are made
In the mortuary trade
 A little to the Left *etc*.

The boat has left its course – No!
The boat is right on course – No!
It's turning round in a circle
Like a demonstration vehicle
 A little to the Left *etc*.

The ship of state is healing
Dismiss that sinking feeling
How dare you say disaster?
It's a national fiesta!
 A little to the Left *etc*.

It's truly orgiastic
A pendulum to mimic
The ruling minds are static
But the balls are swinging frantic
 A little to the Left *etc*.

Drifting, drifting, drifting.
How sweet is simply drifting
I'll see you around
When the ship goes down
    Drifting, drifting, drifting.

How sweet is simply drifting
Drifting, drifting, drifting . . .

PRISONER 2. At least, prison get stability. I sorry too much for all these people wey still dey outside. How den dey manage survive, enh? How anybody dey manage?

WARDER. You've had your fun, right? I heard nothing. I was taking a pee while you were warming up to begin work. The regulations permit a five-minute warming-up session and a five-minute cool-down session per hour. You've used up both. Now get to work. Clean up this pigsty! And don't forget I've got my eyes peeled for any malingerers. Trusty!

PRISONER 1. Oga warder.

WARDER. Take over. (*Goes off some distance and sits down, lights a cigarette.*)

PRISONER 1. Twenty minutes per each, that na the deal wey I make with warder. I take the first shift. All of una, begin work. Clean up the rubbish.

They go off in different directions, picking up debris in the most desultory fashion. PRISONER 1 *moves towards* SANDA, *a broad, expectant beam on his face.*

Oga mi!

SANDA *nods towards* TRADER. PRISONER 1 *moves towards him.*

PRISONER 1. Shey we do justice small to that your conga?

SANDA. Not bad. Not bad.

PRISONER 1. You get new one for us?

SANDA. It's in the welfare package. You'll find the cassette inside the loaf of bread.

PRISONER 1. Trust oga! But make you no forget your promise o. When we commot, you must put us for inside that band you wan' form. We be four wey done begin learn instruments. My own na guitar. Jacko done begin expert for the saxophone wey you buy am.

SANDA. We'll see, we'll see.

PRISONER 1. Mama Put, I dey come o. Make you put me two naira *konkere* at the ready. Two meat. (*Shaking his head.*) When man taste Mama Put *konkere*, e no go believe say na de same bean den dey take make we own *sapagiri* for prison. And one shot of Number One, plus one bottle for takeaway. No worry for hurry, oga warder done give us twenty minute each. Na me take first turn. (*Sees the* JUDGE *for the first time, his mouth open in surprise.*) Ah-ah. But no to we own very judge na in dis?

TRADER. Na im. (*Hands him the packet.*)

PRISONER 1. Why e go do in hair like that come dey frighten person? Abi 'in craze done reach top of television aerial *pata-pata*?

> TRADER *shrugs.* PRISONER 1 *eyes* JUDGE *warily as he moves to* MAMA PUT's *corner.*

Mr Judge, how now? Why you come dey do dis kin' show? E fit frighten person make 'e begin think dey done carry am go back inside court.

> *Reaches out for the bowl of food in* MAMA PUT's *hand but she stretches out her other hand without a word.*

Ah, sorry Mama, I forget say na cash before carry.

> *Loosens the rope of his shorts, manipulates an inner lining and fishes out some money.*

Na seven of us dey come, so make you count am correct o.

> *He begins eating, rapidly, casting dubious glances at* JUDGE.

But Judge, you still dey do your circuit – er – wetin you dey call am now – clinics? Yes, circuit clinics. The one for remand prisoners.

JUDGE. Why not? Any time I encounter the rodents in open air, like today, I let them nibble at the loaf of liberation. I heard your group would be marched here to clean up the neighbourhood. Are you interested in instructions?

PRISONER 1. Me? No. I done receive my sentence long time ago. Only eleven more months to go.

JUDGE. Independence Day is just round the corner. Does that mean nothing to you?

PRISONER 1. Sure. Na dat day dem go put less water and one extra meat for stew and sometime even less stone for inside the *sapagiri*. And of course all the imams and Christian preacher go come nuisance themselves with reformation and redemption and patriotic talk-talk.

JUDGE. Amnesty. Doesn't the gracious wand of amnesty touch some of you on the national occasion?

PRISONER (*hisses*). Oh, that one. Anyone wey want commot prison for that amnesty door go take short cut to lunatic asylum. Wise person no dey hope inside prison. (*Points to the number on his chest.*) That code na my release date. Anything else, I no dey think am.

JUDGE. You're a fool. The prerogative of mercy is always open, and open to all. You only have to ensure that you are noticed, that's all. You must be noticed. You have to undergo a change. Visible change. And there are even more chances under a military regime. A governor's birthday. A hundred days in office. A year's successful tenure. His wife producing a male son – preferably twins. Anniversary of Coup. Christmas, Id-el-Fitr. Rhamaddan. New Year's Day. Army Day. Navy Day. Remembrance Day – you see, the Military have far more to celebrate than your ordinary civilian mortal.

PRISONER 1. En-hen. Thas more like our Judge. When I see you for that dress and wig, I fear you done become real judge, those wicked people wey no dey hear Sorry, I no go do so again, sir. Now you done begin talk like your real person.

JUDGE. What religion are you?

PRISONER 1. Na Christian. At least na inside Christian family den born me.

JUDGE. How often does the prison chaplain visit?

PRISONER 1. It depends. Every Sunday for sure, but e dey come take bible and catechism classes, sometimes three times a week. He can come every day if people get interest.

JUDGE. Then waste no more time. Persuade him that you have begun the journey to souls' kingdom. You're in luck. In me you have found the ideal travelling companion.

PRISONER 1. Wetin dat?

JUDGE. We shall make the journey together. Yours, of course, will be fake, but then your life is already a fake, isn't it? Faking new demons just to get out of prison should be no problem for you. Revelation, that's the key. Let your chaplain believe that you have a revelation.

PRISONER 1 (*sighs*). My time is almost up, Judge.

JUDGE. Eleven months to go, you said.

PRISONER 1. No, I mean this time I get siddon chop for Mama Put. Now now. For this very today. The twenty minute warder allow person make we disappear, go where we want. We fit spend that time with wife or girlfriend, you know. Is all matter of luck. Or arrangement. You get the money, you get assignment to where you want. Sometime those officers, dem dey auction the assignment, give am to highest bidder. De moment I hear say work dey for Broad Street, me I done begin negotiate for am, because I know Oga Sanda go do us well. Now I done chop belleful. Master Sanda's takeaway dey for my hand, and is nearly time to join my mates. All dis one you dey talk. I no get time for am.

JUDGE. You do not wish to take advantage of the Prerogative? Do you realise that it is even higher than the MA-JE-STY of the law. Even I do not yet aspire to such a plane, but I have begun the journey, right from this morning. I offer you the honour of serving as my guinea pig.

PRISONER I (*rising*). Hey, hey, watch your mouth. Na me you dey call pig? You people, make you warn this your Judge enh . . .

JUDGE. Go away. A mere shell of being, nothing more. A no-man's wilderness inhabited by phantoms. Your fate is to become a born-again, the genuine thing. A hideous bore. Revelation will come to you on a forlorn road, and you will clutch it to your bosom, cradling and naming it – so predictably – a jewel of inestimable value. It will come like a Mercedes Benz with blazing headlamps on a pitch dark night. The door will open and a mysterious stranger will invite you in, and you will enter, blind as a bat from the penetration of the lamps. But you will never be in the driver's seat.

Enter another PRISONER, *sees the first and jerks his head towards exit.* PRISONER I *starts to leave, still scowling at the* JUDGE. *He plucks a packet of cigarettes from his parcel and hands it over.*

PRISONER I. Na you and Jacko go share that one. No forget to thank Master Sanda. I done pay Mama Put for all of una. As for that crazeman, if 'e yap you like e just yap me, make you no waste time for reply am. Just dust am one for me because he owe me one. Me, guinea pig. Nonsense!

A ragged procession is reflected on the doors. Men, women and children, carrying baskets, boxes, rolled-up beddings, bed springs, cupboards, chairs, clutching all kinds of personal possessions. Interspersed among them are the occasional lorries, equally laden to the top, with people perched precariously on top and among the loads. Wheelbarrows, omolanke, a tractor with trailer, also loaded with human and domestic cargo, the odd television set and antenna protruding from among baskets and sacks – An animated 'battered humanity' mural of a disorderly evacuation, maybe after an earthquake, from which an assortment of possessions have been salvaged.

JUDGE (*raises his head slowly to stare, like others*). And what is that desolate throng? (*The procession continues, seemingly endless. He seizes a pair of clippers and bangs it thrice on the table, formally.*) Cou-ou-ou-ou-ou-ourt! The witness will answer all questions put to him and address the bench only. I said, what is that dismal throng?

BARBER. Hey, that's my work tool. (*Snatches it off him.*) If you damage it, don't imagine I shan't make you pay for it.

JUDGE. I'll deal later with this act of contempt. Meantime, I want some answers. (*Leaps up and disappears through the auditorium.*)

MAMA PUT. I hoped I had escaped such sights for ever. While the Civil War lasted, oh yes. It was like that for us most of the time. First the Biafrans who insisted we were part of them. We packed our belongings and drifted to the villages. Then the Federal Army came with their gospel of liberation. So we trooped back, just like that. Then the Biafran army returned and back we went on the roads, along bush paths, knee-deep in swamps and foraging for food like beasts of the forests. And yet again, the Federals counter-attacked, and we were told that this time, the enemy was gone for good. Not that the killings ever stopped. Both sides seemed to enjoy playing at judge and executioner. Private scores were settled as former friends and even relations denounced one another.

SANDA. I wish I could answer his question.

TRADER. Which question, oga?

SANDA. The Judge. He asked, who are this throng? This humanity?

TRADER (*puzzled*). But you know who they be, oga, na dem be the people of Maroko wey government force commot this morning.

SANDA. That's a million people, Trader. A million people within a certain environ called Lagos. Do you know them?

TRADER. How can? I no dey live inside Maroko. But we know some of them, oga, you know some of them dey come join us sometimes when we get – er – action and we want reinforcement.

SANDA. That doesn't answer the Judge's question – who are they? That's a million people you know. Look at this small group passing through Broad Street, *who* are they? And the others, drifting all over the face of Lagos. A million, that's mere statistics, but a million *people* – yes, the Judge was right. *Who* are they?

TRADER. Oga, I no sabbe this kind question you dey ask at all.

MAMA PUT (*her eyes on the passing throng*). Don't ever forget this knife, girl, don't ever forsake its history. They teach you history in school but this school is different, and the history I teach you is yours, just yours. It belongs to one one else. Look at it. They call it a bayonet. You've got that? Bay-on-et. You'd think I would hate it, keep away from all things of steel, especially this. But I kept it. You can see I use it to cut the vegetables and the meat. But it was this knife that killed my brother, so I keep it to remind me, yes, just to remind me. Because he died trying to stop them from raping me. The liberators, you know. The ones who came to liberate us. They flung him against the wall, then one of them plunged this knife in his heart. It was a quick death. There was not much to be thankful for during that war, but that was one. A quick death. They left the knife in his body and drove away in his car.

SANDA. The war is over now, Ma Put, the war is over.

MAMA PUT. Is it? Then tell me what is that procession passing through? What force was it that expelled them? Is this a sight one encounters in peace time?

SANDA. Some countries have it every year – Ethiopia for one. Such sights are common enough where droughts ravage the land and governments do not care. The whole world predicts the drought but, it's always news to those in charge.

MAMA PUT. Even that is war, then. It's war of a different kind. It is war of a kind governments declare against their people for no reason. We're too soft. We have to learn to be part of this thing here. If I had my way I'd make my girl take one to school in her schoolbag. We all need something like this lodged in our innocence.

> *A* MILITARY OFFICER *enters from the direction in which the* JUDGE *made his exit, takes the steps two at a time, furiously. At the top he pauses, looks in the direction from which he has just emerged, scowling in rage, straightens out his uniform which is slightly askew, flicks off invisible dust from his sleeves, vigorously rubs off some invisible stain from his shoulder. His* AIDE-DE-CAMP *comes panting up after him from the same direction, and he spins round to face him.*

MILITARY OFFICER. Don't tell me you've done with him already.

ADC. The others are taking care of him, sir.

MILITARY OFFICER. I said you were to take personal charge.

ADC. I did, sir. And I left them very specific instructions, sir. I made sure he was bundled into the car boot before I left. (*Displays car keys.*) I secured the boot myself.

MILITARY OFFICER. You locked him in the boot, then what?

ADC. I thought we'd take him to the nearest police station, sir.

MILITARY OFFICER. On what charge?

ADC. Interference I thought you said, sir. Interfering with your er . . . your control of the evacuees.

MILITARY OFFICER (*between his teeth*). I ought to have you court-martialled. I ordered you to stay and handle it personally. Personally! And you want to take him to a police station where he'll intimidate them and regain his freedom? The fool interfered with my uniform. He touched it – do you understand that? He pulled my sleeve, he placed his bloody civilian hands on my uniform. And all you want to do is take him to the police station? Didn't you hear me say he was to be given the special treatment?

ADC (*salutes*). I'm sorry, sir, I didn't catch that part, there was so much commotion all around. I shall attend to it at once. (*Turns smartly to go.*)

MILITARY OFFICER. Wait. You say you have him in the boot already?

ADC. Securely locked, sir.

MILITARY OFFICER. It won't do to bring him out now and begin giving him a thrashing. There's bound to be one of these busybody upstarts calling themselves journalists who'll start publishing lies about what never happened. (*Points to the cannister hooked onto the soldier's belt.*) Mace him! Open the car boot, spray his face thoroughly and close it back. We'll take him to the barracks afterwards and then he'll begin his course of instructions. Get moving.

SANDA. Is there some trouble, officer? Can I be of help?

MILITARY OFFICER. Just some stupid judge who left his court to come and interfere with my operations.

SANDA. A judge?

MILITARY OFFICER. This section of Broad Street is to be blocked in an hour. I come here to supervise the arrangments and what do I meet? A bunch of Maroko refugees and their filthy loads clogging up the place. So I order them to move on. They are stretched out all the way to the Marina – they must have come up the Marina through Victoria Island – it would take at least an hour at the slow pace they're moving, and some of them are already thinking of camping under the flyway. Under the flyway! The party here is supposed to spill over to the flyover and down to Ita Balogun . . .

SANDA. Yes, yes, officer, this judge . . .

MILITARY OFFICER. He leaves his court and tries to interfere. Maybe he thought I would be impressed by his wig and robes – dirty robes I must say. Says a lot about the quality of judges we have on the bench these days. Probably slipped into the nearest bar for a quick one and couldn't find his way back. Do you know, he didn't even have any shoes on. He was in such a hurry to challenge my authority, he must have left them in the bar.

SANDA (*throws a brief but urgent nod at* TRADER, *who disappears*). Officer, there are no courts in this area.

MILITARY OFFICER. Typical of their judicial hypocrisy. Goes where he's not known to get thoroughly soused. Maybe that's where he holds his clandestine courts – you know, where the real judgements are dispensed. They're all so corrupt they even hold parallel courts. You know, where the only legal argument is naira.

SANDA (*laughing*). That bad?

MILITARY OFFICER. You had better believe it!

SANDA. But surely, officer, not in judicial robes.

MILITARY OFFICER. He was in his robes and a wig, I tell you . . .

SANDA. Are you sure he was not a vagrant? One of those . . . er . . . touched in the head? Maybe even one of the people displaced from Maroko.

MILITARY OFFICER. That would only make the matter worse for him. (*Almost screaming.*) He TOUCHED my uniform. Can you imagine one of those Maroko vermin desecrating my uniform. For his own sake, I hope he is a genuine judge.

SANDA (*smiling*). Well, I hope so too, officer. Imagine, that would really be an *infradig*. A common tramp. Maybe even a lunatic escaped from some institution . . .

MILITARY OFFICER (*taken with sudden recollection*). Wait . . . a . . . minute. He . . . now that I think of it . . . his manner . . . I mean, what was that gibberish running from his mouth? Something about prerogative of mercy but, no, not in any way that made sense. Good God! You mean he could have been one of those street lunatics? He wasn't wearing any shoes and his – er – robes, yes that did look rather tatty. But the wig was clean, well groomed. Still . . . he kept tugging at my sleeve. He kept pawing my uniform!

SANDA. I would put it all out of my mind, officer. Madmen or vagrants or Maroko squatters – all they need is a dose of strong action. So you finally sorted out Maroko?

MILITARY OFFICER (*instantly recovered*). Oh they surely got what was coming to them. They had to go. I mean, even in their own interest. That place was unhealthy for human habitation. The government promised to relocate them but no, their leaders went to see the new locations only to return and incite their people to reject them. Said they were too swampy, too isolated, no infrastructures, too this and not enough that. What did they expect? Four-star hotels? That's when we ordered the police to stand aside and leave the job to professionals. That place should have been sanitized ages ago, but the bloody civilian government kept pussyfooting and allowing technical and pseudo-legal delays to obstruct development plans. That's where a military government is really godsent, whatever anyone says.

SANDA. So Maroko is really gone? Gone for good?

MILITARY OFFICER. Didn't you see the bonfire? We didn't merely bulldoze it, we dynamited every stubborn wall, then set fire to the rubble. That place was disease ridden! No point developing it for decent citizens only to have them die of some lingering viruses from way back. Those squatters might be immune to anything but we have to think of the future residents. We took them by surprise. They woke up as usual but found themselves staring into the muzzles of guns. Few of them had any time to pick up their belongings.

SANDA. They had no warning at all?

MILITARY OFFICER. They've had masses of warning under the civilian regime, even some feeble, half-hearted eviction attempts. But the law courts always interfered. So, as the good book says, the fire next time! If you'd got up early enough you'd have seen the flames against the skyline. Gave Lagosians quite a spectacular sunrise. Lit it up for miles around as if an atom bomb had been exploded on the beach. I tell you, it was worth several weeks of training for our boys – you never know when such experience will come in useful. (*Strains to make out signs of his* ADC.) Now where's my fellow? Doesn't take that long to mace one hoodlum.

SANDA. It's quite crowded out there. He may have problems getting through. But, officer, I hope you don't mind my curiosity . . .

MILITARY OFFICER. Not at all, not at all. What do you want to know?

SANDA. What is Maroko being turned into? The rumour we heard was that the island was sitting on oil.

MILITARY OFFICER. Oh, we know of those rumours. No. Not a drop of the black gold in that area. But it's prime residential area, right on the lagoon. Oh yes, and that was something else — the sea could have risen any time and overwhelmed those stupid residents in their tin and wooden shacks. Think of the scale of the disaster! I mean, they're human beings after all. And some families have lived there over three generations. They deserve something better than a watery grave.

SANDA. You see. The media never mentioned that.

MILITARY OFFICER. The media is prejudiced. Simply prejudiced and irresponsible. But we'll deal with them in our own good time. We've worked out plans to deal with their excesses just as we've perfected plans for holding back the sea from Maroko. End the hundred or so years of neglect and decay, transform it from a breeding ground for armed robbers, drug dealers and all kinds of undesirables. You know, we couldn't even be sure that the people living there are Nigerians. Many of them could jolly well be aliens! Well, that's the end of that national embarrass- ment. You won't recognise it when we've completed the transformation.

SANDA. I'm sure of it.

MILITARY OFFICER. Now where in hell are . . . or — should I say — what the hell!

The ADC has entered, accompanied by another soldier. They look very much the worse for wear. They race up the stairs and salute.

ADC. Permission to make report, sir.

MILITARY OFFICER. I'm waiting.

ADC. I have to report that the prisoner has escaped.

MILITARY OFFICER. Escaped? Didn't I order you to mace him unconscious?

ADC. He was unconscious, sir.

MILITARY OFFICER. Then how did he escape?

ADC. Sorry, sir, I think I put it rather badly. He didn't actually escape, sir, he was rescued.

MILITARY OFFICER. Rescued. (*Mirthless laughter.*) And by whom, may I ask? His pot-bellied colleagues on the bench? Or the Nigerian Bar Association? Yes, just who effected this rescue against a fifty-strong detachment from the crack regiment of the Nigerian army. Rescued in the presence of a fifty-strong military presence? That's nearly company strength, officer.

ADC. It was the Area Boys sir. We were overwhelmed before I could call for reinforcements — you will recall, sir, that we had positioned our men in all the strategic places for blocking off the marked-out sector for the party.

MILITARY OFFICER. Yes, go on.

ADC. I had just given the prisoner three or four solid squirts in the face and of course he was screaming like the civilian pig he is. I was about to close the door of the boot when they descended on the driver and myself. They spirited him away, sir and — er — rough-handled us.

MILITARY OFFICER (*begins pacing up and down*). Fill me in, fill me in. I still don't understand. You had your pistol, major. Why didn't you waste their ringleader? That's an elementary lesson you've been taught often enough. Waste the leader and the rabble will melt away.

ADC. If you will be good enough to observe, sir, I have been disarmed.

MILITARY OFFICER. You were . . . ?

ADC. Disarmed sir. We were grossly outnumbered.

MILITARY OFFICER. Don't talk rot, major! Our Intelligence report had fed us accurately with the strength of the Area Boys in this neighbourhood. An armed soldier is worth at least ten unarmed civilians any day, and there must have been at the very least . . .

ADC. Six of us, sir, counting the personnel in the escort car.

MILITARY OFFICER. Then what story are you trying to tell me? The Area Boys between the flyover and Ita Balogun number no more than sixty-three. That reduces the maximum number around this shopping centre to maybe twenty – make it twenty-four at the outside. Our Intelligence reports were detailed, right down to the muscular make-up of every Area thug. So will you please explain how six armed soldiers from the crack regiment were overwhelmed by twenty-four civilian rabble.

ADC (*points to the reflection in the sliding doors*). The Maroko rabble, sir. No Intelligence report alerted us to their presence here. They joined in, sir. They hemmed us in and cut us off all possible reinforcement. Our colleagues had no idea of what was happening. I doubt if they are aware of it up till now.

> MILITARY OFFICER, *now in a towering rage, strides up and down, slapping his swagger stick against his thighs. Stops, takes a look at his soldiers, grits his teeth and growls.*

MILITARY OFFICER. They shouldn't have done that. They shouldn't have tampered with your uniform. They should not have laid their hands on it. (*Thrusts his fists in the air.*) You should have warned them – DON'T TOUCH MY UNIFORM!!!

> My uniform is sacrosant
> From cap pom-pom to underpant
> It cannot bear civilian touch
> This cloth proclaims: you've met your match!
> The uniform's forbidden grounds
> For bloody civs. it's out-of-bounds
> Don't get me mad, don't make me sore
> Don't challenge my esprit-de-corps
> DON'T TOUCH MY UNIFORM!!!

Inflexible the starch foundation
A glossy boost to chest inflation
The pressing iron leaves on a crease
Of razor. Discipline guarantees
The buttons never lack for polish
Boots wear a gleam that women relish
And epaulettes stand stiff and spry

Straining as if to spring and fly
    DON'T TOUCH MY UNIFORM!!!

A private quarrel? Don't be coy
Our services you may employ
The sight of khaki makes all freeze
We'll take your side for a modest piece
Of the action paid in cash or kind
Just play the game and you will find
The uniform is the talisman
That proves that 'man pass man'
    DON'T TOUCH MY UNIFORM!!!

A Colonel at twenty-four
I've never been in any war
A leveller, that's a *coup-d'etat*
Makes room at the top for a third-rater
A very different breed we are
From foreign slaves to criteria
Like service, sense and competence
Or that bogus word – intelligence
    DON'T TOUCH MY UNIFORM!!!

The uniform means born to rule
The uniform marks the ultimate school.
Superior to the civic bounder
The uniform marks the all-rounder
Know-all, Be-all, Seize-all, End-all
Alpha and Omega, self install
As President and Head of State
Commander-in-Chief, Great Potentate
    DON'T TOUCH MY UNIFORM!!!
    DON'T TOUCH MY UNIFORM!!!
    JUST DO NOT TOUCH – MY UNIFORM!!!

(*His song over, he breathes heavily, then snaps to action.*) I don't
want just the traffic to be stopped. I am not interested in the
usual road blocks. I want this sector sealed up entirely. Not a

mouse goes in or out. Round up every moving object, anything that breathes, walks, looks or stinks like an Area Boy. Look in the local bars and pools shops. Break into the houses and the shops and flush them out. I want nothing less thorough than the Ogoni treatment. Do I make myself clear?

ADC. Orders clearly understood, sir.

MILITARY OFFICER. And that includes the Maroko migrants. They obviously haven't learned from this morning's exercise, so, we'll complete their lesson here. Those miserable items that they managed to salvage – smash them up. Pile them up and make a bonfire of them. If there's any resistance, don't be stingy with the bullets. I want a bonfire sunset here to rival the sunrise we donated to Maroko this morning. Let them know that the Army's fully in charge.

SANDA (*deferential cough to attract attention*). Colonel, sir, if I may put in a word . . .

MILITARY OFFICER. You may not, sir. I am in no mood for any plea for clemency. It's time we introduced some military discipline into these surroundings.

SANDA. Plea for clemency? From me, sir? You are just about to do the store a favour. These Area Boys are the very pestilence. They pester our clientele, intimidate them, extort money from them and vandalise their cars. You are about to make my job here much easier, I assure you, Colonel.

MILITARY OFFICER. Oh. At last some music to my ears. Yes, I'm listening. Play on.

SANDA. The wedding, sir. You're forgetting the wedding.

MILITARY OFFICER. No. I hadn't forgotten. I'm cleaning up the place for the wedding.

SANDA. You'll have a running battle on your hands, Colonel. I know them. I've seen them at work. Hit and run skirmishes will still be going on when the guests begin to arrive. The occasion will be totally marred and er . . . you, I rather suspect, you will be held responsible.

MILITARY OFFICER. Oh. (*Pauses.*) Hm. I must say . . . Maybe we should wait until the ceremony is over? It's expected to go on until dawn, you know.

SANDA. Of course. A dawn operation, just like Maroko. The Management will be particularly obliged to you.

MILITARY OFFICER (*thinks it over briefly*). That's it then. We'll concentrate on herding the Maroko invaders out of here. (*Gritting his teeth.*) In an orderly fashion – for now. If we have to, we'll even *plead* with them. But later, oh yes, later. Right! No further distractions – until dawn. Follow me!

They go off at a brisk pace, watched by BARBER *and others. The* MINSTREL *plucks his box-guitar and sings: 'Maroko'. Towards the end, he is joined by others, including the passing evacuees.*

MINSTREL.

Maroko o. What a ruckus
Over a wretched shanty town.
It was stinking
It was sinking
We were rescued or we would drown.

The lagoon breeze was pestilence
A miasma hung over the horizon.
We were banished
Or we'd be finished
By sheer atmospheric poison.

No electricity or piped water
No sewage or garbage disposal.
Was it decent
To be indifferent?
We must make way for urban renewal.

Come learn from we new relocation
The best nomadic architecture.
Window or roof
Like cattle on the hoof
Will arrive some time in the future.

As for education for our children
Invention is the child of necessity.
In the open air
We'll pioneer
The genuine Open university.

So na here me I come relocate
With every modern amenity.
Food dey for belle
I even save my tele
Some day, we go get electricity.

Maroko! What an illusion
To make a home in the middle of the ocean
But the waters
Never hurt us
It was government with the Final Solution.

The light has been changing gradually to onset of dusk.
TRADER *enters with the departure of the soldiers, nods to*
SANDA *and begins to pack up his wares. So do* BARBER *and*
MAMA PUT *at a brisk pace. Enter a group of* SOLDIERS, *armed,*
aggressive. They charge the various stalls, throwing merch-
andise, pots and pans in every direction. Protestations. MAMA
PUT *goes wild, picks up her bayonet and dares them. Three*
guns are levelled at her. SANDA *finally makes himself heard*
during this stand-off.

SANDA. Cut it out! Did you hear me? I said, put those guns away!
Do you realise you're disobeying the orders of your superior
officer?

SOLDIER. Which officer? Our orders are to demolish all illegal
structures.

SANDA. And I'm telling you the Colonel was here just now, and he
expressly said that no stall around here was to be touched.

SOLDIER. Nobody mentioned any exceptions. Our orders were to
tear down all illegal structures. Everything goes in the bonfire.

SANDA. I don't care what your orders were, but go ahead if you like. Go on, smash up one more item and see if you don't end up in the guardroom.

SOLDIER. But she tried to attack us. Look at her, still threatening my men with that knife. Nobody does that to my men and gets away with it!

SANDA. That's not a knife, you blind recruit. That's a bayonet. I told you she's an army wife. How else do you think she would be in possession of a bayonet? She has a gun too, you're lucky she chose not to use it.

SOLDIER (*cranes his neck to obtain a closer look*). Oh. It's a bayonet.

SANDA. Of course it's a bayonet. And she is an army wife. That's why the Colonel exempted this area. Now put everything back as you found it and I'll forget about this assault.

SOLDIER (*salutes* MAMA PUT). Sorry, ma'am. It was all a mistake. Thank you, sir. We'll put it all back. Come on, you two. Get moving.

They scamper round, trying to restore everything as before.

MAMA PUT. Leave it, leave it. Just leave it and leave us alone. Go away. Get out of here!

SOLDIER. Sorry, ma'am. Very sorry. Squad, Fall out! (*They stumble out over one another, the leader making imploring gestures to* SANDA *to the last.*)

TRADER. As I bin say before, oga, you sabbe tink quick quick for your feet.

BARBER. Mama Put, so you done become army wife now. Which barracks make we come dey look for you?

MAMA PUT *simmers down slowly, begins to repack up her things.*

SANDA. If you're going home to change for the party, you'd better get cracking yourself.

BARBER. Me, I don't need much time. A quick wash and a new

agbada, and no one can tell the difference between me and a retired General. I tell you, an *agbada* is the greatest leveller in the history of clothing. Of course the material can make all the difference but, the difference doesn't show that much at night.

SANDA. You're thinking of changing your trade to tailoring? Don't take too long, everybody. You're all coming in on my invitation. I'm reserving a table for you right here so I can make sure you get served to bursting.

TRADER. Me, my stomach done ready since yesterday.

SANDA. How is Judge?

TRADER. Na bad ting dat gas wey dem put for in face. 'E still not fit see when I leave am for house na but different ting 'e done begin talk now. 'E say 'e done make de journey wey e tell me about, and at last 'e discover the colour of the soul, and na pitch black 'e be. But e say 'e no sure if na in own soul 'e see, or that of Lagos, or even that of the whole nation. But everything there, e say na black with small small spots.

MINSTREL *sings:* '*Ka L'owo L'owo, Kaa R'ayafe*'.

In a series of fussless, well coordinated moves:
The cleaners enter, sweep. Others begin to erect a marquee.
A carpet is rolled from the interior of the store down the steps.
A high table is set up, with plush chairs. Guest tables follow.
The major-domo *indicates where they are to go – and that is seemingly among the audience. The tables make their way downstage, down the aisles and out of sight.*

A 'juju' band enters, with instruments. The BAND LEADER *pats the* MINSTREL *on the shoulder.*

BAND LEADER. Good talk, colleague, your choice couldn't be more appropriate. This is one wedding that doesn't lack for cash or clout. (*Goes up to* SANDA.) Hallo, friend.

SANDA. You're welcome.

BAND LEADER. You don't happen to know where we're to set up, do you? We're The Benders, from Ibadan.

SANDA. I know you. Your group will play from the balcony. I'll take you there myself.

He leads them off, using the exit to the side. From now on, the sliding doors will remain firmly closed. The preparations continue, with the workforce responding to the lyrics, joining in and giggling at the suggestive sections. The caterers enter with huge tureens, covered dishes, warmers and coolers. The band begins to tune up their instruments. Soon, they take up the MINSTREL's *song and throw in their full instrumentation.*

The sliding doors reflect cars arriving, depositing GUESTS, *driving off.* SANDA *returns. He has changed his uniform for a buba and soro. Strolls round to make routine checks, impassively.* GUESTS *arrive.*

Finally, the party of the BRIDEGROOM *appears, heralded by a small combo of High Life musicians, led by a trumpeter. They are ushered to the High Table by the* MASTER OF CEREMONIES. *Once seated, he shoos off the group who disappear in the same direction as the 'juju' band, whose music again resurfaces in the background.*

A siren tears the evening apart, and a convoy of cars is reflected in the sliding doors. Car doors opening, stamp of boots etc. The MASTER OF CEREMONIES *nearly falls on his face as he rushes to the foot of the steps to usher in the august guest. A few moments later and a portly figure in uniform, brimming with medals ascends the steps and is duly placed at the head of the table, his ADC standing at attention behind him. The table rises to scrape and bow. The band strikes up the national anthem and all stand at attention. The* MC *is beside himself.*

MC. Your Excellency the Military Governor, your Excellencies honourable members of the diplomatic corps, my Lords spiritual and temporal, your Royal Highnesses the Emirs, Obis, Obas, Chiefs and other titled dignitaries, revered families of the Bride and Bridegroom, friends of the families of Bride and Bride-groom, distinguished guests, ladies and gentlemen, and all other protocols observed, it is my great honour and privilege to formally declare open this engagement ceremony between the illustrious families of Chief Honourable Surveyor Kingboli, BSc. Cantab., Order of Merit, honorary doctorates and chieftaincy titles too numerous to mention – and Professor Sematu, BA, MA, DSc., former Minister of Oil and Petroleum Resources and Ambassador Extraordinary to many nations in his long and illustrious career. Please put your hands together for the living heads of these two families, whom God has spared to be among us on this august occasion to witness the sealing of the bond of happiness between their charming offsprings. Put your hands together please.

> *Enthusiastic clapping, accompanied by fanfare.* MC *gestures to the two family heads to rise and take a bow. They do.*

Your Excellencies, my Lords Temporal, distinguished guests, ladies and gentlemen, all other protocols observed. Although my humble self will be taking charge of the proceedings, it is necessary at this stage to announce and welcome the chairman of the occasion. Yes, we dared invite. Yes, we dared our interme-diaries. Yes, we dared nurse expectations. Yes, we dared trepi-dations. Yes, we dared anticipate and yes, we dared hope and behold – his Excellency is here in person, the Honourable Military Governor of Lagos State . . . (*Clapping. Fanfare. The* MILITARY GOVERNOR *rises, and acknowledges.*) Your Excel-lency, it is an honour. On behalf of both families, I thank you profoundly for taking time off your busy schedule to honour us with your presence at this ceremony, and even more, to preside over the occasion.

Your Excellency the Chairman, honourable members of the diplomatic corps, my Lords Temporal and Spiritual, all other protocols observed. As we proceed, I shall have the honour to recognise some of our distinguished guests – yes, the list increases all the time, and I promise that all necessary recognitions will duly take place. However, I regret to say that, thanks to the crisis in the nation, fomented by some disgruntled elements, his Excellency our Chairman is obliged to take a plane to Abuja this very evening for an emergency meeting of the Armed Forces Ruling Council. His time with us is therefore very short, and without further ado, we shall proceed to the heart of the business that has brought us here tonight. Needless to say, it is an all night affair for the rest of us who do not have to keep watchful vigil on the affairs of the nation. We shall carry on till daybreak. You will notice that at the bottom of your invitation cards, are the initials RSVP. Well, for those of you who do not know what that means, it simply says:

GUESTS. Rice and Stew Very Plenty.

MC. Need I say more? And of course, that other one which is taken for granted – Bar . . .

GUESTS. Inexhaustable.

MC. This is obviously a highly sophisticated gathering, which is only to be expected. And now . . . (*Signals towards the balcony. Fanfare.*) Please put your hands together for the bridegroom.

> BRIDEGROOM's *entry, accompanied by drummer. He is followed by an attendant who carries an outsize briefcase. He stops at the foot of the steps.* MC *signals the band to stop.*

Stop! Wait a minute. What is this? Ladies and gentlemen, I think we have a little mystery here. This is not an office. The bridegroom is not going on a business trip. Our son is not absconding. He is not attending a board meeting. I thought we had all been invited to his betrothal. That he should arrive with a basket of kolanuts would be in order. That he should be trailed by bolts of *akwete* cloth would be no surprise. That he should be trailed by a lorry load of male yams, palm oil and bags of salt would be answering true to his origin. Or cases of *oyinbo* wine and champagne – why not? Don't we know that he was trained in

Toronto, Paris, and Budapest? So why not? But a briefcase! I am bewildered, mystified, confounded, disconcerted, and discombobulated.

Cries of 'More! More! Fire on! Finish the vocab!' Plus applause.

Ladies and gentlemen, I think we are about to witness something rarer than the sight of an elephant giving birth. We are about witness the secrets of the other side of the moon. At the end of a fruitless hunt, we sighed and got ready to make do with a wild tuber. When we pulled it from the hot ashes what did we find? A whole roast antelope! And they say the age of miracle makers is gone? We plunged our calabash into the animal's drinking hole and found it filled with frothing palm wine. They told us there were no leaves on the tree because it was harmattan, but they had reckoned without the perennial rain tree. Undoubted son of your father, do as your father has been known to do! Outdo your ancestors as your father did in his time! If you see me tomorrow morning with lockjaw, say I brought it on myself. Say it was I who said to the miracle masquerade: Surprise me!

With an indolent motion, the BRIDEGROOM reaches into the briefcase with the left hand, pulls out a fistful of naira notes, scatters them on the carpet behind him as he ascends each step. The GUESTS go wild, the drummer ecstatic. He repeats this all the way to the top, so that the carpet is overlaid with another carpet of banknotes. When he reaches the high table, he bows. The table rises to greet him, led by the MILITARY GOVERNOR who even throws him a salute.

The BRIDEGROOM then proceeds to the bench placed to one side for his party, again carpeting the way behind him with notes. Takes his seat to thunderous applause. The attendant turns the briefcase upside down, waves it above his head to show it has been emptied.

The MOTHER OF THE DAY *has taken the place of the* MASTER
OF CEREMONIES.

MOTHER OF THE DAY. Enh, forgive me, our elders, but it was the
cockatoo who pecked too deep inside iroko wood pursuing a
worm, that is why its beak is bent till today. You see me here
because that man who was here before, jeered that there were no
more tricks in the masquerade's pouch. The masquerade said,
'Turn your head and look behind you.' The man turned to look
but he saw nothing unusual. 'I don't see anything,' he said.
'That's the trick,' said the masquerade. Till today, you can
encounter the man still walking about with his head turned this
way, the rest of his body that way. When he recovers, he'll be
back with us. Meanwhile, well, the fact that the drum is at rest
doesn't mean that the legs won't tap. The rhythm of yesterday
still lingers in the head of the trained dancer, and this gathering
with all due respect, contains some of the best trained citizens of
this nation – you only have to look at the quality of the presence
we have on our high table, and all around.

Yes, that rhythm. Our dear Excellency the Chairman and
Military governor, ladies and gentlemen, I dare say that you may
have missed something when our prime young elephant showed
his mettle on the way to take his place. Did it not seem contrary
to familiar usage? Our forefathers say that the wise one always
throws his water forwards because whoever moistens the
ground before him will surely tread fruitful earth. And don't we
all pray to place our feet on earth that is bursting with fruit? But
our young son kept nourishing the ground behind him. Now, I
ask you, what could that mean? Is he being chased by hired
assassins or armed robbers? Was that a way to slow them down?
Or did he think he was on his village farm where you walk
backwards to sow the guinea corn? Or could it be – yes, I
wonder, I wonder with delicious anxiety – could it just be that he
– that he, he is laying a trail for someone to follow. A trail that
must lead eventually to himself. A trail of love. Of devotion. A

trail of – shall I say it? Shall I seat it on the ground and seal it with a prayer? A trail of . . . *omo jojolo*. Of children, and grandchildren, and great grandchildren . . . ?

Fanfare. Enter the BRIDE, *with attendants. The* GUESTS *rise. She steps on the carpet of notes all the way to the high table. She turns to the right, as if about to follow the trail of money but is stopped by the* MOTHER OF THE DAY.

MOTHER OF THE DAY. No, miss! Over there.

She is led to the opposite bench. The MOTHER OF THE DAY *feigns displeasure.*

Hng-ngh-ngh! I don't know what is wrong with the children of this modern age. Did you see that? She couldn't wait. She just couldn't wait. I have a mind to send her back to the village where she can be properly educated. (*Laughter. The* BRIDE *is seated.*) That's better. If you are in a hurry, we are not. If you and your hus . . . sorry o, you see, even I have caught the hurry-hurry disease. Yes, if you and your – intended – are thinking of packing up the food and drinks to stock your new home, you've got another think coming. We are not leaving here until the last drop has been drunk and the last speck of food licked off the plate. When we are done, you will think that an army of soldier ants invaded this place because when we've given you away – *if* we do give you away – we don't know when next we shall be invited to see the contents of your soup-pot. Now – (*She signals offstage. A maid appears with a well polished gourd and calabash cup, places it down before the* BRIDE.) Well, there it is. I hope it is not too heavy for you to carry. It had better not be, because you'll be carrying something heavier before long – that's if you are not carrying it already. One never knows. After all we seem to live in a hurry-hurry age.

I hope you know what to do. There are your parents. There are all these witnesses, all men and women of – as we say – timber and calibre. Let's go. (BRIDE *rises. The attendants place the gourd in her arms.*) We've only heard that there is a man who wants you for a bride – as if there is anything surprising about that – but we don't know him. We don't even know what he's like. All we know is that he must have a good pair of eyes in his head. There – (*She waves towards the audience.*) – as you see, there are plenty of fishes in the sea. Go and see if your man is there. When you start pouring him a drink, we'll know that he is no stranger.

Band: 'Meta Meta L'ore o'.

BRIDE *comes down the steps and scans the faces of the audience. Entering into the game, she makes a pretence of being about to set down the gourd before one man, then another, but veers off at the last moment, teasing the victim. Festive reactions as she feints off each expectation. She returns to the* MOTHER OF THE DAY, *shaking her head negatively.*

MOTHER OF THE DAY. What? No sign of him there? Well, some people are really choosy, I must say. Oh, I see. Sometimes, you know, we miss the obvious. I had forgotten we had some real cream of society seated over there. (*Points at the high table.*) All right, so that's where he is enh? Go and serve him his palm wine so we can all go home. I'm getting tired of all this and you're keeping us from the food and drinks.

The smiling BRIDE-TO-BE *goes to the High Table, scans all the faces, looks closely at the the* ADC, *frowns and shakes her head, then makes to set down the gourd in front of the* MILITARY GOVERNOR. *Mock horror from the* MILITARY GOVERNOR. *She glides smoothly away just before the gourd touches the table. Applause. She returns to the* MOTHER OF THE DAY. *She waves her off 'angrily', goes and plonks herself in the* BRIDE's *seat.*

MOTHER OF THE DAY. No. I have nothing more to do with you? We've looked at everybody and still you're not satisfied. Am I

now to put an advertisement in the papers to find someone
suitable for you? Or start combing farmsteads and thorough-
fares? Or travel overseas – oh yes, maybe you're one of those
who dream of marrying a foreigner. A white man. You think we
don't have enough milk in our cocoa, not so? (BRIDE *stands
forlornly before her.*) Well, don't just stand there like a drenched
chicken. Look around and see if there is any rooster hiding in
some corner of the barn. Sleeping, maybe. Or hiding. Playing
hard to get. Or maybe he thinks it's him we're planning to
slaughter and serve up to our guests. Of course there is also the
military around. Maybe he thinks they're here to whisk him
away into detention. The poor creature is probably frightened to
death. Starving. Thirsty. See if you can find him and revive him
with a drink. Don't come back here until you've found him!

The BRIDE *goes off, follows the money trail. As she reaches the
High Table, she appears to slow down, pauses, looks in the
direction of the* BRIDEGROOM. *She walks slowly in his direction. A roll of drums begins softly, welling up. She reaches
the* BRIDEGROOM, *begins to set down the gourd. Just before it
touches the ground, she straightens up again and turns
around. The* BRIDEGROOM *smiles broadly – it's all still part of
the game. His supporters tease him, and the* GUESTS *applaud.
The* MOTHER OF THE DAY *turns to the High Table and
audience in a mock appeal.*

Only gradually is the change of expression on MISEYI's *face
noticed. It has become set. She comes down the steps, looks
slowly around, then breaks into a run.* SANDA *is the most
surprised person when she runs up to him, plonks down the
gourd before him and turns round defiantly to face the High
Table.*

For a few moments there is stunned silence. Then the BRIDE-
GROOM *leaps up, breathing heavily.*

TRADER (*dolefully*). Sai! E done sele! I done warn oga make e get ready to dodge. As I watch how dat woman dey yap am dis morning, enh . . .

BRIDEGROOM. This — is an insult! This — is an unpardonable insult!

CHIEF KINGBOLI (*incoherent with rage*). Who — is — that — man?

MILITARY GOVERNOR (*leaping up*). Arrest him! (MILITARY GOVERNOR's ADC *leaps into action.*)

MISEYI. What for?

CHIEF KINGBOLI. My family has been insulted. Publicly insulted.

BRIDEGROOM. I want him castrated.

> MILITARY GOVERNOR's ADC *advances towards the couple,* MISEYI *standing protectively in front of* SANDA. TRADER, BARBER *and* MAMA PUT *emerge and surround them.* TRADER *puts his fingers to his lips and lets off a loud whistle. A stand-off between* ADC *and the group.*

CHIEF KINGBOLI (*rounds on* MISEYI's *father*). You were in the know. You planned to humiliate me in public. You've never forgotten that oil contract you lost to my company.

MILITARY GOVERNOR (*panicky*). No, not here. Not in public.

CHIEF KINGBOLI. Why not? Because you backed him in cabinet? I knew you had an interest in his firm but I won the contract anyway. He's never forgiven or forgotten, neither had you. So you both plotted to inflict this disgrace on my family?

MILITARY GOVERNOR. S-sh! Stop it! Let's go to my residence and sort this out. Let's all keep a cool head.

CHIEF KINGBOLI. Just remember I have friends and partners among your superiors!

MILITARY GOVERNOR (*places his arms round him*). Let's go, let's go. You've got it all wrong. I am just as shocked . . .

BRIDEGROOM. All I want is to see him castrated. Publicly!

MILITARY GOVERNOR (*seeing the stand-off at the* MISEYI *end*). Send for reinforcements, Major!

> *From under her wrapper,* MAMA PUT *whips out her bay-onet.* ADC *freezes. The* MILITARY GOVERNOR *stares aghast.*

Confusion as the GUESTS *scatter. The* MILITARY GOVERNOR
knocks back his chair, and moves down.

Leave them be. Let's go. We'll deal with them later. Get the
outriders started. (ADC *salutes and runs out.*) Come on, gentlemen, to my residence. Let's go over this in my place calmly. It's a
family affair, so let's stay calm. This is the time to keep our
heads. Let's talk family to family. We'll all ride in my convoy.

BRIDEGROOM (*follows the High Table* GUESTS. *Signals to his
retinue to gather up the money*). Pick up every last naira.

TRADER (*steps forward and wags his finger*). Oh-oh.

BRIDEGROOM (*hesitates. But the* MILITARY GOVERNOR's *party is
already out of sight. Turns to* SANDA). You'll need it. You'll need
it for your medical bills. Because if it's the last thing I do in this
world, I'll cut off your genitals!

BARBER. Did you hear that? With all his money, he still wants to
make more – and using his rival's genitals!

BRIDEGROOM *storms off. Several moments silence.*

SANDA (*sighs*). I do not recall proposing.

MISEYI. Neither do I.

SANDA. I am not prepared for marriage.

MISEYI. Neither am I.

SANDA. So what the hell did you do that for?

MISEYI. As the something said to the other, it seemed a good idea at
the time.

SANDA. So what happens now?

MISEYI (*facing him*). Well, there is a feast.

SANDA. The guests are gone.

MISEYI. Oh, I don't think so. Trader.

TRADER. Yes, Miss Bride.

MISEYI. Do you think this feast will be wasted for want of guests?

TRADER. I get locusts plenty for outside, miss. Save for food or
drink to waste, na dem belle go burst.

SANDA. You'd better first take care of that money, Trader. We've
got to store it up rightaway. I'm not sure even I can control the

boys if they set eyes on it, and it's got to be given back. Barber, Boyko . . .

They begin sweeping up the money, joined by MAMA PUT.

TRADER. Enh? You say we go give 'am back, oga?

MISEYI. No, he didn't mean that.

SANDA. I do. It's not yours.

MISEYI (*sighs*). I forgot, these differences in cultures. Among my people, tradition makes the money – mine. For us, that is asking money. It is show-off money. It isn't bride price or dowry or anything like that. It enters the bride's home, and it stays there whatever the answer is. It can be one coin, one yam tuber, some woven cloth or jewellery, or a wad of tobacco. None of that is refundable. It's like the running expenses for the ceremony.

SANDA. But what on earth made you change your mind. I thought you were all set for domestic bliss. The merging of two powerful dynasties.

MISEYI. I don't know. I just knew I couldn't go through with it. Look, let's talk of more serious business. I know what you think you've been doing, I approve, but I think you've been going it the wrong way. Look at Boyko for instance, he should be in school.

SANDA. As a matter of fact, I've been giving it some thought. I've been reshaping my ideas lately, it's just that no sooner does one appear to see light, than a new cloud of questions obscures one's vision. Look at Maroko today. What answer does one have to that? What remedy does one apply? Before a new crisis is over, another has been hatched. Before Maroko it was . . . wait one second!

MISEYI. What is it?

SANDA. Get a move on, Trader. Quick, quick, everybody! They'll be back. You bet they'll be back. Once they've escorted the governor home safely, they'll be back. And that colonel, when he gets to hear about what happened here – and he's probably being briefed at this very moment . . . Come on, come on! Not a moment to lose. Get all the food and drinks into the banqueting room. It's soundproofed and air-conditioned. (*Stops and thinks fast. Looks around.*) Here, Boyko . . .

BOYKO. Yes, Mr Sanda.

SANDA (*grabs a fistful of notes and gives it to him*). You'll stay behind. They must find a pile of this with you – you know what to do. They'll snatch it off you. You'll burst into tears. You'll plead with them, saying that it's all you were left by the Area Boys who grabbed the rest of the loot. Now where did they go with it? Where?

BOYKO. I heard them say they were going to Anikulapo's nightclub to celebrate.

SANDA. Can't you think of somewhere much further off?

BOYKO. The Good Time Bar in Ikorodu.

SANDA. Good lad! Just sit there in all innocence and play on that flute.

MISEYI. Sanda!

SANDA. He'll go to school, I've promised. This is just a routine service for his old school. A last service, sure. No use wasting acquired skills. My friend Barber, can you handle the police bit?

BARBER. Trust me. You want the Kill-and-Go, the Mobile?

SANDA. None other. Those ones with permanent fire in their eyes and holes in their pockets. Use the basement entrance when you get back.

BARBER *goes off.*

MISEYI. Now what was that all about?

SANDA. Greed. Rivalry. Barber will lodge a formal complaint to the police that some soldiers made off with a few hundred thousands from the party and have gone to celebrate at the Good Time Bar. After the clash, there will be the usual commission of enquiry.

MISEYI. My God. Is this all you have been learning since you abandoned college?

SANDA. No. It's the way I've learnt to apply all I learnt. Both in there where we both were, and out here. Outside is one great learning place, Miseyi.

MISEYI (*the penny finally drops. She looks shocked. Turns slowly to inspect* TRADER *and the few remaining hangers-on more carefully*). Wait a minute. I know what you've become. You are not just a *megadi*, not just a security guard. You are one of them. An Area Boy. King of the Area Boys!

SANDA (*bowing*). At your service – if you prefer to put it that way.

MISEYI. Those bullies? Enforcers and extortionists? Thugs, yes, sheer thugs. Ready to serve the highest bidder. They make potholes in the middle of the road, then extort money from motorists for their – public spirited – service in filling them up. They break your windscreen if you don't pay up or slash your tyres. They rip the necklace off your neck in a traffic hold-up or snatch your watch. They're robbers. Daylight robbers. No better than armed robbers. That's the kind of people you consort with? Or is it worse? How much further have you sunk? Drugs? Cocaine pushing? Tell me the lot, what else?

SANDA. No-o-o, I am not that far up on the social ladder. Certainly not on the same rung as your father, or your would-be father-in-law for that matter. You heard them and the Military Governor at their bickering. I am not a pen robber. I don't lift oil illegally. I have never traded off import licences and I have never looted the treasury.

MISEYI. You dare impute . . . !

SANDA (*quietly*). I do.

> MISEYI *bristles, then wilts. She plonks herself down on the steps.*

Let's face it. You didn't meet me after all these years and fall in love with me. You fled your fiancé with the gourd because I reminded you of the values you once held. When you were not afraid to admit or speak the truth about anything – including your family. I don't say I am right in everything I've done since then but, we did remind each other of a little of our real selves. Wasn't that what really happened?

MISEYI. Oh, I am confused. What do we do now?

SANDA. First, move into safety. I am sorry, but I'm used to being practical. I have become used to having many people in my charge, and their welfare comes first. The heavier issues of the nation must wait for now, there'll be plenty of time to discuss them. Let's join the others in the banqueting hall.

MISEYI. Is it safe?

SANDA. I'm in charge of the plaza.

MISEYI. But what's the use of a wedding banquet without a wedding? I don't really feel like partying for the sake of partying.

SANDA. We-e-e-ll, I've been doing some thinking. (*Pulls her up.*)

MISEYI. But now you don't even have a job. I hope you realise that.

SANDA. I see you also have been doing some thinking.

MISEYI (*pulling sharply away*). I am not in love with you. What I did then was just – just – impulse. Sheer impulse.

SANDA (*puts his arms around her and leads her upstage*). I know. I've just had an impulsive idea myself. We could settle down with the Maroko people in one of the new locations. It will be cheap, and we would be among the founding members. There will be a lot of demand on us. We could work with them, take up their case, maybe get them compensation – that at least . . .

MISEYI. And what do we live on in the meantime?

SANDA. We-e-ell, to tell you the truth. I was already planning to leave this job. Leave this place altogether. I know I was searching for solutions but, well, this isn't it. So, I've been quietly putting a band together. We can eke out a reasonable living from that.

MISEYI. From subversive music? Because I can already guess . . .

SANDA. Come on, of course we'll diversify. The right music for the right occasion. Maybe you'll even pick up the old xylophone and join the band. But the real work will be with Maroko, not just that Maroko, but the Maroko all around, the eternal nightmare of a Maroko into which one wakes every day.

MISEYI. What can one do with the military still around?

SANDA. They won't always be there.

MISEYI. Who is going to remove them?

SANDA. You see, there is already plenty for us to think about. And plan towards. And two heads are better than one . . .

MISEYI. I've always wanted to found something worthwhile.

SANDA. Well, here's your chance. Why don't we go in and raise a toast to that?

> *They go off in the same direction as the others. Except for* BOYKO *playing his flute, the stage is empty. Enter* JUDGE, *in dark glasses. He listens.*

JUDGE. Who's in there?

BOYKO. Just me, Judge. (JUDGE *turns, and stumbles against a chair.*) Careful, Judge. Are you all right?

JUDGE. Fairly so. Fairly so. Just the little mystery of these wandering souls. I was certain I'd caught up with mine at last, and it was a void without features, mottled as the conscience of a tyrant. I know him by the way. I was locked up in the boot of a car but I heard them talking. Before I was gassed. What didn't they do to Maroko! Boastful bastards! So it was they who faked that sunrise. Dislodged a million people to rival my own labour of the spirit. Damn! I was so sure it was my own handiwork.

BOYKO. You don't seem all right.

JUDGE. It's getting light again, as if they've all begun to reform. But that I'll believe when I see it.

BOYKO. Oh. You must leave quickly, Uncle. The soldiers will be back any time.

JUDGE. Animals!

BOYKO. Judge, you must hurry.

JUDGE. I close the book of the prerogative of mercy against them. And their kind who masquerade in sheep's clothing. For ever!

BOYKO. Come, Judge, I think I can hear them already. Hurry!

JUDGE. Where to? Has this not always been our space?

BOYKO. Mr Sanda says you must come with me. At once.

JUDGE. That's different. That Security man appears to know what's what. A very sensible young man.

Snatching up the pile of notes, BOYKO *rushes him up the steps. As they reach the level of the High Table, soldiers break into the area.*

SOLDIER. Stop!

BOYKO. Come on, Judge!

A shot rings out. JUDGE *pitches forward, falls.*

Judge!

SOLDIER (*gun levelled at* BOYKO). You! Come here!

BOYKO *looks down on the prone figure of* JUDGE *and hesitates.*

If you don't want to join him, you'd better bring yourself here.

BOYKO (*slowly raises his arms, the money held in both hands*). Why did you have to shoot him? Judge has never harmed . . .

SOLDIER. Shut up! I said, com . . . (*His eyes pop.*) What's that you've got in your hands?

BOYKO (*sniffing*). That's all they left him, and me.

SOLDIER (*moving on him*). Who? Where's the rest? And where are the others? (*Snatches the money. The others crowd round them.*)

BOYKO. They went off to celebrate. They took everything.

SOLDIER. Where? Come on, you wretched little thug? Where did they go?

BOYKO. I heard one say The Good Time Bar, Ikorodu. They said they wanted to get as far away from here as they could.

SOLDIER (*shoves him violently away*). Let's go. Move it, move it!

They rush out. SANDA *looks in round the corner. Enters, followed by* MISEYI, TRADER, MAMA PUT, BARBER *etc.*

SANDA. What happened? We heard a shot.

BOYKO (*weeping*). They killed him. They shot him in the back.

JUDGE (*groans*). Here I go again. In the kingdom of lost souls.

BOYKO. Judge, are you still breathing?

MISEYI. Oh, thank goodness. We must get him to a hospital.

SANDA *rushes to his side. Kneels and turns him over. Examines him.*

SANDA. He's not bleeding. Judge, what happened?

JUDGE. Someone knocked me down, gave me a powerful blow on the back.

SANDA. What's this? (*He feels under the robe and exposes some thick, quilted material. Props him up into a sitting position.*) He didn't have this on when he left. Judge, where did you find this?

JUDGE. The waistcoat? In the boot of the car where they locked me. I've always wanted a waistcoat to go with the robe. It should be black of course, a judicial black, with a golden chain. I've had the chain hidden away for a long time, but not all my foraging could turn up a waistcoat – until I found myself in the boot. Not much to do in there, so I poked around. Foraging becomes a habit you know, and there is plenty of room in a Mercedes boot. You'd be astonished what other items I discovered.

SANDA (*he has taken off the robe and the waistcoat. Holds up the latter. Shakes his head, laughing*). This is a bullet-proof vest, do you realise that? A bullet-proof vest! You lead a charmed life, Judge, that's all I can say.

JUDGE. Bullet-proof? (*Feels himself frantically.*) You mean I'm not dead? I thought I was already at destination. I must confess I was rather pleased to find you all there. I never doubted you. I was certain none of you lacked soul, it was only a matter of finding out where it was hidden. (*Struggling up. Winces.*) My back is sore.

SANDA. You're lucky it's no worse. Come. I'll bring you where the others are. The programme has changed slightly, but the party continues till daybreak.

JUDGE (*as he is led off*). Ah yes, daybreak. Another sunrise to plan, this time, make it foolproof, keep those vandals from interfering and rivalling my prerogative with a bestial conflagration . . . I shall never forgive them. Never!

> TRADER *groans and disappears with* BARBER *ahead of the others.* MINSTREL's *voice in the distance, singing: 'B'orombo Ta Bo'. The band joins in. The set is left empty.*

GLOSSARY

agabada	loose traditional gown (male)
akara	bean cake
akwete	a locally woven cloth
alawada	clown
bosikana	food-shack
buba	loose female blouse
ewa	bean
gari	farina
haba	come on!
juju	magic, supernatural powers
kain-kain	distilled palm-wine (usually around 80% proof)
konkere	bean pottage with farina
megadi	security guard
molue	locally built passenger bus
oga	boss
omo jojolo	treasured child
omolanke	locally made, commercial luggage cart
oyinbo	white man
patapata	absolutely, entirely
saka-jojo	shadow-play; silent film
sapagiri	prison version of konkere (*see above*)
sawa-sawa	whitebait (peppered)
so-o-say	problem-free
soro	straight-leg trousers
wahala	trouble
wayo	fraud, con game

TRANSLATIONS FOR PRISONERS' SONGS

Left – Right – Left. Left – Right – Left.
Be it warder, be it prisoner
Both of them are one.
Be it soldier, or policeman
Irredeemable thieves
Who gets caught is the one we browbeat
The real thief's on the loose.
The robber is dressed in khaki
The General a robber
The Major a bandit
Slaps you round and snatches your wife
Twists your arm and seizes your home
Bribery left, corrupt right
Your place is reserved right here
Your place in the prison yard
Left – Right – Left. Left – Right – Left.

Left – Right – Left. Left – Right – Left.
The river is fearless. Left – Right. I'm in goal
Left – Right. I have climbed up, I have plunged
Faka–fiki faka fi
The forest depths are nothing, the savanna holds no surprise
Does the bridge not leap over the gorge?
Watch the prisoner leap over his days
I have gone in, I've collected my number
The bean pottage is firm in my stomach
Be it the river, be it the ocean
The wind leaps over them both
The railway merely boasts; there is nothing new to the eye
The Sanitary Inspector is a liar
The dungheap is ever a dungheap.
Mosquito larvae still inhabit the waterpot
Even if you strain harder than the last year
Left – Right – Left. Left – Right – Left.
Soldier politician, incorrigible robber
Father of mayhem, you no longer bear arms
You fight no wars but chase contracts all over the place.

Methuen World Classics
include

n Anouilh (two volumes)
n Arden (two volumes)
den & D'Arcy
ndan Behan
hra Behn
tolt Brecht (six volumes)
chner
gakov
derón
ton Chekhov
ël Coward (five volumes)
uardo De Filippo
ax Frisch
rky
rley Granville Barker
(two volumes)
nrik Ibsen (six volumes)
rca (three volumes)
arivaux

Mustapha Matura
David Mercer (two volumes)
Arthur Miller (five volumes)
Molière
Musset
Clifford Odets
Joe Orton
A. W. Pinero
Luigi Pirandello
Terence Rattigan
W. Somerset Maugham
(two volumes)
Wole Soyinka
August Strindberg
(three volumes)
J. M. Synge
Ramón del Valle-Inclán
Frank Wedekind
Oscar Wilde

Methuen Modern Plays
include work by

For a Complete Catalogue of Methuen Drama titles
write to:

Methuen Drama
215 Vauxhall Bridge Road
London SW1V 1EJ